Faces of Latin America

FACES

of

LATIN

AMERICA

Duncan Green
with Sue Branford

MONTHLY REVIEW PRESS

New York

Library of Congress Cataloging-in-Publication Data
available from the publisher.

U.S. ISBN: 978-1-58367-324-9 (paper)
U.S. ISBN: 978-1-58367-325-6 (cloth)

Published in North America by:
Monthly Review Press
146 West 29th Street, Suite 6W
New York, New York 10001
www.monthlyreview.org

Distributed in the UK by:
Latin America Bureau
Enfield House, Castle Street
Clun, Shropshire SY7 8JU, UK
http://www.lab.org.uk/

UK ISBN: 978-1-899365-76-0 (paper)

5 4 3 2 1

Contents

For Catherine, Calum, and Finlay

Acknowldgements

This new edition was updated by Sue Branford, in consultation with Duncan Green (who is just getting too rusty on things Latin American to do it himself). She would like to thank Nick Caistor and Javier Farje for their help in this task. And Duncan would like to also thank Tito Castro, for taking the trouble to set him on the right road on the shores of Lake Titicaca back in 1981, and to Jenny Pearce for providing the initial inspiration for this book. All opinions and errors are of course, the authors' own.

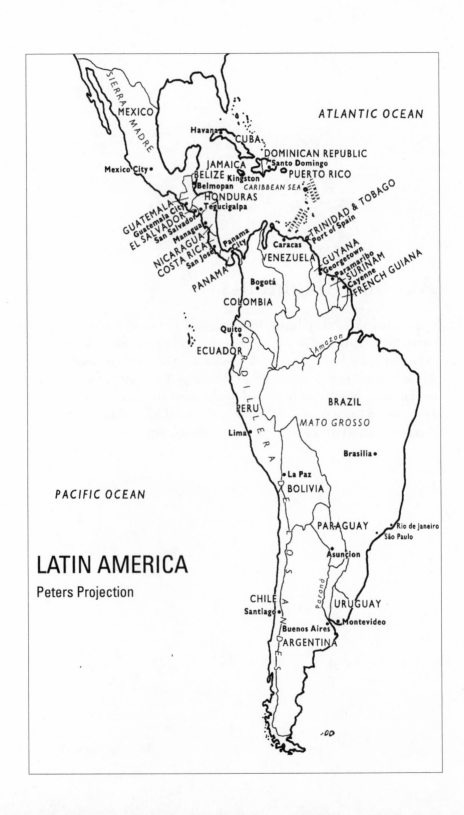

SIERRA MADRE

MEXICO

ATLANTIC OCEAN

Havana

CUBA

DOMINICAN REPUBLIC

Mexico City

JAMAICA
BELIZE
Belmopan
Kingston
CARIBBEAN SEA
Santo Domingo
PUERTO RICO

HONDURAS

GUATEMALA
Guatemala City
EL SALVADOR
San Salvador
Tegucigalpa

TRINIDAD & TOBAGO
Port of Spain

Managua
NICARAGUA
COSTA RICA
San José
Panama
City

Caracas

GUYANA
Georgetown
Paramaribo
SURINAM
Cayenne
FRENCH GUIANA

PANAMA

VENEZUELA

Bogotá

COLOMBIA

CORDILLERA

Quito

ECUADOR

Amazon

PERU

BRAZIL

MATO GROSSO

Lima

Brasília

La Paz

PACIFIC OCEAN

BOLIVIA

PARAGUAY

Rio de Janeiro
São Paulo

Asunción

LATIN AMERICA

Peters Projection

Paraná

ANDES

CHILE
Santiago

URUGUAY

Buenos Aires
Montevideo

ARGENTINA

.00

Introduction

Latin America has long been portrayed to the outside world through stereotype and myth. It started back in the sixteenth century when El Dorado, the mirage of a golden king in a golden city, first excited the Spanish *conquistadores'* greed. Back in Europe, idealized accounts of the Inca and Mayan civilizations inspired Thomas More's *Utopia*. The West has both plundered and been dazzled by Latin America ever since. Some of the greatest Latin American writers, such as Mario Vargas Llosa, Isabel Allende, and Gabriel García Márquez, were, in the words of one critic, "the equivalent of the Amazon rainforest, providing oxygen for the stale literary lungs of the developed world."

But recently Latin American writers, weary of magic realism, have turned their attention away from the sleepy rural world of García Márquez's Macondo to the drugs and violence that face so many Latin Americans in their daily lives. Chilean author Alberto Fuguet ironically brands the new genre "McOndo," yet another Latin syncretic combination of old and new, external and internal influences.

This book tries to paint a picture of this complex and often contradictory society. It is about Latin Americans: not just presidents and businessmen, some of them among the richest in the world, but the millions of faces of the shantytowns, small farms, mountains, rain forests, factories, and plantations. It explores the processes that have shaped people's lives, the jobs they do, where they live, and how they see and want to change their world. Through the lives of its inhabitants, the book attempts to capture the everyday ebullience and dynamism of Latin America, a world away from the cynicism and corruption of much of its formal political life.

Far from being the passive victims of circumstance, ordinary Latin Americans possess depths of courage and creativity, enabling them to confront with humor and grace a seemingly endless array of problems: how to feed and educate their families, find a home, improve their neighborhood. Many such attempts at self-help have in recent years been led by women, struggling to free themselves from the stifling values of *machismo*. The indigenous peoples of Latin America have also belied their reputation for passivity by fighting vigorously to defend their ways of life.

Today the region is imbued with a new feeling of optimism, despite the dispiriting number of obstacles it still faces. The last two decades of the twentieth century saw a debt crisis usher in a devastating sequence of market reforms, bequeathing a harsh world where economic growth did not create jobs, and the gulf between rich and poor grew ever wider. Since then, however, a series of left-of-center governments have gained power in much of the region and the economy has rebounded. In some countries modest progress has been made in combating the region's age-old scourge of income inequality, the worst in the world.

Yet many are asking whether the region has found a sustainable way forward. It remains heavily dependent on the export of primary products, in some countries even more than in the past. The rural poor are still struggling for a plot of land on which to feed their families in an environment devastated by deforestation, soil erosion, and unregulated mining and industrial development. Unemployment and violence, much of it related to drug-trafficking, remain high in the shantytowns that encircle the region's cities.

Old problems perhaps, but also a new vitality. The return of civilian rule to almost all the region has imbued many Latin Americans with the belief that they can and should have a say in determining their country's future. Through social media they are creating new forms of protest, new ways of organizing. This book aims to help you understand the roots of this new Latin American effervescence.

Faces of Latin America was first published in 1991, in the run-up to the 500th anniversary of Christopher Columbus's first voyage to the Americas. Much has happened since then and this fourth edition, covering developments up to 2012, has been extensively rewritten as a result. With this new edition, the mood of the book has also evolved. As the traumas of dictatorship, civil war, and economic collapse recede, a more positive story emerges: the rest of the world has much to learn from the vigor, imagination, and courage of millions of Latin Americans as they struggle for a better future.

—DUNCAN GREEN
and SUE BRANFORD, 2012

1.
The Curse of Wealth: Economics

History and Power

What is Latin America?

From Tijuana in the north to Cape Horn in the south, ringed by islands in the Caribbean Sea and both Pacific and Atlantic Oceans, Latin America is a region defined by shared colonial experience. Colonialism's most obvious legacy is linguistic. From Mexico southward, Spanish, Portuguese, and, in a few cases, French put the "Latin" into Latin America (the English-speaking islands of the Caribbean and a few mainland ex-colonies such as Guyana are not included). Even the name "America" comes from conquest, derived from that of Italian explorer Amerigo Vespucci.

Pre-Latin America

The apparent facial similarity between Andean villagers and the nomads of the Mongolian steppes is no accident. People first came to the Americas from Asia, crossing the frozen seas of the Bering Strait to Alaska and the west coast of North America. This migration probably began around forty thousand years ago, although large swathes of the "New World" remained uninhabited until much later.

Driven by a search for food and the pressure of new waves of arrivals, the Americas' first peoples moved slowly south, sparsely populating the entire continent as far as Tierra del Fuego. Some remained as hunter–gatherers, but others discovered agriculture, enabling them to settle in towns and develop diversified societies.

Many small urban civilizations sprang up and disappeared, either defeated by warlike neighbors or absorbed into a surrounding culture. Some early societies left vast, complex ruins like Teotihuacán in central Mexico, a series of pyramidal structures to rival those of Egypt; others left almost nothing.

The Maya were a nation of astronomers and architects, already in decline before the Spaniards came. They were brilliant mathematicians, developing the concept of zero long before any other civilization, and making astronomical calculations of astonishing accuracy. Their ornate temples are still being rescued from the jungles of Central America, and it is not yet clear what caused the Mayan Empire to go into a sudden decline around 1000 CE.

In the mid-thirteenth century, an itinerant warlike people known as the Mexica settled in the area now called the Valley of Mexico. Over the next two hundred years, through conquest, tribute, and cultural domination, the Aztec Empire was created around the great capital of Tenochtitlan. This city was built in the middle of Lake Texcoco, accessible only by long causeways from friendly territory or allied city-states. From this stronghold, the Aztecs were able to subdue their rivals; by 1500, they ruled virtually all of central Mexico as well as parts of Guatemala. The empire was fueled by a tribute system that required conquered societies and allies to send goods and slaves to the metropolis. Human sacrifice was a key element of the political and religious system, and by the late fifteenth century the Aztecs began to make war with their neighbors with the sole objective of capturing future victims.

At the same time, the Incas were forging a huge empire in South America, and by 1400 had emerged as the dominant culture of the Andes. Less brutal and more practical than the Aztecs, the Inca political philosophy was more pragmatic than spiritual. Defeated enemies were conscripted rather than sacrificed, and conquered cultures were integrated into the social hierarchy. The Incas introduced a vast road network throughout the Andes, along which relay runners took messages as swiftly as modern buses. The cultural and political system established by the Incas brought unity to a huge, disparate region; unlike that of the Aztecs, the Inca legacy was looked upon favorably and inspired several popular uprisings against the colonial authorities after both civilizations had been overwhelmed by the conquistadors of Spain.

Despite their greatness and the differences between their political systems, both Aztecs and Incas rapidly succumbed to a handful of European adventurers in the decades following the landfall of Columbus in 1492. In one of history's most extraordinary collapses, hundreds of thousands of armed indigenous warriors were overwhelmed by Spanish muskets, cannon, horses, and Old World diseases to which the indigenous peoples had no immunity.

Conquest and Colonization

The late fifteenth century was a period of expansion and conquest for the dominant Spanish kingdom of Castile. Ferdinand and Isabella had pushed

**Table 1.1: Estimated Indigenous Population of America at the
Time of European Contact**

	Estimated Population (millions)	Percent of Total
North America	4.4	7.7
Mexico	21.4	37.3
Central America	5.65	9.9
Caribbean	5.85	10.2
Andes	11.5	20.1
Lowland and South America	8.5	14.8
TOTAL	**57.3**	**100.0**

Source: William M. Denevan, ed., *The Native Population of the Americas in 1492* (Madison: University of Wisconsin Press, 1976).

the muslim Moors back to the Mediterranean in what became known as the "Reconquest," and the exuberant king and queen saw no need to limit their belligerent Christianizing mission to the Iberian peninsula. The Genoese explorer Cristóbal Colón (Christopher Columbus)—better known in exploring circles for his bluster and greed than for his seafaring talents—received the monarchs' blessing to seek a westward trading route to the Indies. Colón first sighted what he believed to be the Indies in October 1492—they were, in fact, the Bahamas, part of the Antilles Island chain that also includes Hispaniola and Cuba, discovered soon after. These lands were claimed for Spain with the approval of the Pope (although Portugal submitted a successful counterclaim for most of Brazil, where they landed in 1500 and charted and settled over the next hundred years). Over the next three decades, many expeditionary forces crossed the Atlantic to the Caribbean, aiming to settle and Christianize the newly charted territory in the name of the Spanish throne.

When the first Europeans arrived, the Aztecs and the Incas were the two great city-dwelling civilizations in the region. Initial contact, however, was limited to the small, relatively primitive tribes of the Antilles Islands in the Caribbean, where little resistance was encountered either to the extraction of surface gold or to the enslavement of the indigenous population. The limited potential of these islands for the production of precious metals soon pushed adventurers toward the continental mainland.

Hernán Cortés led the conquest of Mexico. His strategy depended on alliances with local enemies of the Aztecs, and, by playing the indigenous factions off against each other, was eventually able to capture Tenochtitlan. Francisco Pizarro, against incredible odds and with only a few dozen men, brought the Inca Empire to its knees. Like Cortés, he made use of spies and gathered accurate intelligence; both were also aided by the devastating effects of European viruses that ravaged the local population. Pizarro ably exploited divisions in his enemies' ranks—his invasion coincided with a war of succession between two Inca princes. In 1532 at Cajamarca, Peru, Pizarro captured the emperor Atahualpa and, without losing a single man, defeated an Inca army of many thousands. The initial unfamiliarity of gunpowder and horses, along with prophecies of the providential return of white-skinned gods, may have led the inhabitants of the New World to see Cortés and Pizarro and his lieutenants as supernatural, although this theory is contested. Even without fear of godlike powers, native weaponry was no match for metal armor or shot.

History is written by the victors, and partisan chroniclers frequently romanticized the subjugation of Mexico and Peru, usually on the grounds that the Aztec and Inca civilizations were unusually cruel and barbaric. The conquests were portrayed as Christian civilizing missions, and there is little doubt that the conquistadors—and the missionaries who accompanied them—put a great deal of effort into the conversion of the local population. Yet some of the invaders subsequently experienced remorse. The conquistador Mansio Serra de Laguizamón recalled: "We found these realms in such order that there was not a thief, nor a vicious man, nor an adulteress . . . we have destroyed by our evil behavior such a government as was enjoyed by these natives."

Whatever their religious motives, the conquerors were utterly rapacious in their pursuit of wealth, and the extraction of the abundant indigenous riches.

What the Spaniards Found

On the Aztecs

And when we saw all those cities and villages built in the water and other great towns on dry land, and that straight and level causeway leading to Mexico, we were astounded. Those great towns and buildings rising from the water, all made of stone, seemed like an enchanted vision from the tale of Amadis.

On the Incas

I say again that I stood looking at it, and thought that no land like it would ever be discovered in the whole world, because at that time Peru was neither known nor thought of. But today all that I then saw is overthrown and destroyed; nothing is left standing.

—Bernal Díaz, *The True History of the Conquest of New Spain*, trans. J. M. Cohen, Harmondsworth, Penguin, 1963

Bernal Díaz, a chronicler among the conquistadors, recalled the obsession with treasure and bounty: "Moctezuma's treasure chamber did not contain many jewels or golden ornaments, because all the best had been extracted to form the magnificent offering that we had sent to his majesty."

The attentions of the colonial bureaucracy soon became focused upon the silver-rich regions of New Spain (Mexico) and Peru (which also included modern-day Bolivia). In both areas, silver ore could be mined by an abundant supply of indigenous slave labor, providing a steady source of income for the Spanish crown.

By about 1600, the boundaries of Spanish America were drawn, and the mapping of Brazil followed soon after. British, French, and Dutch colonies were founded in the previously unexplored area east of Venezuela, though later attempts by these countries to expand their influence and territory were largely unsuccessful. Having been among the less wealthy and successful European powers, Spain and Portugal now began to benefit from the labor and products of their resource-rich colonies. Thanks to the alliance between the white colonial elite and the locally born creoles (those of European descent but born in Spanish America), Spain and Portugal were able to maintain vast empires with relatively little manpower. The general population, a mixture of indigenous and mixed-race (*mestizo* and *mulatto*) peasants, was taxed and policed.

Once the center had been removed, Spanish viceroys replaced the emperors as the supreme authority and the former empires fell into their hands. Where indigenous groups were less advanced and centralized, the Spanish encountered much greater difficulties. In southern Chile and Argentina the native Mapuche peoples successfully resisted the colonial forces well into the nineteenth century, finally losing their fight to the new Chilean and Argentine armies following Latin America's independence from Spain. Argentine schoolchildren now learn the names of the heroes of the "War of the South," a nineteenth-century campaign to exterminate indigenous people, during which soldiers were paid a reward for each pair of testicles they brought in to their commanders. The extermination of the indigenous people opened up the south of Argentina for sheep and cattle ranching.

An enduring legacy of the conquest was the misnomer "Indian," dating from Columbus's first landfall in the Americas, when, thanks to a miscalculation of the circumference of the globe, he was convinced he had reached Asia. In the furor surrounding the Columbus quincentenary in 1992, many indigenous Latin Americans rejected the term "Indian," which in Spanish carries distinctly derogatory overtones. This book instead opts for the rather clumsy alternative, "indigenous people."

For the indigenous peoples everywhere in the continent, the conquerors' military victory was only the beginning of the process of extermination.

Indians having their hands chopped off for failing to meet the gold dust quota. From a book by Bartolome de las Casas entitled *Spanish Cruelties* published in 1609.

Within a century of the conquest, as much as 90 percent of Latin America's indigenous population were wiped out in what became known as "the Great Dying." In the Caribbean, the Arawak peoples who first greeted Columbus with delight soon rued the day they had paddled their canoes out to his ships, bearing gifts for the exhausted sailors. Enslaved to the Spanish lust for gold, those who survived smallpox, influenza, measles and other new diseases committed mass suicide by poisoning and hanging. Mothers even slaughtered their newborn babies to prevent them being enslaved by the Spanish. Within twenty-five years of Columbus's arrival, only 3,000 Arawaks remained of an original population of 600,000, and by the mid-sixteenth century they were extinct. Five centuries later, the youth of Brazil's Kaiowa people met the same threat in the same way. In 1990 alone, twenty boys and girls from the threatened tribe, all aged between 13 and 18, killed themselves by hanging or poisoning. Thirty others tried but were saved. On February 3, 1991, 15-year-old Maura Ramírez hanged herself from a tree. Her mother said, "She was sad. She dreamed Helena was calling her." Helena, Maura's elder sister, had committed suicide three months earlier. Psychologists blamed the deaths on the dislocation caused by leaving home to work on the sugar plantations.

Although more indigenous people fell victim to the diseases introduced by the Spanish and Portuguese than died in the mines, plantations, or battlefields, the level of economic exploitation and misery inflicted by the Europeans was at least partially responsible for making them so vulnerable to illness. Millions were literally worked to death. The colonial authorities adopted various systems for exacting tribute and labor from their indigenous "vassals." During the initial period the *encomienda* (forced agricultural labor) system rewarded Spanish officers and favorites with entire indigenous communities. In return for supposedly bringing their allocated vassals to Christianity, the *encomenderos* were authorized to demand tribute and unpaid labor. In the densely populated regions of Mexico and the Andes, this left Indian villages more or less intact. In more sparsely peopled regions, the *encomienda* system degenerated into raiding parties to abduct slaves. European writers and theologians put forward a variety of ideological justifications to show that the natural inferiority of the indigenous people made their enslavement both necessary and an act of mercy.

As the centuries passed, racial boundaries became blurred. Since men far outnumbered women in the European colonial communities, indigenous women were frequently obliged by their owners to have sex with them, and the subsequent intermingling of blood created a growing mixed-race population, known as *mestizos*. Other indigenous people abandoned their traditional dress and learned Spanish, often moving to the cities. Over time, cultural criteria, rather than physical characteristics, became the means of identifying ethnic background. An "Indian" wore non-European dress and spoke little or no Spanish, whereas a "mestizo" adopted both the white language and Western dress. In the coastal regions of Latin America, indigenous groups were swiftly wiped out on the plantations and were replaced with African slaves, who added a further ingredient to the continent's racial mix. By the time independence came in 1825, 12 percent of Latin Americans were black, 28 percent were mestizo, and only 42 percent were indigenous. The remaining 18 percent were white.

This racial mix continues to characterize the region. Statistics are even more unreliable than in the case of indigenous groups, but by one calculation, the black and mulatto (mixed race) population of Latin America (that is, excluding the English-speaking Caribbean, United States, and Canada) is around 150 million, significantly exceeding the indigenous population. The largest black population by far is in Brazil, where almost half of the country's 180 million inhabitants are directly descended from slaves, followed by

Colombia, Haiti, and Cuba. Racial integration has not brought social equality. Although slavery was abolished in 1888, Afro-Brazilians remain at the bottom of the social pyramid, often living in shantytowns, with minimal power or representation in national political life.

The Commodity Trade

The Indians have suffered, and continue to suffer, the curse of their own wealth. That is the drama of all Latin America.

— EDUARDO GALEANO, *Open Veins of Latin America*

Fourteen thousand feet up on the Bolivian plateau, Cerro Rico (Rich Hill) looms high over the bleak mining town of Potosí. A giant rust-red spoil heap, it tells the story of Bolivia's cruel past and impoverished present. For two centuries after the Spanish *conquistadores* marched into the Andes and defeated the Inca Empire, a stream of silver ore flowed down the slopes of Cerro Rico, through the furnaces and mints of Potosí and over the sea to Spain. Hundreds of thousands of press-ganged indigenous laborers died bringing out the ore. The silver rush made seventeenth-century Potosí into the largest city in the Hispanic world and earned Cerro Rico a place on the Bolivian national flag, but today only some fine colonial churches recall the days when the streets were literally paved with silver. For the Corpus Christi procession of 1658 the authorities ordered that the cobbles in the center of the city be removed and replaced with solid silver bars. Boomtown Potosí was a chaotic, brawling city of 160,000 people, including, according to a census in 1601, 800 professional gamblers and 120 prostitutes. Today, some Latin Americans still describe immense wealth with the phrase "worth a Potosí," first coined by Cervantes in *Don Quixote*. But behind the splendor of the churches and the antics of the Spaniards lay the grim reality of the *mita*, the Spanish-imposed system by which each indigenous community had to send a portion of its able-bodied men to work in the mines, working shifts of up to 36 hours, only to be swindled of what little wage they were due.

Cerro Rico is now an anthill of 5,000 tunnels, where self-employed miners scratch a perilous living from what the Spanish left behind. "In the old days the veins were a yard thick. Now they're half an inch," says Marco Mamani, a young indigenous miner. "It's like a tree—the Spaniards took the trunk and left us the twigs." For many years, Potosí has been the poorest region of the poorest country in South America.

Potosí's path from poverty to riches and back to even greater poverty is an extreme example of the process that has dominated Latin American development—the commodity trade. Although the exact definition varies, commodities are the raw materials that drive the world's economy. They include natural resources, such as oil and copper, and agricultural products like wheat or coffee. Europe's insatiable appetite for commodities was the driving force behind the centuries of colonial expansion, which left the largest part of what is now called the Third World under the rule of competing European powers.

Ever since the Conquest, Latin America has produced commodities for export—coffee, tin, oil, sugar—and used the proceeds to import manufactured products from industrialized nations in Europe, and later from the United States, Japan, and China. The richer nations used their power to keep commodity prices low, playing one desperate producer country off another and when necessary using military and technological might to reinforce their supremacy. In human terms the unequal struggle between commodity producers and industrialized powers has condemned millions of the Third World's people to lives of suffering and want. Only in the twentieth century did the larger countries like Brazil and Mexico develop large-scale industry, and even then much of it was under foreign control.

Over the five hundred years since the arrival of the Spanish, the commodity trade has exacted enormous social costs. In the mines the Spanish forced indigenous laborers to work in inhuman conditions until hundreds of thousands died from the dust, poor food, and disease.

The Mita

Without Indians there can be no mines, because there is no one else to work them and their shortage has caused more damage than war or plague.

—Bernal Díaz, *The True History of the Conquest of New Spain,* trans. J. M. Cohen, Harmondsworth, Penguin, 1963

The day of departure is very sad. These victims of obedience line up before the priest who awaits them in his robes at the door of the church, with a cross held high. He sprinkles them with holy water and says the usual prayer and a Mass which they pay for, to implore the All Powerful for a successful return. Then they go to the square with their parents, relatives and friends. Embracing each other with many tears and sobs, they say goodbye and, followed by their women and children, take the path out of the village crushed with sorrow. This mournful scene is accentuated by the sound of their drums, and the bells which are beginning to ring for prayers.

—Gabriel René Moreno, nineteenth-century Bolivian historian

In the countryside the introduction of each new export crop led to more land coming under the control of big landowners and more peasants being expelled. The onward march of export agriculture helped drive the tidal waves of displaced peasants that broke over the continent's cities during the second half of the twentieth century, creating the sprawling shantytowns that surround the continent's "First World" city centers. By allowing peasant farmers, who generally grow food crops like maize and beans, to be driven out to make way for export crops, many countries lost their self-sufficiency in food production—Mexico, where maize was first cultivated, now imports it from the United States. On a national level the commodity trade proved an unreliable basis for Latin America's development. In the long term, commodities suffered from two main problems: a long-term decline in prices and a tendency to boom-bust cycles, rather than steady growth. Prices fell over the long term because supply rose faster than demand, driven by technological improvements and new entrants. Vietnam's rapid rise as a coffee producer in the 1980s created a global glut and a price collapse that ravaged the Latin American coffee industry. Prices are also affected by dumping: when Latin American farmers compete with crops also grown in the rich countries, northern governments rig the rules by pouring subsidies into their agriculture, enabling firms to flood Latin American markets with food exported at below the cost of production. With the North American Free Trade Agreement (NAFTA), Mexican maize farmers have become one of dumping's most notorious casualties.

Overlaid on the long-term decline are the boom-bust cycles characteristic of commodities. When prices rise, farmers plant more, leading to oversupply, a glut, and a subsequent price collapse. The problem is worse when there is a long lead time between planting and harvesting, as in the case of tree crops like coffee. When prices fall, farmers take land out of production, leading to a shortage; prices rise, and the cycle begins all over again. Volatility is exacerbated by changes in patterns of demand. In recent years the taste for better coffee in Europe and the United States has increased demand for high-quality beans from Central America and Colombia, and reduced demand for lower-quality Brazilian beans. Throughout Latin America's history entire commodity sectors have flourished and then disappeared, in some cases due to technological innovation such as the discovery of synthetic dyes in the nineteenth century, which wiped out the indigo industry. In other cases, mineral deposits have been exhausted, as occurred with Bolivian silver, or the soil has become impoverished, as befell the sugar plantations of northeast Brazil.

The price fluctuations common to commodities make planning extremely difficult. To make matters worse, countries are often dependent on one or two commodities, exacerbating their vulnerability to any sudden fluctuations. Even when prices rise, economies have difficulty coping with the windfall. Governments often use the money to increase public sector spending. Though this could, in theory, lay the basis for future economic development through improving health and education, sudden and unplanned public sector growth has often in practice encouraged corruption and inefficiency.

In the 1970s, in an attempt to avoid the problems of price fluctuations and trade wars between producer nations, many Third World countries joined forces in setting up price stabilization agreements. But even when they succeeded in guaranteeing more stable prices, these agreements have often merely encouraged producer nations to increase production, eventually leading to oversupply, a price war, and the collapse of the agreement.

Many Latin American governments recognized the pitfalls of commodity dependence and tried to avoid them. One obvious path was to develop local industry that would replace dependence on foreign imports. For fifty years, from the Great Depression of the 1930s to the debt crisis of the 1980s, Latin American governments turned to import substitution as their new development model, while still relying on commodities to bring in most of their export earnings. After 1982, the continent largely returned to its historical reliance on commodities, as neoliberal reforms across the region put industrialization into reverse and gave new emphasis to "export-led growth" based on commodities and cheap labor. The exception was Mexico, where a Free Trade Agreement with the United States (NAFTA), which came into force in 1994, led to a boom in manufactured exports of increasing sophistication. In many ways, NAFTA split off Mexico from the rest of Latin America, turning it into a cheap labor enclave of the U.S. economy. Further south, the emphasis has been on reviving traditional areas such as mining and agro-exports such as soybeans, cotton, and sugar, while diversifying into new, luxury crops such as fresh fruit and cut flowers.

Commodities continued to exert a powerful grip on the region. In Bolivia, rows over the export of natural gas produced presidential resignations; in Venezuela, high oil prices have propelled Hugo Chávez into a role as regional leader and benefactor. Within Latin America commodities enriched chiefly those engaged in exporting them abroad. Export crops such as cotton or sugar were more profitable when grown on large plantations, so the expansion of cash crops led to a concentration of landownership and wealth in the hands of a few very powerful individuals. Mining interests were historically controlled by entrepreneurs like Simon Patiño (1868-1947), Bolivia's greatest tin baron, who rose from poverty to become one of the ten wealthiest men on earth. From the luxury of his European home, Patiño could make or break Bolivia's governments, acting as an absentee landlord toward an entire country.

The fabulous wealth of a few commodity exporters failed to "trickle down" to the poor majority, since it was either invested abroad or used to

The Spaniards and Gold

Of gold is treasure made, and with it he who has it does as he wills in the world and it even sends souls to Paradise.

—Christopher Columbus, logbook from his first voyage, 1492

They lifted up the gold as if they were monkeys, with expressions of joy, as if it put new life into them and lit up their hearts. As if it were certainly something for which they yearn with a great thirst. Their bodies fatten on it and they hunger violently for it. They crave gold like hungry swine.

—Indigenous (Nahuatl) text from the time of the Conquest

'Look what a stupid idol these savages are worshipping'
'Father it's made of gold'

Source: *América La Patria Grande*

import luxury goods. Farmers could make more money growing crops for export than by growing food to sell at home. The commodity barons felt no need to create a domestic market by redistributing wealth more evenly, since this would have meant giving up some of their privileges. The source of their wealth and power lay overseas; all they required at home was cheap, docile labor. When the workforce in their mines or plantations demanded better wages or living conditions, the commodity magnates were quite prepared to use the most extreme violence to prevent them winning. In El Salvador during the 1980s, the heads of the coffee-growing families ran the "death squads" that killed tens of thousands of peasant activists and trade unionists.

White Gold

The European colonists pursued different commodities depending on the soil, climate, mineral deposits, and accessibility of each region. On his second voyage to the Americas in 1493, Christopher Columbus brought sugarcane to Hispaniola (now the Dominican Republic) and it flourished. Sugar subsequently fueled Brazil's first and greatest commodity boom.

Per acre, "white gold" produces four times the food energy of potatoes and ten times that of wheat, and sugar was in great demand to feed Europe's new industrial working class. Brazil's sugar boom was centered in the northeast, around Salvador de Bahia.

Sugar is a capital-intensive crop, requiring substantial investment to process the cane immediately after cutting, before it can be shipped off to foreign refineries. In Brazil, the Dutch West Indies Company initially financed the sugar industry. The monotonous cane fields rapidly spread across Brazil's northeast, squeezing out food crops such as beans and maize, so that even in the best years of the sugar boom there was chronic malnutrition.

The Dutch later expanded into the Caribbean, which was nearer to the European market. In Brazil, the soil was already losing its fertility through overuse. By the eighteenth century, the Caribbean had completely eclipsed northeast Brazil: Haiti's exports to Europe at that time exceeded those of all thirteen North American colonies put together. As production rose, prices fell, and Brazil's northeast became one of the most deprived areas of the continent. Refugees fled its famine- and drought-stricken lands and headed for the next commodity boom—the gold rush in the south. Sugar also left its mark on Brazil's racial composition. The plantations were worked by African slaves, victims of a deadly but lucrative trade dominated by British slavers. Today the people are largely a blend of black African and white European immigrant stock, with an unmistakable "pigmentocracy." Although the Brazilian government denies claims of racism, most black people are poor, most rich people are white.

In the 1990s Brazilian sugar had a revival as the government struggled to overcome its dependence on imported oil by encouraging a switch to ethanol (a sugar-based alcohol). By 2005, with oil prices at record highs, ethanol was up to 55 percent cheaper at the pump, and major economies, such as the United States and China, were looking to Brazil for lessons in reducing oil dependence. Since then, however, the situation has changed. The production of sugar has stagnated in Brazil, largely because of competition over land for other crops. Brazil has been faced with an ethanol shortage and has even imported ethanol from the United States. At the same time, Brazil made a major discovery of oil in 2006. It will not be easy to explore this oil because

---

Britain and Latin America

Take his whole equipment—examine everything about him—and what is there
not of raw hide that is not British? If his wife has a gown, ten to one it is made
in Manchester; the camp-kettle in which he cooks his food, the earthenware he
eats from, the knife, his poncho, spurs, bit, are all imported from England.

—Description of Pampas *gaucho* (cowboy) by British consul in La Plata. Sir Woodbine
Parish, *Buenos Ayres and the Provinces of the Rio de la Plata,* London: J. Murray, 1839

In all of Brazil's haciendas the master and his slaves dress in the products of
free labor, and nine-tenths of them are British. Britain supplies all the capital
needed for the internal improvements in Brazil and manufactures all the utensils
in common use, from the spade on up, and nearly all the luxury and practical
items from the pin to the costliest clothing.... Great Britain supplies Brazil with
its steam and sailing ships, and paves and repairs its streets, lights its cities with
gas, builds its railways, exploits its mines, is its banker, puts up its telegraph
wires, carries its mail, builds its furniture, motors, wagons.

—James Watson Webb, U.S. Ambassador in Rio de Janeiro, c. 1865

---

it is located at an astonishing 7,000 meters below the ocean bed off the coast
of Rio de Janeiro but, if the technical problems can be resolved, it should turn
Brazil into a leading world oil exporter. It will be tempting to the authorities
to neglect more sustainable alternatives.

Even so, it is unlikely that the Brazilian government will completely abandon ethanol. It has acquired a great deal of technical expertise about its production, more than any other country in the world, and is now using this
knowledge to increase its economic and diplomatic influence abroad. Trade
missions are encouraging countries like Botswana, South Africa, Angola,
Zambia, Tanzania, Zimbabwe, and Mozambique to work with Brazil to overcome their dependence on imported oil by producing ethanol.

Booms and Busts

Gold was discovered in the Brazilian state of Minas Gerais in the 1690s, and
came onstream just as Portugal signed a trade agreement with Britain. Brazil's gold duly underwrote British industrialization, and the accumulated gold
reserves later paid for Britain's war against Napoleon.

Although Brazil's boom-bust cycles have been the most spectacular, they
have occurred at regular intervals all over the continent right up to

the present day. In El Salvador the indigo industry collapsed following the discovery of synthetic dyes in nineteenth-century Germany. In the northern deserts of Chile, the nitrate fields that had provided fertilizers for Europe's agriculture, and over which Chile had fought a war with Peru and Bolivia, became worthless overnight in 1909 when a German chemist discovered how to make artificial fertilizers. In the 1990s, the bottom fell out of the coffee market as new producers such as Vietnam flooded the market and coffee processors developed new techniques for producing high-quality coffee from low-quality beans.

Some commodities have produced better longterm results than others. Demand for temperate-climate products such as meat and grain is steadier than that for tropical products such as coffee and sugar, whose prices therefore swing more wildly. In Argentina, the cattle and grain trades laid the basis for significant economic development, which made Argentina perhaps the tenth-largest world power in 1914. In Brazil, the coffee boom that gave the country 50 to 70 percent of the world market between 1850 and 1950 made São Paulo into the economic powerhouse of the strongest nation in Latin America. The commodity trade has shaped both European and Latin American history. The flow of gold and silver through Spain and Portugal to the manufacturing nations of Holland, France, and Britain financed the early stages of their development as world industrial powers. After most Latin American nations won their independence in the early nineteenth century, Britain rapidly became the dominant economic influence. In 1824 the British foreign minister, George Canning, wrote to a friend, "The deed is done, the nail is driven, Spanish America is free; and if we do not mismanage our affairs sadly, she is English."

The first fifty years after independence were a time of political and economic chaos, but from the 1870s onward, a new commodity boom took off, lasting until the Great Depression of the 1930s. Beef and grain from the Argentine pampas, Chilean copper, Brazilian coffee, Central American bananas, Peruvian silver, and Cuban sugar led the way in a continental export boom that made many fortunes, many of them British. British investment in Latin America, concentrated in railways and telecommunications, went up nine-fold between 1870 and 1913, by which time it represented two-thirds of all foreign investment in the region. When necessary, the British government used its political clout to give its businesses a helping hand. In 1879 when Chile embarked on the War of the Pacific against Peru and Bolivia, the then U.S. secretary of state, James Blaine, commented, "One shouldn't speak of a Chilean-Peruvian war, but rather of an English war against Peru with Chile as an instrument." Britain's reward lay in the hostile deserts that Chile seized from Peru, where British capital bought up the world's greatest deposits of nitrates, used as fertilizers in agriculture.

The Banana Man Comes

Among those theatrical creatures, wearing riding breeches and leggings, a pith helmet and steel-rimmed glasses, with topaz eyes and the skin of a thin rooster, there arrived in Macondo one of so many Wednesdays the chubby and smiling Mr. Herbert, who ate at the house. . . . When they brought to the table the tiger-striped bunch of bananas that they were accustomed to hang in the dining room during lunch, he picked the first piece of fruit without great enthusiasm. But he kept on eating as he spoke, tasting, chewing, more with the distraction of a wise man than the delight of a good eater, and when he finished the first bunch he asked them to bring him another. Then he took a small case with optical instruments out of the toolbox that he always carried with him. With the suspicious attention of a diamond merchant he examined the banana meticulously, dissecting it with a special scalpel, weighing the pieces on a pharmacist's scale, and calculating its breadth with a gunsmith's calipers. . . .

On the days that followed he was seen with a net and a small basket, hunting butterflies on the outskirts of town. On Wednesday a group of engineers, agronomists, hydrologists, topographers and surveyors arrived who for several weeks explored the places where Mr. Herbert had hunted his butterflies. Later on Mr. Jack Brown arrived in an extra coach that had been coupled to the yellow train and that was silverplated all over, with seats of episcopal velvet, and a roof of blue glass. Also arriving on the special car, fluttering around Mr Brown, were the solemn lawyers dressed in black.

—Gabriel García Márquez, *One Hundred Years of Solitude,* trans. Gregory Rabassa, London: Jonathan Cape, 1970

By the early twentieth century, Britain had been overtaken by the United States as the major continental power. Washington's hemispheric ambitions began with the Monroe Doctrine of 1823, which declared that "the American continents, by the free and independent condition which they have assumed and maintained, are henceforth not to be considered as subject for colonization by the European powers." Though ostensibly to protect these newly independent states from the designs of Old Europe, in practice the Monroe Doctrine provided a convenient cover for the United States' own interests. The United States steadily expanded its economic strength and political influence throughout the nineteenth century and came of age after its decisive defeat of Spain in the Cuban-Spanish War of 1898. The victory marked a symbolic changing of the guard, ushering in the "American century" in Latin America. From the 1960s, European and Asian countries such as Japan, Germany, Spain, and China rose to become major economic influences, but they did not dispute U.S. political dominance in the region. The only country that may eventually compete for dominance with the United States, at least in South America, is China. Its economic influence has grown apace over the last decade, partly because of the opening of new trade routes across the Pacific, but so far it has carefully avoided any confrontation with the United States in political and military matters.

Rise of the Multinationals

Up to the late nineteenth century, European and U.S. businesses used their capital and control over transport, processing, and marketing to ensure they obtained a low price from local growers of agricultural commodities. However, at the end of the century increasingly powerful U.S. companies decided to take over production as well in order to achieve "vertical integration"—control over each stage of production, transport, and marketing in their chosen product. The pioneers were the banana companies like United Fruit and Standard Fruit, which acquired so much power over domestic politics in countries like Honduras and Guatemala that these countries became pejoratively known as "banana republics." In the 1920s, one banana baron boasted of his company's control over local politicians, observing that "in Honduras a mule costs more than a deputy," and in 1954 United Fruit played a key role in the overthrow of Guatemala's reforming president, Jacobo Arbenz, an event that would spark a brutal and long-running civil conflict in that country. Since then the multinational companies have steadily extended their grip to most key areas of Latin America's economy, including virtually all mineral extraction, the most dynamic areas of industry, and many agricultural commodities.

Multinationals' heavy-handed behavior led to a backlash in the shape of trade union mobilization and occasional government attempts to nationalize their holdings. This prompted a rethink, and agricultural multinationals increasingly prefer to concentrate on the transport and marketing of a product, which are the most profitable areas. For example, just 10 percent of the final retail value of a banana finds its way back to the plantation owners, and only 1.5 percent to the plantation workers that grow them.

Since the Second World War, multinationals have steadily increased their influence, through a combination of new investment, buying up local companies and, since the late 1980s, scooping up a large number of state companies privatized in so-called structural adjustment programs. Today, multinationals dominate the region's exports (e.g., minerals and cereals), domestic production (e.g., cars), and services (telecoms, airlines, supermarkets, and, increasingly, public utilities such as water). Multinational companies such as Philip

Morris (tobacco), Nestlé (coffee), Chiquita and Dole (bananas), and Cargill (grain) make up an informal coalition with Western banks and commodity brokers that exerts a powerful grip on the world market in each product. Their sheer size also places them in a strong bargaining position with Third World governments competing for sources of jobs and investment and with producers seeking better prices. Recently, a new element has emerged. The government of the most powerful economy in the region—Brazil—is carefully promoting its own "national champions," that is, corporations that can compete on an equal footing with the world's largest multinationals. Indeed, Brazilian companies have come to dominate important sectors of the world market, such as the beef industry. The Brazilian giants are not seeking to force other multinationals out of the region but to find a *modus vivendi* with them. They want a seat at the table, too.

Black Gold

Petroleum is the greatest commodity of all. As a fuel and source of plastics and chemicals, it drives world industry (increasingly along with natural gas). Latin America contains major world oil and gas exporters, such as Mexico and Venezuela, and many other less fortunate countries condemned to dependence on oil imports. Over the last seventy years, control over oil has become a politically explosive issue. In 1938, Mexico became the first Latin American country to nationalize its oil industry, and in the decades that followed other countries followed suit, weakening the grip of the seven great U.S.- and European-owned oil multinationals, known as the "seven sisters." Such was the importance of oil that governments were willing to incur U.S. displeasure in the process, as when General Velasco's military government in Peru seized the installations of the International Petroleum Corporation in 1968.

In 1960 Venezuela joined Saudi Arabia and five smaller producers to found the Organization of Petroleum Exporting Countries, OPEC, which became the king of commodity cartels. Mexico refused to join for fear of U.S. trade sanctions, but both countries cashed in when OPEC shocked the industrialized world with large price rises in 1973–74 and 1978–79, taking oil from US$2.70 to US$40 a barrel. The oil producers paid the price for their defiance, as recession cut demand for oil and consumer countries responded to higher prices by investing in alternative sources of energy and energy conservation. In 1986 the ensuing price collapse took oil back down to US$10 a barrel.

State oil companies such as Petrobrás in Brazil, Pemex in Mexico, and Venezuela's PDVSA became giants, wielding great economic power and channeling large amounts of cash back into exploration and development of

Oil in Venezuela

In December 1922, Venezuela struck vast reserves of oil, changing the country's destiny overnight. Oil multinationals swiftly began operations, and by 1936 export earnings from oil were nine times those of coffee, Venezuela's other main commodity export. Yet oil wealth did not bring development. As dollars poured in, Venezuela's currency became overvalued, destroying the competitiveness of its other exports. Cheap imports undercut and wiped out domestic industry. Venezuela became an oil junkie, a consumer culture that produces nothing, its fortunes tied indissolubly to the international price of oil. When prices rocketed in the 1970s, government spending and corruption rose and the government nationalised the industry in 1976. When they fell back in the 1980s, Venezuela slumped into a debt crisis; then, following a sharp rise in international prices in the 1990s, oil was once again able to prop up the state. Now Venezuela's state oil company, PDVSA, is among the five largest oil companies in the world and a key supplier to the U.S. market, and is once more a strong voice in OPEC. Against the advice of the IMF, the Chávez government has earmarked increased oil revenues for a literacy campaign and other social programs. Venezuelans appear at last to be reaping the benefits of their subsoil wealth, but any slump in oil prices is certain to wipe out such progress. . . .

Today, Caracas is a supersonic, deafening, air-conditioned nightmare, a center of oil culture that might pass as the capital of Texas. Caracas chews gum and loves synthetic products and canned foods; it never walks, and poisons the clean air of the valley with the fumes of its motorisation; its fever to buy, consume, obtain, spend, use, get hold of everything leaves it no time to sleep. From the surrounding hillside hovels made of garbage, half a million forgotten people observe the sybaritic scene. . . .

[Lake Maracaibo] is a forest of towers. Within these iron structures the endlessly bobbing pumps have for half a century pumped up all the opulence and all the poverty of Venezuela. Alongside, flames lick skyward, burning the natural gas in a carefree gift to the atmosphere. There are pumps even in houses and on street corners of towns that spouted up, like the oil, along the lakeside—towns where clothing, food and walls are stained black with oil, and where even whores are known by oil nicknames, such as 'the Pipeline,' 'The Four Valves,' 'The Derrick,' 'The Hoist.'

—Eduardo Galeano, *Open Veins of Latin America*

new oil reserves, as well as funding the burgeoning public sector. Oil transformed Venezuela from a rural backwater to one of Latin America's wealthiest nations, although the poor did not always share in the bonanza. The price of success was pollution and debt, as Venezuela borrowed heavily on the strength of its oil reserves. In Mexico, Pemex had run up a debt of US$15 billion by the early 1980s.

State companies ensured national control over a vital resource and were able to use profits to benefit their countries. By investing in exploration, they managed to quadruple Latin America's known reserves between 1974 and 1988, as countries such as Colombia and Brazil became significant new oil producers. Yet they were also plagued by problems; a shortage of qualified managers was aggravated as governments made political appointments within the bureaucracy. Corruption and inefficiency reduced economic benefits, while nationalization risked closing the door to the oil multinationals' modern technology.

Even during the debt crisis of the 1980s, as neoliberal reforms obliged governments to privatize state assets, they were reluctant to sell off state oil companies. Oil's enormous political significance has, over the years, prompted huge domestic opposition to the sale of national oil enterprises, leading to the downfall of presidents in Bolivia and to strikes by oil workers in countries such as Brazil and Peru; meanwhile the upturn in oil prices from the late 1990s onward sustained the Chávez government in Venezuela and has allowed him to finance a wide range of social reforms. Yet most governments badly need injections of foreign capital and technology in the oil and gas sector. As a result, they have opted instead for slowly opening up the oil sector by granting exploration and production licenses to multinational oil companies, and in some cases going into joint ventures with them.

Cocaine—Just Another Commodity?

Were it not for the drug's effect abroad, coca would be lauded as an ideal export crop.
—*Financial Times*, 1990

For centuries, the leaves of the coca bush have been chewed by the peoples of the Andes, providing a mild stimulant that also stilled hunger pangs. Over the last thirty years, however, coca production has surged, as a booming market has developed for the leaves. Cocaine has provided Latin America's latest commodity boom. Although figures in this area are never more than informed guesswork, by 2005 the annual wholesale cocaine trade was estimated at US$70 billion in the United States alone, exceeding revenues of large corporations like Starbucks; it is the second most valuable commodity in the world (after oil). Every gram is produced from coca leaves grown by Latin American peasants.

In the Andean countries of Peru, Bolivia, and Colombia, thousands of small farmers depend on the scrubby coca bushes for their livelihoods. Many of them semi-process the leaves by treading them in pits filled with kerosene. The resulting coca paste is then smuggled to clandestine laboratories, where it is turned into refined cocaine powder before being shipped to the United States, Europe, and Japan. According to the U.S. State Department's 2011 International Narcotics Control Strategy report, 90 percent of the cocaine seized in 2010 by the U.S. authorities came from Colombia.

The cocaine boom began in the early 1980s, even though the drug had been known for over a hundred years and was used in various forms by such illustrious figures as Sigmund Freud and Queen Victoria. For the peasants, coca is a dream crop—its leaves can be harvested several times a year, and it needs minimal attention; buyers come to the peasants, solving the difficulties of getting the product to market that dog other crops in the remote areas where coca is grown. Moreover, its illegality ensures that big companies will not enter the market to compete and drive prices down.

However, coca's illegality has fueled corruption and criminality, in some cases undermining Latin America's political stability. In Colombia, right-wing paramilitary groups and left-wing guerrillas fund themselves with the proceeds from the cocaine trade; in Paraguay the general in charge of the country's anti-drug unit was gunned down while preparing to release evidence linking businessmen, military officers, and the police to drugs.

Over the last ten years the drug business has become more atomized, as high-profile barons such as Colombia's Pablo Escobar were captured and replaced by more diffuse, shadowy networks. The trade's general influence has changed in the process, from having a direct, tangible impact on politics—Colombia is the best example—to something more subtle, integrated into society at a much more grassroots level. Drug money has driven both the "informalization" of the economy and an alarming crime wave. Drug gangs and drug use are both on the increase; in Rio, local drug lords effectively run many *favelas* (urban shantytowns).

Internationally, the story of drugs remains one of the few about Latin America that regularly makes headlines, chiefly because of its domestic importance within the United States. Since 1986, successive U.S. presidents have made the "war on drugs" a national priority. By 2011, it was estimated that the United States was spending over US$100 billion a year on all the various programs, including the arming and training of Latin American governments and security forces to eradicate crops and intercept shipments, the funding of alternative crop programs in producer areas, and the running of international interdiction efforts. Indeed, since President Nixon declared his war on drugs in 1971, it is estimated that the United States has spent about US$1 trillion on its efforts to eradicate illegal substances. Yet all the money and publicity have achieved remarkably little: cocaine use in the States has not fallen; the street price of cocaine is at or near an all-time low; and the trade has expanded into Europe and the former Soviet bloc.

Within Latin America the impact of the "war on drugs" has been largely negative. Most of the profits from the drug trade remain in the consuming countries of the north. Meanwhile, U.S.-sponsored forced eradication and aerial herbicide spraying programs have hit poor peasant farmers hardest. Involving local armies in the drug war has both boosted their influence and corrupted many officers at a time when Washington was avowedly intent on consolidating human rights and democracy in the region. For all the high-profile eradication efforts, the number of hectares planted with coca remains remarkably resilient.

Drug policy analysts liken the drug trade to a balloon: squeezing it in one area merely causes it to expand in another. Crackdowns on producers in Peru and Bolivia have merely encouraged production in Venezuela, Panama, and particularly Colombia, which has become the region's largest producer, ahead of Peru and Bolivia. The civil war in Colombia has allowed paramilitaries and guerrillas to take over and expand the production and taxation of drugs, running a narcotic economy with military efficiency. The United States has reacted with "Plan Colombia," a military aid and crop eradication program that has achieved only limited results, despite an outlay of US$5 billion between 2000 and 2010. About four-fifths of the money has been used to finance military and security forces, giving credence to claims that it is a counterinsurgency measure disguised as an anti-drug program in order to make it more politically palatable in both the United States and Colombia.

While new drug mafias have sprung up in Bolivia, Peru, Venezuela, and Brazil, the most powerful newcomers are the Mexican cartels. They have taken great advantage of Mexico's 2,000-mile-long border with the United States and the increased cross-border traffic resulting from the North American Free Trade Agreement (NAFTA). Not surprisingly, violence has increased as the government has sought to rein in the gangs. At least 40,000 people have died since President Felipe Calderón started his war on drugs in 2007.

One of the most alarming consequences has been the rippling out of violence across the country. Until 2008, drug-related violence was concentrated in a few cities in the north of the country, such as Ciudad Juárez and Tijuana. By 2010, violence had spread to the states of Nuevo León, Tamaulipas, Guerrero, and Durango. And today states such as Jalisco and Morelos, which used to be relatively peaceful, have also been affected. Violence has also extended to groups that have nothing to do with drug trafficking. Many illegal migrants, who cross Mexico on their way to the United States, have suffered. According to the Mexican Human Rights Commission, 11,000 migrants were abducted in 2010 alone. Many were snatched in an attempt to extort money from them, while others were forced to work for the cartels. Human rights activists have also become victims of the drug war, with the murder of 27 activists between 2005 and 2010.

Money-laundering operations and transshipment routes have also spread to every corner of the continent, creating growing headaches for U.S. drug control efforts. The drug trade's resilience has been extraordinary. The death of the infamous drug baron Pablo Escobar in a shootout in 1993 led to the dismantling of the Medellín cartel in Colombia, which U.S. officials in the 1980s claimed was responsible for 80 percent of the cocaine entering the United States, yet it had no discernible impact on the supply of the drug.

Moreover, the drug cartels have become extremely skilful at adapting to new circumstances, displaying what the *The Economist* has called "all the acumen and professionalism of the big international tobacco companies." In the 1980s, individual "mules" were replaced by large-scale shipments by air and sea, but then cartels set their sights even higher: in 1997 a Miami businessman was caught trying to import a Piranha-class nuclear submarine from the Kronstadt naval base in St. Petersburg in Russia. According to U.S. Drug Enforcement Agency (DEA) officials, the plan was for Colombian cartels to use the submarine to bring shipments to California.

Although U.S. drug policy has failed, few viable alternatives are on offer. Every so often a courageous or foolhardy official suggests that drugs should be legalized, arguing that most of the drug trade's most damaging impacts on society would disappear by breaking the link with criminality. Argentina's President Cristina Fernández de Kirchner is the latest high-profile official to put forward this argument. She and others have pointed out that after the end of prohibition in the United States the control that gangsters like Al Capone had over the alcohol trade crumbled overnight. Legalization would also allow governments to tax drugs, a tantalizing prospect for any administration trying to reduce its budget deficit. Even so, given the dogmatic refusal of many Americans even to discuss such a step, it is hard to see how legalization could come about in the near future. However, it is worth considering the effect it would have on the cocaine trade: coca would become a normal commodity like tobacco, big farmers could move in and take over production from the peasant producers, who currently cultivate the coca bushes; the Colombian and Mexican cartels would suddenly be faced with stiff competition from leading multinational companies; and the U.S. and Latin American governments would no longer have to waste hundreds of millions of dollars in fruitlessly trying to combat the well-equipped and powerful drug cartels.

The other option is for the United States to recognize that as long as demand comes from the hundreds of thousands of cocaine users there, then the supply will surely follow. That would involve a substantial shift from supply-side to demand-side policies, focusing on public education within the United States, perhaps as part of a broader program of inner-city regeneration aimed at breaking the cycle of poverty and exclusion that creates new generations of drug users. Yet such a strategy is unlikely given the current state of U.S. politics. Extra funding in recent years has been directed at faith-based programs for addicts as well as stricter policing. Until a shift in the political agenda occurs, it seems unlikely that Congress will act as an open and rational forum for debate.

Silent Revolution:
Market Economics

Growing Pains: Industrialization, the Debt Crisis, and Neoliberalism

São Paulo is made of cheap concrete. Millions of tons, poured in a hurry, spewed forth to make houses, tower blocks, factories, and flyovers. Within a few years rain and sun leave it stained and crumbling, but quantity matters more than quality, for dilapidated buildings can always be replaced by bigger and newer constructions, using yet more concrete. The flood of concrete that created the great megalopolis of São Paulo is part of Brazil's rush for industrialization, a titanic effort that has turned a relatively primitive coffee exporter into an industrial power, the fifth-largest economy in the world. However, like the concrete, Brazil's industrial development is flawed and vulnerable. To pay for it, the national economy ran up huge debts in the 1970s, driving the country to the verge of bankruptcy during the debt crisis of the 1980s. State-led industrialization also failed the Brazilian people. In the main thoroughfares of São Paulo, the rush hour is a stampede of the well-heeled, the manicured, and beautiful beneficiaries of Brazil's growth. On the street corners the losers, the old and unemployed, earn a pittance working as human billboards. Standing in bored clumps all day, they wear T-shirts saying "I buy gold," with a phone number. Thanks to a much enhanced social welfare program, implemented over the last decade, far fewer Brazilians go hungry than in the past, but the country's industrial sector still provides relatively few jobs. It has not become the economic powerhouse that many Brazilians dreamed of.

For half a century after the Great Depression of the 1930s, Latin Americans saw industrialization as the path to development. The satanic mills whose fumes now choke Caracas or Mexico City may seem unlikely saviors, but the region's planners pointed to the experience of the rich countries, like the UK, United States, or Japan, where the growth of industry had led to a rise in both political power and the standard of living. Industrialization, they argued, offered Latin America a way out of its crippling dependence on commodity exports, and its humiliating reliance on foreign governments and multinational companies for aid and manufactured goods.

Latin America's industrial quest started late. During the colonial period, the Spanish and Portuguese governments did everything they could to prevent the growth of domestic industry, which they feared would disrupt the continent's dependence on commodity exports. In 1785 a royal decree from the Portuguese crown banned all industry in its Brazilian colony, ordering all textile looms to be burned. When independence arrived in the early nineteenth century, Britain's cheap manufactures soon undercut what little local industry had arisen as the colonial ties weakened. Nevertheless, most countries managed to achieve a first stage of industrialization; they semi-processed agricultural crops and minerals for export, and local industries produced simple goods like soap, clothing, and bottled drinks. European immigrants set up many of the first local industries—in Argentina and Uruguay British immigrants built slaughterhouses, freezer plants, and tanneries to serve the beef export industry, while Germans set up Peru's beer industry and controlled 90 percent of Brazil's textile production by 1916.

Despite these primitive local industries, Latin America remained a commodity exporter, dependent on manufactured imports, until the late 1920s. By then, the cattle and grain trade had made Argentina the fifth-richest country in the world, and coffee had established São Paulo as Brazil's economic heartland. In 1929 the Wall Street crash and the ensuing Depression in the industrialized world rudely awoke Latin American governments to the perils of commodity dependence. Brazil's exports fell by 60 percent between 1929 and 1932, and the country suddenly had no hard currency with which to import manufactured goods. Latin America learned its lesson. Just like the U.S. government under Roosevelt's New Deal, or the followers of John Maynard Keynes in the UK, they concluded that the state had to play a much greater role in running the economy if future crashes were to be avoided. In Latin America, as local entrepreneurs moved in to start producing simple manufactured goods to plug the gap left by the import collapse, several governments began looking at ways to encourage "import substitution." By the late 1930s they were taking the first steps to improve transport, electricity, and water supplies for local factories. When the Second World War came, the dilemma of the Great Depression was reversed; the industrialized nations were now desperate for Latin America's exports, but had fewer manufactures to spare as factories were converted to war production. The largest Latin American economies accumulated great wealth during the war, and afterward used it to begin import substitution in earnest.

Besides improving national infrastructure, countries such as Argentina, Brazil, and Mexico set up state-owned companies in strategic industries such as iron and steel, and raised taxes on imported manufactured goods. These tariff barriers were essential to protect fledgling local industries from being undercut by cheap imports. At the same time, governments encouraged multi-national companies to set up factories on Latin American soil, arguing that this would create jobs while providing the technology and capital that the region lacked. Volkswagen built its first factory in Brazil in 1949, with other car producers from the United States, West Germany, and Japan hot on its heels. By 1970, 80 percent of the country's cars were assembled in Brazil itself.

The initial results of import substitution were impressive. Between 1950 and 1970 Latin America's Gross Domestic Product (GDP, a measure of all goods and services produced) tripled, and even in per capita terms it rose by two-thirds. In the mid-1950s, Latin America's economies were growing faster than those of the industrialized West. By the early 1960s, domestic industry supplied 95 percent of Mexico's and 98 percent of Brazil's consumer goods. By this time, however, there were already clear signs that the model was approaching exhaustion, as state-led development in Latin America began to suffer much the same fate as the state-run economies in Eastern Europe. Protected industries had no need to invest or innovate, and fell behind the rest of the world in technology and productivity; political interference encouraged corruption and incompetence, as people were appointed to run state companies on the basis of political favoritism rather than merit. The ever-growing state sector began to outspend meager revenues (rich Latin Americans have always been adept at avoiding taxes), generating growing inflation.

In social terms, import substitution also failed. Latin America and the Caribbean have always had hugely unequal societies, and import substitution further aggravated the situation. In order to keep wage costs down in industry, governments held down food prices, penalizing the peasant farmers who grew the food and creating poverty in the countryside. Millions of peasants gave up hope of earning a living from the land and drifted to the cities, where they joined the armies of job seekers in the shantytowns that sprang up on the edges of the continent's cities. Some achieved their ambition of a steady, waged job, but most ended up as street sellers, domestic servants, or doing odd jobs.

The local market for manufactured goods was limited because most people in Latin America were too poor to buy more than the most basic necessities. This prevented industry from growing and reducing costs through mass production. Even Brazil, the most populous country in the region, faced this problem, although there was at least a significant middle class to buy locally produced goods, enabling Brazilian industry to outperform its Spanish American counterparts. The problem of a small domestic market could have been solved if wealth were redistributed to allow more people to buy goods, but that option was ruled out by the wealthy elite.

Initially, governments responded to the lack of an internal market by establishing a variety of free trade agreements with other Latin American nations. Organizations such as the Latin American Free Trade Association and the Central American Common Market, both established in 1960, soon foundered, however, because the smaller countries opened their markets to the more industrialized nations in the agreement, but received little in return.

The Dance of the Millions

Many Latin American governments were forced to adopt austerity programs to cope with the slowdown in growth. In Brazil and Argentina, military governments seized power in order to implement such unpopular policies. They used both the law and brute force to suppress trade unions and lower the living standards of the poor majority. The major economies then set off in pursuit of the elusive third stage of industrialization, the move from import substitution to becoming an exporter of manufactured goods. This meant large-scale investments, which had to be funded by foreign capital. Latin America turned to the international loan sharks. The initial results were astonishing. In just thirteen years, from 1967 to 1980, Latin America's manufactured exports increased in value forty-fold, from US$1 billion a year to US$40 billion.

Brazil led the field in both industrialization and the race for foreign loans. In 1958, it overtook Argentina as the region's leading industrial power. By 1961 it was self-sufficient in electric stoves, refrigerators, and television sets. Vehicle production boomed from 31,000 in 1957 to 514,000 in 1971. In 1968 Brazilian industry finally outstripped agriculture as the major wealth producer in the country. By 1988 Brazil's industrial output was twice that of Mexico, and nearly five times that of Argentina, and by 1996 four of Latin America's top five companies were Brazilian. The onetime coffee producer had become the region's superpower.

As the factories multiplied, so did the foreign debt. The big borrowers were the state corporations that dominated the politically vital areas of steel, petroleum, and electricity production. By the early 1980s, Mexico's petroleum corporation, Pemex, had run up a debt of US$15 billion. State and private banks also borrowed heavily abroad, in order to re-lend to local businesses.

The "dance of the millions," as the round of frenzied foreign borrowing became known, took off after the oil price rise in 1973–74. OPEC oil producers recycled their new wealth to Western banks, which in turn were anxious to find outlets for their "petrodollars." Latin America seemed the ideal borrower; it had decades of steady growth and industrialization already behind it, and countries such as Mexico and Venezuela were sitting on huge oil reserves. Foreign bankers fell over themselves to lend as much as possible, as fast as possible. Since they assumed that governments could not go bankrupt, they paid little attention to where the money was actually going. In practice, it went into a number of unproductive areas, such as capital flight, in which government officials and business leaders siphoned billions of dollars out of the country back into U.S. bank accounts; prestige "megaprojects" such as hydroelectric dams and roads; and arms, as military governments went on a spending spree for the latest hardware for their troops. In all, US$60 billion in foreign loans entered Latin America between 1975 and 1982. Sixty percent of the money went to Brazil and Mexico, as they and Argentina became the Third World's top three debtors. In Mexico, the rain of dollars funded exploration and development of the oil industry; in Brazil it fueled the country's further rise as an industrial power. Brazil was the only country to successfully make the leap to the third stage of industrialization as an exporter of manufactured goods. Between 1970 and 1978 it doubled its proportion of the region's exports, becoming a producer of a vast range of goods, from computers to aircraft.

The dance of the millions ended abruptly in August 1982, when the Mexican government announced that it could no longer pay the interest due on its foreign debt. Many U.S. and other banks suddenly realized that what had seemed a safe and lucrative loans business in Latin America could drive them into bankruptcy if other countries followed Mexico's lead. The announcement sent a shudder through the international banking community, raising fears of a run on the banks and a possible collapse of the world financial system. The following weeks established the pattern for years to come. The banks and creditor governments worked together to find a solution—not to the problem of Mexico's excessive debt repayments, but to remove the threat to the banking system. The initial remedy was a hastily improvised affair whereby the financial system would reschedule debt repayments and lend Mexico new money, purely so that it could give it straight back as interest payments. This would avoid the banks having to write off Mexico's loans as bad debts, which would in turn have damaged their profits and sent their shares plunging on the stock market.

By early 1984, every Latin American nation except Venezuela, Colombia, and Paraguay had been forced into similar rescheduling deals. Cuba and Nicaragua also avoided such agreements, since Washington was imposing an effective financial boycott on both left-leaning governments. In each case the creditors stuck together, but insisted on negotiating with each debtor nation separately. Rescheduling was good business for the banks, since they could exact particularly high interest rates in exchange for deferring repayments. In return for rescheduling US$49.5 billion in loans, the banks earned an extra US$1.7 billion. At the same time, they ended virtually all new lending to Latin American nations, other than that needed to enable them to keep up with interest payments on the original loans.

The immediate cause of the debt crisis was the sudden rise in U.S. interest rates announced by newly elected President Reagan in 1981. Since Latin America's debts had been largely contracted at floating interest rates, this meant a massive increase in its interest payments. Each time the international interest rate rose by 1 percent, it added nearly US$2 billion a year to the developing countries' bills. At the same time the austerity policies of "Reaganomics" and the second OPEC price rise of 1979 produced a

Figure 1.1: Total Foreign Debt and Capital Flows to and from Latin America and the Caribbean, 1975–2004

*Net incoming capital minus net payments on utilities and interest.
Source: UN Economic Commission for Latin America and the Caribbean.

sharp recession in the industrialized nations, which cut demand for Latin America's manufactured exports and sent commodity prices tumbling. Latin America earned less hard currency for its exports, just as it needed to pay more interest on its debt.

The role of the West's debt collector went to the International Monetary Fund (IMF), a multilateral funding agency controlled by the wealthy industrialized countries. Its role in the debt crisis earned the IMF another name: the Institute for Misery and Famine. For Sir William Ryrie, a top World Bank official, the debt crisis was "a blessing in disguise." It forced Latin America into a constant round of debt negotiations, providing the Reagan government, along with the IMF and the other international financial institutions, with all the leverage they needed to overhaul the region's economy, in alliance with northern commercial creditor banks and the region's home-grown free marketeers. The state-led model was discredited, monetarism was in the ascendant with champions in the White House and Downing Street—and Latin America was ripe for a free-market revolution.

From then on, almost all of Latin America and the Caribbean followed a similar path. In the initial stage of reform, known as "stabilization," the IMF and banks pressured governments both to crack down on inflation by cutting spending and to keep up their debt repayments by cutting their imports and generating a trade surplus. At the same time, commercial banks decided Latin America had become a bad risk, and stopped lending. Throughout the 1980s, capital flowed out of Latin America, destined for the rich countries of the north. This perverse flow of wealth from the poor to the wealthy squeezed out US$218.6 billion, over US$500 for every man, woman, and child in the region.

With time, reforms moved on to a broader process known as "structural adjustment," involving a relentless assault on the state's role in the economy, including cuts in social spending, privatization, and deregulation of everything from trade to banking to employers' abilities to hire and fire at will. The aim of such measures was to move Latin America and the Caribbean rapidly to a dynamic market-based economy, but for many years the panorama was largely one of recession and austerity.

Silent Revolution

Everyone smoked in the Mexican stock exchange, a beautiful new 20-story mirror-glass building shaped like a box cutter, slicing into the smog of downtown Mexico City. It was 1992, and on a roundabout in the street below a grimy statue of an Aztec emperor cut a forlorn figure, marooned in the traffic. Inside, away from the glare of the sun, the disciples of the new economic order rushed to and fro: well-groomed men shouting orders to shoulder-padded peroxide-haired women. On the trading floor, green computer screens were the only color to break the gray and silver monochrome of business suits and stainless steel fittings.

Efraín Caro was the exchange's director of international affairs. He was thirty-three, but looked younger. On the wall of his office a *Wall Street Journal* cartoon showed an executive being told by his boss, "It has come to my attention that you're not under enough stress." The following week, Efraín was hosting a worldwide conference for representatives from sixty stock markets, and he had stress to spare. Chain-smoking, grabbing phones, shouting orders to subordinates even younger than himself, he spared ten minutes to rattle off figures in perfect English: in 1992 the Mexican stock market was booming, pulling in a total of US$22 billion in foreign investments, 80 percent of it raised on Wall Street. That day's papers carried vital news from the presidential campaign in the United States: "Clinton Says Yes to NAFTA." Efraín believed the dollars would be coming forever.

By 2005, it was clear that Efraín had mistaken a brief boom for Latin America's eternally elusive sustained prosperity. The Mexican economy crashed in 1994, requiring a massive US$54 billion bailout from the U.S. government and the IMF. No sooner was the region back on its feet than a series of crashes in Asia and Russia led to a crisis in Brazil, and effectively ended the era of easy

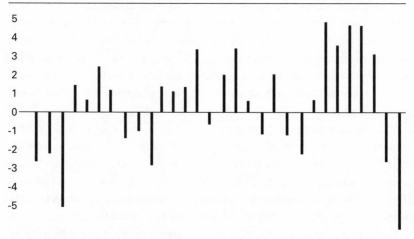

Figure 1.2: The Latin American Roller Coaster: Percentage Increase/Decrease in GDP Per Capita, 1982–2010

Source: UN Economic Commission for Latin America and the Caribbean.

access to capital. A global recession didn't help. Over the last twenty years of the twentieth century, Latin America's growth and investment curves looked like a particularly violent roller coaster.

The slump in Latin America's economy precipitated by the debt crisis contributed to one war and several bloody anti-IMF riots. Argentina's military leaders invaded the Falklands/Malvinas Islands to divert attention from a collapsing economy, while riots, protests, and looting afflicted cities across the continent. Prior to the 1980s, Latin Americans were accustomed to a growing economy. In every year between 1964 and 1980, the regional economy grew by more than 4 percent, making the recession that hit in 1982 all the more painful. In 1982 Latin America's economy shrank in real terms for the first time since the Second World War. Chile was the worst hit, with per capita GDP falling by 14.5 percent in a single year. The despair of Chile's unemployed workforce was captured in the lyrics of one of its top rock bands in the late 1980s, Los Prisioneros:

> They're idle, waiting for the hands
> that decide to make them run again.
> The mist surrounds and rusts them. . . .
> I drag myself along the damp cement,
> remembering a thousand laments.
> Of when the misery came, when they said
> don't come back, don't come back, don't come back.
> The factories, all the factories have gone.

The cause of the collapse was the austerity programs implemented under IMF pressure to keep debt repayments flowing. The extraction of wealth from the region left a large hole in the economy in the form of an investment collapse. Governments forced to adopt IMF austerity measures found it less politically costly to cut public investment than to sack employees in the middle of a recession (although many did that as well), while the private sector was deterred from investing both by the impossibility of borrowing abroad and by the recession and high interest rates at home, as governments lifted interest rates to fight inflation. Foreign investors also took flight. Across the region, gross domestic investment (which includes both local and foreign investment) collapsed from US$213 billion in 1980 to US$136 billion in 1983. The level of investment is crucial to any economy's prospects; Latin America was mortgaging its people's future to pay its debts.

Falling investment and the domestic recession brought about by austerity programs provoked an industrial collapse. By 1983, the degree of industrial development in Latin America had regressed to the levels of 1966. In Argentina and Peru it was back to 1960 levels, while in Chile and Uruguay it was more like 1950.

The 1980s were a period of recession and false starts, as governments desperately sought a way out of the debt crisis and continued to send billions of dollars to overseas creditors. By 1991, the capital tide had turned. Although debt repayments continued, foreign investors rediscovered the region, and started pouring money in again. They did so partly because pickings were thin elsewhere, partly because they were lured in by the latest component of Latin America's neoliberal reforms: from the late 1980s governments had been privatizing the state assets built up over fifty years of import substitution.

The pressures on governments to privatize seemed irresistible. The growing fiscal crisis of the state sector, provoked by both foreign and domestic debt payments, forced governments to increase revenue or cut expenditure; privatization achieves both, shedding loss-making companies while raising substantial amounts of cash. In Argentina, President Carlos Menem's selling spree raised US$9.8 billion in cash, and enabled the government to lop a further US$15.6 billion off its foreign debt between 1989 and 1993 as transnational corporations bought up paper debt and swapped it for a stake in the newly privatized companies. In Mexico, the family silver raised a total of US$13.7 billion in 1990–91, during which time privatization receipts provided just under a tenth of government revenues.

Privatization was also part of the broader ideological shift, since neoliberals believe in cutting back the state and passing ever larger chunks of the economy over to the private sector. Once privatized, they argue, management will be able to take decisions based on economic efficiency rather than politics, and a company's performance is bound to improve. The rhetoric employed was the same as in Margaret Thatcher's Britain, the only country to surpass the large Latin American economies in its privatizing zeal. In Latin America, privatization provided a juicy carrot with which to attract foreign investment back into the region after the capital famine of the debt crisis. Transnational corporations were expected to introduce capital and new technology into a region starved of both.

State airlines and telecommunications companies went on the block throughout the region, but only Argentina and Bolivia allowed the rush to market to sweep away their state oil companies. Elsewhere, governments were reluctant to hand over such strategic or highly profitable companies, preferring instead to encourage joint ventures with transnational corporations to attract technology and investment while retaining some degree of overall control. In recent years, public opinion has moved heavily against privatization of national and natural resources, and this has been reflected in government policies. Argentina has set up a new state oil and gas company. Bolivia has imposed tough new operating conditions on private companies, including a measure of renationalization. Operating conditions for foreign investors have also been tightened in Venezuela and Ecuador.

The track record of privatization varied enormously. Areas that urgently required injections of capital and cutting-edge technology, such as telecommunications, clearly benefited, but critics of the privatization process argue that governments missed the chance to divide up giant companies and introduce competition, and were lax in regulating the newly privatized companies. There was often a lack of transparency and accountability in the privatization process, and corruption undermined public support even further. Privatization programs were, however, extremely good news for the local business class with the capital (often through joint ventures with foreign companies) to snap up the bargains. Mexico's stock of billionaires rose from two to twenty-four during the privatizing presidency of Carlos Salinas de Gortari (1988–94), all of them with close ties to the ruling Institutional Revolutionary Party (PRI). In another echo of the British experience, Chile's pioneering privatizers in the 1970s operated a highly questionable revolving-door system, moving from government posts in which they oversaw the privatizations to top jobs in the big conglomerates who cashed in on the sell-offs.

In Mexico and Argentina, the sudden inflows of dollars produced a short-lived rerun of the dance of the millions, as governments abandoned austerity in favor of reducing inflation by using the exchange rate. Overvalued currencies made imports artificially cheap, keeping prices down at home. Not surprisingly, imports boomed, but governments were able to use the incoming capital, as long as it lasted, to cover the resulting trade gap. It lasted until 1994, when a series of political crises, including the Zapatista uprising in Chiapas and the assassination of the PRI's anointed successor to Carlos Salinas, made foreign investors reassess Mexican risk. Capital flows to Mexico fell away, producing a run on the peso, a devaluation, and a devastating recession, costing two million jobs over the course of 1995. In what was called the "tequila effect," foreign investors also pulled out of Argentina, which was pursuing a similar policy to that of Mexico, provoking massive recession and unemployment there during 1995. Capital inflows recovered their pre-tequila levels in 1997 only to fall away again, slowly at first and then spectacularly in the wake of the Argentine crisis of 2001. Under pressure from global financial institutions, governments had little option but to return to the more painful 1980s style of adjustment.

By disposing of loss-making companies and pulling in one-off windfalls, the privatization bonanza did, however, play a crucial part in curbing governments' spending deficits and getting inflation down in many Latin American countries in the early 1990s. Inflation in the region as a whole peaked

Soft Fruit, Hard Labor

Orchards fill the Aconcagua valley northeast of Santiago in Chile. Parallel rows of peach trees stretch off to infinity, playing tricks with the eye. The monotony is punctuated by the occasional fat-trunked palm tree or weeping willow, shining with new leaf on a cold and dusty spring day.

Carlos Vidal is a union leader, president of the local *temporeros,* the temporary farm laborers who plant, pick and pack the peaches, kiwi fruit and grapes for the tables of Europe, Asia and North America. A shock of black curls streaked with gray fringe his round, gap-toothed face. A freezing wind off the nearby Andes blows across the vineyards as Carlos tells his story:

"On this land there were 48 families who got land under [former president] Allende. We grew vegetables, maize and beans together, as an *asentamiento* [farming cooperative]. There were a few fruit farms then, but we planned them. After the coup [in 1973] the land was divided up between 38 families—the others had to leave. Then it started to get difficult, we got the land but nothing else; the military auctioned off the machinery.

"Then the *empresarios* [entrepreneurs] started to arrive, especially an Argentine guy called Melitón Moreno. The bank started taking people's land—foreclosing on loans—and Moreno bought it up. Three *compañeros* [comrades] committed suicide here because they lost their farms. Melitón got bank loans and bought yet more land and machinery. He planted nothing but fruit—grapes at first, then others.

"My father was a leader of the *asentamiento.* The first year after the coup we were hungry; lunch was a sad time. We began to sell everything in the house, then we looked for a *patrón* to sell us seeds and plough our land for us, and we paid him with part of the harvest. Next year we got a bank loan and managed to pay it off, but the following year they sold us bad seed. We lost all the maize and the whole thing collapsed. We had to sell the land and Melitón Moreno bought it.

"Of the 38 families, most are now *temporeros.* We all sold our land but kept our houses and a small garden to grow food. Trouble is, even the gardens are no good, the water's full of pesticides from the fruit. This area used to be famous for watermelons and now they don't grow properly any more. They chuck fertilizer and pesticide everywhere; it doesn't matter that the earth is dead because the fruit trees live artificially. No one grows potatoes or maize any more—it's cheaper to buy the imported ones from Argentina."

—Duncan Green, *Silent Revolution: The Rise and Crisis of Market Economics in Latin America* at around 1,200 percent in 1989 and 1990. After that privatizations, further government cuts in spending and investment, and improved tax collection all helped to get fiscal deficits down. By 2000, inflation was down to single figures and the hyperinflationary nightmares of the previous decades were starting to fade.

Regional Integration

The region's shift away from import substitution toward the merits of "export-led growth" also saw a renewed interest in free trade agreements. Within Latin America dozens of bilateral and multilateral agreements have been signed since the late 1980s, the largest being the Southern Cone Common Market, Mercosur, which came into operation in 1995, bringing together Argentina, Brazil, Uruguay, and Paraguay.

The best-known free trade agreement in the region, and the only one in the world between the First and Third Worlds, is the North American Free Trade Agreement (NAFTA), between Mexico, the United States, and Canada, which came into force in 1994. By 2009, NAFTA had phased out almost all trade tariffs and restrictions on foreign investment between the three countries. Its many critics argue that it is little more than a "charter of corporate rights," working to the benefit of large corporations at the expense of the poor. Big companies in the United States relocated to Mexico in order to cut wages, thereby increasing unemployment in the States. Although some Mexicans found jobs in the new factories, far more have suffered the impact of ending tariffs on imported maize, which is produced on heavily subsidized commercial U.S. farms at a fraction of the cost of Mexican-grown maize. Mexican business reports claim that 1.3 million jobs have been lost in the agricultural sector as a direct result of the treaty. Meanwhile, the purported benefits of NAFTA—capital inflows, factory relocation—began to fall off dramatically as U.S. firms turned to China for cheap labor and high productivity.

In 2005 the Central American Free Trade Agreement (CAFTA) came into force. It reduced trade and investment barriers between the Central American republics (plus, bizarrely, the Dominican Republic) and the United States. Like NAFTA, it is an agreement between profoundly unequal players that allows consumers in the poorer countries to enjoy the benefits of cheap food imports, the latest computer technology, and even the dubious delights of an invasion of U.S. fast-food chains, but it also condemns them to trade on their comparative advantage (cheap labor and raw materials) rather than allowing them to upgrade their industry, as South Korea and Taiwan did so successfully in the second half of the twentieth century. Such industries struggle to emerge when a free trade agreement (FTA) forces the economy to remain open to competition from already established U.S. companies.

Both NAFTA and CAFTA have been highly controversial. Critics have argued that they have not brought improvements in the standard of living of most of the people but have only deepened economic and social inequalities that existed prior to these agreements. Partly as a result, the U.S. dream of turning Latin America, Central America, and the Caribbean into one vast free trade area, to be called the Free Trade Area of the Americas (FTAA), has been shelved, after widespread protests by leaders and members of the general public. Instead, Latin America has pushed ahead, albeit cautiously, with the expansion of its alternative trading bloc, Mercosur, to stand as a counterweight to NAFTA and CAFTA. Founded in 1991, it now has ten members. Progress has been slow, partly because of fears among some countries that Brazil may try to use the body to impose its dominance. More recently, the region has also felt the need to set up a political body, outside the influence of the United States, to represent the region, called the Community of Latin American and Caribbean States (CELAC). At the same time, the Organization of American States (OAS), which used to be the leading regional body and includes the United States and Canada (but not Cuba), has been losing credibility, largely because it is widely seen as a mouthpiece for Washington. All these developments are indicative of the growing independence of the region or, more accurately, of some important countries and trading blocs within it, from the United States.

The Lost Decade

The Third World War has already started—a silent war, not for that reason any the less sinister. This war is tearing down Brazil, Latin America and practically all the Third World. Instead of soldiers dying there are children, instead of millions of wounded there are millions of unemployed, instead of destruction of bridges there is the tearing down of factories, schools, hospitals, and entire economies.

—LUIZ INÁCIO LULA DA SILVA,
Brazilian labor leader (later president), 1985

The profound economic transformation of Latin America in the 1980s and 1990s was only achieved at enormous social cost. Throughout the region, after decades in which the percentage of Latin Americans living in poverty had been falling (though not their actual number), poverty was once again on the rise. By 2002, more than 70 million new names had joined the grim roll call of the poor, leaving 44 percent of the population—more than 220 million

Dollarization

In response to the economic volatility of the 1980s and 1990s, some of the smaller Latin American economies concluded that the luxury of a national currency could no longer be justified, and opted for the U.S. dollar instead. Ecuador (2000) and El Salvador (2001) joined Panama, which had been dollarized since 1903, in abandoning their currencies. In so doing, they relinquished much of their ability to manage their economies, along with the income that governments gain from printing money, known as *seigniorage.* Without their own exchange rates, their interest rates are effectively determined by the U.S. Federal Reserve, plus whatever risk premium global markets attach to the country in question, leaving only one of the three main levers of economic policy (fiscal, i.e. public finances) still available to these governments. That means that governments running into any kind of trouble have little option but to cut spending.

The argument for dollarization is particularly strong for smaller economies, where floating exchange rates have traditionally proved more volatile and currency fluctuations have a more direct effect on inflation. Ecuador, however, also demonstrates the perils. Following dollarization, it proved unable to get inflation down to U.S. rates, leading to a steady loss of competitiveness. Although this was masked to an extent by new oil finds, which continued to bring in dollars, without the option of devaluation the government faced the prospect of a severe domestic recession, which would at some point get prices back in alignment.

Dollarization is just the latest twist in an economic conundrum for Latin American governments—what to do about exchange rates? Dollarization is also political. For many citizens, the loss of their familiar national currency is a compelling symbol of a loss of power and sovereign identity. These days the received wisdom in Latin America is that there are only two options: dollarization or floating exchange rates. Any attempt to find a middle ground, for example, by pegging currencies temporarily to the dollar in order to ride out fluctuations, merely offers global market speculators a juicy incitement to gamble on being able to force countries to a devaluation. This was a factor in, for instance, the economic collapse in Argentina in 2001–2.

—Duncan Green, *Silent Revolution: The Rise and Crisis of Market Economics in Latin*

people—living in poverty. In rural areas, particularly in Central America, this figure rose to as much as 70 percent. Almost half of Latin America's poor, around 97 million people, were indigent, barely existing on an income of less than a dollar a day. As the poor got poorer, the rich got richer, especially the very rich: according to *Forbes* magazine, the number of Latin American billionaires rose from 6 in 1987 to 42 in 1994 and to 51 in 2011.

Neoliberal reforms exacerbated poverty and inequality in numerous ways. According to a UN report at the time, the main cause of increasing poverty and inequality was the "massive decline in real wages ... the rise in unemployment and ... the number of people employed in very low productivity jobs." State cutbacks, recession, and unemployment all combined to suppress wages, as did adjustment policies designed to "flexibilize" the labor market. In practice, this has meant cracking down on trade unions and making it easier for managers to hire and fire employees, enforce part-time work, and cut costs by subcontracting work to smaller companies, often little more than sweatshops.

Women bore the brunt of adjustment. Many of the new low-waged or part-time jobs generated by adjustment went to women, while many men lost their role as family breadwinner, as full-time waged jobs disappeared, or wages fell so far that a single income became insufficient to feed a family. On top of this "double day" of work and running the home, the deterioration of social services, especially in urban areas, forced women into a third role: taking responsibility for running their communities, fighting or substituting for inadequate state services in schools, health, drainage, water supply, or roads.

Adjustment made all these tasks more vital to the family's survival and more exhausting: "flexibilization" often meant lower wages, longer hours, and greater insecurity, just as cuts in state subsidies brought steep price rises in basics like food and public transport. One study of women in a shantytown in Guayaquíl, Ecuador, gave a graphic picture of the impact of adjustment on women. The research found that the women were affected by adjustment in three different ways. About 30 percent of the women were coping, juggling the competing demands of their three roles in the workplace, home, and community. They were more likely to be in stable relationships with partners who had steady jobs. Another group, about 15 percent of the women, were simply "burnt-out," no longer able to be superwomen 24 hours a day. They were most likely to be single mothers or the main breadwinners and were often older women, physically and mentally exhausted after the effort of bringing up a family against such heavy odds. They tried to hand over all household responsibilities to their oldest daughter, while their younger children frequently dropped out of school and roamed the streets. The remaining 55 percent were described as simply "hanging on," sacrificing their families by sending sons out to work or keeping daughters home from school to help with the housework.

Although curbing inflation undoubtedly improved the quality of life of the poor, adjustment policies also exacerbated poverty by removing food subsidies and other price controls. The combined impact of changes to prices and the labor market under adjustment shifted poverty from the rural to the urban areas.

The Argentine Crash

Neoliberalism in itself did not guarantee immunity from severe economic crisis. Argentina under President Carlos Menem (1989–99) was governed according to strict neoliberal dogma and yet this did not prevent Menem from creating the conditions for a disastrous economic collapse, which finally erupted in late 2001 and led to a horrific decline of 11 percent in economic output in 2002. The roots of the crisis go back to the country's problem of runaway inflation, which was finally resolved in 1991, when the government pegged the peso to the dollar. This step, which effectively prevented devaluation, meant that the government could issue pesos only if they were backed by dollar reserves. In the event of a fiscal deficit, the government's only option was to borrow dollars to cover the gap, thereby adding to its foreign debt.

And fiscal deficit there was, but the cause was not so much government profligacy or corruption as pension privatization. Urged on by the World Bank and IMF, Argentina moved rapidly from a state to a private pension system. The problem was the transition period, during which the government no longer received pension contributions, but still had to pay out pensions guaranteed under the old system. In addition, bungled and corrupt privatizations, often at the behest of the IMF, led to a high-cost economy, with tariffs for phones and electricity raised to ten times international rates. All this led to the peso becoming severely overvalued, but it could not be devalued, as it was pegged to the U.S. dollar. With hindsight, Argentina should have gradually loosened the bond (as happened in neighboring Brazil, which had also ended inflation by pegging the local currency to the dollar). As it was, the overvalued currency and the trade liberalization led to a surge of imports that destroyed the country's industry and inflated the trade deficit.

The vulnerability of the economy was finally exposed by the slump in international capital flows after the Asian crisis of 1997–98. The government staggered on, raising interest rates in a vain effort to pull in the dollars needed to service its escalating debt, but collapse was inevitable and, when it arrived, spectacular. A cascade of protests, falling presidents (three in a week—one declared the biggest sovereign default in history, on public-sector debt of US$80 billion), and bank closures prompted Latin America's greatest-ever peacetime economic slump, before the left-of-center government of Néstor Kirchner to office. The economy bounced back quickly, with Argentina being the fastest growing economy in the Western Hemisphere for a few years. Cristina Fernández, Kirchner's wife, was elected as his successor in 2007 and then reelected in October 2011.

Globalization

Globalization describes the process whereby individuals, groups, companies, and countries become increasingly interconnected. This interconnectedness occurs in several arenas:

FOREIGN DIRECT INVESTMENT: The inexorable rise of giant transnational corporations (TNCs) lies at the heart of globalization. Brand names, from Nike to Coca-Cola, have become some of the most widely recognized images on the planet. In 2011, Walmart's sales came to $419 billion, more than the GDP of all 35 low-income countries put together or of major economies such as Argentina, South Africa, or Norway.

TRADE: Between 1990 and 2000, world trade in goods and services rose from US$4.3 trillion to US$8 trillion. By 2010, that number had jumped to US$18.9 trillion. Poor countries concentrated on raw materials, clothes, footwear, electronics, and food—in the UK, a trip down the aisle of the local supermarket reveals asparagus from Peru, mangoes from Brazil, and wine from Chile and Argentina.

An anti-U.S. demonstration in Caracas, Venezuela (Latinphoto).

TECHNOLOGY: The accelerating pace of innovation in information technology (IT) is driving globalization. The cost of a three-minute phone call from New York to London fell from US$245 in 1930 to US$3 in 1990 and to less than 20 cents in 2011. Using 24-hour email, companies can split up their assembly lines between countries on different sides of the globe, sending designs and orders down the phone line and shifting components from one country to another to minimize costs. IT can cut costs and create a global village, but has awakened fears of a growing "digital divide" between the haves and have-nots.

CAPITAL FLOWS: Capital flows, increasingly disconnected from any real trade or investment, grew enormously from 1990. By 2010, the average daily global turnover in traditional foreign exchange markets stood at US$4 trillion, 80 times the volume of global exports (goods and services). In contrast to the "real economy," financial transactions move around in the Alice-in-Wonderland world of swaps, derivatives, futures, and currency trading. Globalization's supporters argue that capital flows can provide much-needed investment. However, such massive capital flows have caused severe social and economic crises in Thailand, Korea, Indonesia, Russia, and Argentina. The World Bank has found that these crises tend to hit the poor hardest, while subsequent recoveries benefit the better off, ratcheting up inequality.

The Search for a New Paradigm

Until the beginning of the twenty-first century, Latin America seemed fairly resigned to the neoliberal model foisted upon the region by the United States, the IMF, the World Bank, and the World Trade Organization in alliance with foreign investors, the global money markets, and home-grown neoliberals among the region's elites. The neoliberal agenda survived, relatively unscathed, three enormous economic collapses—Mexico in 1994–95, Brazil in 1999, and Argentina in 2001–2. Since then, however, memories of runaway inflation have dimmed and the population has grown tired of the social cost of the harsh neoliberal model. Many countries have elected left-leaning governments, which have sought to bring some degree of social and economic justice to the millions of Latin Americans who have been excluded from the benefits of neoliberal economic growth. How successful have these attempts been?

Brazil, the largest country in Latin America, has tried to combine some of the benefits of the neoliberal reforms, such as increased efficiency and

Cartoneros

A stroll in downtown Buenos Aires is bound to include the fabled Avenida Corrientes, alive with lights and people 24 hours a day. In 2003 it was still possible to follow the avenue towards the river at midnight and find open bookshops to browse in after coming out of a theatre or restaurant. Locals—*porteños*—can tell that the facades are shabbier and the bookshops fewer, and they miss the crowds that used to throng here. Yet to the untrained eye, this is a city center where all sorts of people come to enjoy themselves.

The avenue has other uses too. Late at night, when most people have gone home after their play and their meal, when only a few shops and news kiosks cast their light on the broken pavement, a fleet of coaches arrives. Out step entire families who have travelled from the city's vast reaches that spill over from the capital into the province of Buenos Aires. They are collecting anything that might be worth selling, mostly cardboard and papers. They populate the avenue in their hundreds, filling it with their work and the voices and play of children. Several hours later they are gone, back to the jobless neighbourhoods. They are known as *cartoneros*, and are the embodiment of the poverty that has overtaken millions of Argentinians. Most *cartoneros* had jobs until a few years ago. The older ones are skilled workers, but the very young have never known regular employment—there may be as many as 40,000 working the streets of Buenos Aires alone. Their haunting presence is at odds with the uniformed waste collectors who also clean the city daily. They work from new trucks provided by the private companies contracted by the state—cleaning up the capital is worth some US$160 million a year.

Argentina in the 21st century appears to exist in different dimensions: in the "official" world, there are formal institutions to deal with public services from rubbish to education or health. Yet there is a growing dimension where the links between the state and people's everyday lives have been severed and a great proportion of the population has been cast adrift. In less than a generation, the country has gone from boasting the largest middle class in Latin America to having over half of the population—some 16 million people— below the poverty line.

Until recently, the families who today find no safety net had access to education and health insurance and owned homes and businesses. In just a few decades, Argentina has changed from being a land of immigration and promise to being one of net emigration, with nearly half the economically active population underemployed or entirely excluded from the job market.

—Marcela López Levy, *We Are Millions: Neoliberalism and New Forms of Political Action in Argentina* easy access to the world's capital markets, with a much better deal for the poor. The change started in October 2002, when a former trade unionist, Luiz Inácio Lula da Silva, was elected president on his fourth attempt. Expectations ran high and millions of Brazilians took to the streets waving the red flags of Lula's Workers' Party (PT). In fact, change came far more slowly than these delighted supporters expected. Indeed, circumstances had already combined to leave Lula very little room for maneuvering. In the run-up to the election, when it was becoming clear that Lula would win, the Hungarian-American financier George Soros predicted "chaos" for Brazil. In panic, foreign bankers pulled US$60 billion out of the country and default loomed. Many feared that Brazil would have the same fate as Argentina, Brazil's neighbor to the south, where a year earlier, in the wake of a default, the economy had collapsed and hundreds of thousands lost their jobs. To avert a similar disaster, Lula published an "open letter" promising financial orthodoxy, thus tying his hands even before he was elected. The strategy worked, in that panic subsided and the IMF gave Brazil the largest standby credit it had ever supplied, of US$30 billion.

However, economic stability came at a price and little of the far-reaching change that the PT originally promised came to pass. The government did not carry out a radical program of agrarian reform, nor did it take hard-hitting measures to redistribute income. Instead of eradicating pork barrel politics, it learned to play the old corrupt political game. Even so, the Lula years (2003–11) brought real advances for the country's poorest families, largely because the government greatly improved the system of social welfare. About 20 million families were lifted out of absolute poverty, providing Lula with a solid bedrock of support, that guaranteed his reelection in 2006. As well as this, Brazil's least educated president turned out to be the most daring on the world stage, turning Brazil into a world economic and political power, something that most Brazilians had long thought to be the country's manifest destiny but had proved frustratingly elusive. He finally rendered obsolete the old joke that "Brazil is the country of the future and always will be." Lula became a tireless traveler, going on twenty foreign trips in just his first year of office. Turning old diplomacy on its head, he did not travel frequently to the United States or Europe but gave priority to countries in the south. Everywhere he went he promoted trade, investment, and closer diplomatic links. At the top of his agenda was China, which duly displaced the United States as Brazil's main export market in 2009.

During his administration Brazil enthusiastically promoted the Initiative for the Integration of the Regional Infrastructure of South America (IIRSA). The name is a mouthful and the organization keeps a low profile, but it is an important multi-billion-dollar initiative, involving twelve countries for the construction of an extensive network of highways, river networks, hydro-electric power stations, and ports, through which the countries will be able to export their raw materials, particularly minerals, grain, and soybeans, to the rest of the world. The main beneficiary is undoubtedly Brazil, which is gaining a shorter and cheaper route to Asia, as well as winning many of the construction contracts in neighboring countries. Lula also provided hefty financial incentives for Brazil's big companies to merge and to expand abroad. The results have been impressive. Today some of the world's most powerful corporations, particularly in the fields of civil construction and food process-ing, come from Brazil. At the same time, he developed Brazil's own indepen-dent foreign policy, one no longer subservient to the United States. Brazil has become a voice on the world stage and has been particularly active in foster-ing south-south relations. Even so, huge problems remain. Social inequality has declined but Brazil is still one of the most unjust countries in the world, with daunting social problems. About 40,000 people are murdered each year, many of them by the police. Poor people still lack access to decent public health and education services. The country's dependence on commodities remains marked.

Argentina and Brazil were not the only countries to elect left-of-center governments as a reaction to neoliberalism. Apart from Venezuela, which is a case apart and will be discussed in the next chapter, a flurry of other reformist presidents came to power in the following years—Tabaré Vázquez (Uruguay, 2005), Evo Morales (Bolivia, 2006), Rafael Correa (Ecuador, 2006), Daniel Ortega (Nicaragua, 2006), Michelle Bachelet (Chile, 2006), and Fernando Lagos (Paraguay, 2008). In many of these countries policies have been intro-duced to tackle the social crisis. On average, social spending rose from 12 percent of gross domestic product (GDP) during 1990–91 to 18 percent dur-ing 2007–8. This spending bore results. Poverty rates for Latin America and the Caribbean as a whole fell significantly between 2002 and 2008. While 44 percent of the population was unable to satisfy basic nutritional and non-nutritional needs in 2002, the percentage had fallen to 33 percent by 2008. Indigence, which is the level of poverty at which people cannot satisfy their basic food needs, also declined, from about 19 percent in 2002 to less than 13 percent in 2008.

However, social inequality—that is, the gap between the rich and the poor—continues to be severe. It is true that there has been a slight improve-ment: in 2002 the average per capita income of the richest 10 percent of households in Latin America and the Caribbean was 20 times more than that of the poorest 40 percent, but by 2010 it had fallen to about 17 times. Even so, it remains very high by global standards. It is this inequality, together with the growth in drug trafficking, that is fueling the current epidemic of violence and crime in the region. In 2004 Central America and South America had, respectively, 29.3 and 25.9 murders per 100,000 people, among the highest rates in the world. These figures compare with 6.5 for North America and 5.4 for Europe. Each year, 200 million people in Latin America and the Caribbean—one-third of the region's population—are victims, directly or through their immediate family, of a criminal deed.

Deindustrialization and the Return of Commodity Exports

Under a neoliberal regime, countries are encouraged to trade on the basis of their "comparative advantage"—economic jargon for sticking to what you are good at. In the case of Latin America, this still means raw materials and cheap labor. In a return to the course of development followed since the Conquest, Latin America has gone back to being primarily an exporter of commodities, both traditional products such as minerals and oil, and a whole range of new, nontraditional exports, covering everything from cut flowers to fresh salmon. As a result, industrial development has stalled. As can be seen in Table 1.2, industry's share in economic output declined in many countries, notably Brazil, Mexico, Colombia, Chile and Peru, from 2001 to 2009. Moreover, the recovery in its exports since 1982 has been matched by a flood of imports, following blanket trade liberalization, bankrupting potentially competitive local producers and raising fears that the "opening" has undermined the region's industrial future. Furthermore, the boom in nontraditional exports has been achieved at a high social cost, exacerbating inequality and undermining the region's food security, while assembly plants and pesticide-intensive agriculture damaged the environment

Not surprisingly, the decline in industrial might has been accompanied by an increasing reliance on commodity exports. Brazil, widely seen as one of the emerging world powers, is the most surprising case. Although it is still a leading exporter of some important manufactured goods, such as aircraft, the share of commodities in its total exports actually increased during the Lula years. This is largely because of China's voracious appetite for many of Brazil's commodities, particularly soybeans and iron ore.

Mexico is the main exception, for its dependence on commodity exports is much less (25 percent) than in other countries, thanks to strong exports of manufactured goods, usually low-tech products such as shoes or textiles. The prominence of *maquiladoras* (assembly plants), strung along the U.S.-Mexican border, where imported components are assembled by cheap Latin American labor, also boosts manufactured exports. In 2000, these *maquiladoras* were employing around 1.3 million people in Mexico, and many more in

Table 1.2: Deindustrialization in Latin America

	GDP (US$bns*)	Industrial Output as % of GDP	
	2009	2001	2009
Brazil	885.7	19.7	12.8
Mexico	719.8	20.4	17.8
Argentina	398.1	15.4	16.5
Venezuela	157.0	14.5	15.4
Colombia	140.0	13.4	12.7
Chile	103.6	15.4	14.1
Peru	85.0	14.4	13.8
Dominican Republic	36.8	16.4	18.2
Uruguay	27.7	17.5	11.9
Ecuador	24.1	24.0	15.8
Costa Rica	23.3	20.6	20.7
Guatemala	23.2	18.1	11.0
Panama	19.8	6.1	6.6
El Salvador	15.8	22.8	24.1
Bolivia	11.6	13.8	16.2
Honduras	10.4	20.2	19.2
Paraguay	9.1	13.2	14.9
Nicaragua	5.0	17.0	14.0

*In constant 2000 prices.
  Source: *ECLAS, Statistical Yearbook on Latin America and the Caribbean*, 2010 and 2001.

factories dotted around Central America and the Caribbean. Since then, however, even cheaper Chinese labor has begun to encroach upon Latin America's *maquiladora* sector, despite Mexico's proximity to the U.S. market. It was estimated that between 2001 and 2003, one-third of Mexican *maquiladoras* relocated to China, where labor costs were often less than half as much.

But is the return to the old dependence on commodities bad news? Some economists, including those of the World Bank, think not. They have expressed cautious optimism that the region may be breaking out of the miserable pattern of boom-and-bust, accompanied by long-term exploitation of the labor force, which in the past characterized Latin America's dependence on commodities. They say that, rather than a curse, Latin America's commodity wealth is finally becoming a basis for lasting prosperity. The most recent commodity boom, which went from December 2001 to June 2008, was the longest lasting and most comprehensive in the region's history. It brought real

Table 1.3: The Region's Share in the World Commodity Market

	Latin America and the Caribbean's Share of World Exports (%, 2010)
Corn	30
Soybeans	52
Cocaine	100
Wheat	7
Rice	7
Beef	44
Poultry	42
Pork	17
Bananas	70
Sugar	45
Coffee	45
Oil	20

Source: World Bank, *Natural Resources in Latin America and the Caribbean: Beyond Booms and Busts?*, 2010; *The Economist.*

wealth to the region and many analysts believe that commodity prices will never return to the dismal lows of past eras. With the planet fast running out of new land to cultivate, they expect food prices to soar in coming decades. Moreover, the region is no longer so dependent on its huge neighbor to the north—the United States—to take most of its commodities. Exports to Asia are growing fast, with China's share of the region's commodity exports increasing tenfold in the first decade of the twenty-first century. Latin America's abundant natural resources, they say, are finally being recognized as the precious asset they are.

But it is too soon to celebrate. Nowhere in the world has heavy reliance on commodities yet proved to be a firm foundation for lasting prosperity. Successful economies still produce computers, not kiwi fruit. Though it is true that many countries in the region—and most particularly Brazil—are investing billions of dollars in new roads, hydroelectric power stations, and port installations to facilitate the export of millions of tons of iron ore, bauxite, soybeans, beef, and other commodities, this expansion is causing serious damage to the environment. Moreover, just as in the past, most of the region's poorest people are still excluded from the benefits. Whether the new commodity trade is turned into a lasting force for good in the region will depend on the ability of today's largely democratic governments to regulate the sector, to limit the environmental damage, to ensure that the wealth is used to improve education, and to invest in sectors that can truly provide the foundations for sustainable growth. So far, the signs are not encouraging.

Table 1.4: **The Dependence of Latin America and the Caribbean on Commodity Exports***

	Main Commodity Exports	Commodity Exports as a % of Total Exports
Argentina	soybeans, oil, wheat, corn	68.0
Belize (2008)	sugar, bananas	98.6
Bolivia	natural gas, zinc, tin, silver	92.9
Brazil	soybeans, corn, sugar, iron ore, crude oil, coffee	60.9
Chile	copper, fruit, fish, paper and pulp	88.2
Colombia	oil, coffee, coal, nickel, emeralds	72.6
Costa Rica	pineapples, coffee, melons	37.6
Eduador	bananas, oil, shrimp	90.9
El Salvador	coffee, sugar	47.0
Guatemala	coffee, sugar, oil	66.3
Honduras	coffee, bananas	66.5
Mexico	oil, silver, copper, tomatoes	24.9
Nicaragua	coffee, cattle	90.9
Panama	bananas, shrimp, sugar	90.7
Paraguay (2008)	soybeans, cotton, beef	92.1
Peru	copper, gold, zinc	87.8
Uruguay	beef, wheat, corn, dairy	74.8
Venezuela (2006)	oil	92.7

*Figures are for 2009 unless stated otherwise.
Source: *ECLAS, Statistical Yearbook on Latin America and the Caribbean*, 2010.

2.

Ballots and Bullets: The State, the Military, and Politics

The State and the Military

In August 2004, the president of Venezuela, Hugo Chávez, overcame a recall referendum on his government, resoundingly defeating a powerful home-grown U.S.-backed opposition that was prepared to use every means to get him out of office. Six million Venzuelans, 58 percent of the votes cast, backed Chávez to remain in office; the 70 percent turnout was unprecedented for an election in Venezuela.

When Chávez was elected for the first time in 1998, his call for radical change was the exception in a region ruled by conservative leaders: the dicta-tor Hugo Banzer in Bolivia; the free marketeer Carlos Menem in Argentina; Ernesto Zedillo from the Partido Revolucionario Institucional (PRI)—the "perfect dictatorship"—in Mexico; even Brazil's Fernando Henrique Car-doso, once a progressive sociologist, had embraced the free-market model.

Chávez, meanwhile, promised his electorate a "peaceful, democratic" revolution, inspired by his hero, Simon Bolívar. His policies and, even more, his flamboyant, confrontational style of government, aroused deep passions. Some saw Chávez as a breath of fresh air, a genuinely popular politician, who was shaking up the old elitist political system. Others, who briefly overthrew him in a coup in 2002, related a darker story: Chávez's democratic posturing and promise of a new constitution was a ploy—he was an autocrat, ruling by personal charisma and for personal prestige alone, a perfect example of the Latin American *caudillo*, or strongman.

The controversy surrounding Hugo Chávez is the latest stitch in an old pattern. The twin threads of democracy and authoritarianism run through Latin America's history since independence, sometimes alternating between periods of democratic and dictatorial rule, at other times combining to pro-duce hybrid forms of authoritarian democracy.

The authoritarian tradition stems from the Conquest. The Spain from which Columbus set sail in 1492 was a militarized, crusading society, emerg-ing victorious from a seven-century battle with Islam and greedy for new lands. Power lay with the Catholic monarchs, whose authority came directly from God, as they ruled by "divine right," in alliance with the Pope. As late as the 1970s, the Spanish dictator, General Franco, claimed to rule "by the grace of God." In their new colonies, the Spanish implanted a hierarchical system, enslaving the indigenous people. Ironically, the empires they replaced in Mexico and the Andes were if anything even more authoritarian and centralized than the Spanish. Absolute power resided in the Aztec or Inca emperor (at the time of the Spaniards' arrival, Moctezuma II in Mexico and Atahualpa in Peru), allowing the Spaniards to defeat far more numerous rivals by first seizing the emperors, then replacing them at the top of the social pyramid.

In Brazil, Portuguese rule was rather more lax. No gold or silver was discovered for the first two centuries, and Portugal concentrated on its other, more profitable ventures in the East Indies. Rather than develop an all-encompassing bureaucracy, it left the Brazilian colonists more to themselves, contenting itself with taxing Brazil's exports.

The colonies were fairly stable until the mid-eighteenth century, and continued to provide vast amounts of precious metals and luxury goods to Spain and Portugal. Both France and the Netherlands attempted to gain footholds in Brazil, but were repelled by the Portuguese. However, following tax reforms in the 1760s, rebellions began to break out throughout Spanish South America. Protests by frustrated *criollos* (creoles), taxed without representation, were manageable, as the colonial bureaucracy could count on their support in the final analysis. More dangerous were the lengthy rebellion of Atahualpa II in Bolivia (1742–52) and the occupation of Peruvian and Bolivian cities by Tupac Amaru II in 1780–82. These indigenous rebellions aimed to reestablish the Inca Empire, and posed serious threats to the material hierarchy of the colonies. For the three decades following the defeat of Tupac Amaru II, the colonial authorities were supported by the creole elite, now terrified of a potential peasant uprising.

The feared peasant outbreak, led by two priests, Hidalgo and Morelos, did take place in the hitherto stable colony of New Spain, which was the name for the land conquered from the Aztecs. Huge armies of indigenous and *mestizo* peasants defeated the colonial army, then lost the support of sympathetic *criollos* by carrying out vengeful atrocities on the inhabitants of occupied cities. The Mexican rebellion, as well as the earlier outbreaks of violence in Peru, went some way to determining the course of independence. These incidents frightened the creole elite, who recognized the dangers of a temporary alliance with the masses. When opportunities to break free of the imperial state did occur, the wealthy were determined to create independent nations controlled by a strict hierarchy. Although republicanism was the dominant political ideology, democracy was not a priority, and *criollos* tended to put their faith in strong, authoritarian governments.

Independence came suddenly to Spanish America, and almost by accident. In 1808 Napoleon invaded Spain and installed his brother on the throne. *Criollos*, already restive at Spanish rule and Spain's insistence on monopolizing foreign trade, seized the moment to declare independence. The monarch was now the enemy, and the American and French revolutions were still recent memories, so republicanism appeared the obvious alternative to many of the rebels (although some still supported an independent monarchy). As would come to be the case throughout the modern period, Latin Americans imported the latest political fashion from outside and attempted, unsuccessfully, to graft it onto their own traditions.

The greatest of Latin America's freedom fighters, Simón Bolívar (1783–1830), epitomized the process. His beliefs were a complex and often contradictory mixture of authoritarianism and Enlightenment-inspired republicanism. Shortly before his death, disillusioned by his compatriots' lack of experience in government and the chaos unleashed by the independence wars, he wrote the Bolivian constitution. In it, Bolívar created a president-for-life, able to choose his own successor, thereby avoiding "the changing administration caused by party government and the excitement which too frequent elections produce."

Bolívar's dream of a United States of Latin America soon foundered on the rivalries and geographical and cultural differences that helped divide the region into today's republics. In the year of Bolívar's death, "Great Colombia" disintegrated into Venezuela, Colombia, and Ecuador; the former "kingdom of Guatemala" splintered into the numerous feuding Central American republics. Each act of division took Latin America further from the path to prosperity and power that had been followed by the United States to the north.

Republic after republic approved high-sounding democratic constitutions that had little connection with political and social reality. The wars against Spanish rule were won on the battlefield, and in the aftermath of independence, the economic elite of large landowners opted out and retired to their remote haciendas, leaving politics to the former military leaders, who became the feuding local *caudillos*, who have been a feature of Latin American political life ever since.

The *caudillos* were often charismatic, paternalist figures who became the real authority in many rural areas. As one Venezuelan *caudillo* wrote to Bolívar, "The people bring me all their problems—how to build a house, whom to marry, how to settle a family dispute, and what seeds to plant." In Latin America's rigidly stratified society, the military offered one of the few vehicles for ambition and social mobility, and *caudillos* and their personal retinues fought endless wars. In *One Hundred Years of Solitude*, Gabriel García Márquez portrays the fictional life of a classic *caudillo*, Colonel Aureliano Buendía:

Colonel Aureliano Buendía organized 32 armed uprisings and he lost them all. He had 17 male children by 17 different women and they were exterminated one after the other on a single night before the oldest one had reached the age of 35. He survived 14 attempts on his life, 73 ambushes, and a firing squad. He lived through a dose of strychnine in his coffee that was enough to kill a horse. He refused the Order of Merit which the President of the Republic awarded him. He rose to be Commander-in-Chief of the revolutionary forces ...

Some of the strongmen managed to take over a whole country, such as Argentina's Juan Manuel de Rosas, or Mexico's Antonio López de Santa Anna, while others ruled over regional enclaves.

Brazil, meanwhile, followed a different path. When Napoleon invaded, the British fleet shipped the Portuguese court *en masse* to exile in Rio de Janeiro. Portuguese rule had been less restrictive than that of the Spanish, producing less anti-royalist feeling, and in 1822, without violence or economic destruction, Brazil became an independent monarchy under Emperor Dom Pedro I. Although Dom Pedro I faced a difficult few years marked by political division, rebellions, and the loss of what became Uruguay after a war with Argentina, his son, Dom Pedro II, succeeded in uniting the nation, ruling for nearly fifty years and fending off the division, chaos, and economic decline that afflicted the Spanish American colonies after independence. The Brazilian monarchy survived until 1889.

By the 1850s the *caudillo* period was coming to an end, as the economic elites emerged from relative seclusion to reimpose order. Modern nations started to emerge from the wreckage as British capital and technology flooded in, building railways, ports, and telegraph networks. *Caudillos* gave way to administrators, commercial agriculture expanded (often displacing indigenous communities), and exports began to rise. By the 1880s, Latin America had become integrated into the world economy, setting the scene for half a century of economic boom based on agro-exports.

Politics at this point was a preserve of the rich. This was the heyday of landowner rule, either running the government themselves, as in Argentina or Chile, or via the imposition of dictators, as in Mexico, Venezuela, and Peru. Unlike the squabbling *caudillos* of the first half of the century, this new brand of dictator, exemplified by Mexico's Porfirio Díaz, were modernizers intent on building up their nations through foreign investment and economic growth.

The key political issues of the time were reflected in the endless battles between liberals and conservatives. Although the ideological distinctions between them were frequently less important than the personal ambitions of their leaders, conservatives tended to be pro-Church and supported a centralized system of government that favored the big cities, while liberals tended to be anti-clerical and federalist. As often as not, they conducted their discussion on the battlefield; nineteenth-century Colombia witnessed eight national civil wars, 14 regional civil wars, and countless local disputes between the two parties.

Although many countries had universal male suffrage by the mid-nineteenth century, the elite proved adept at preventing this from posing a threat to their rule. Using everything from ballot-box stuffing to free beer they managed to stifle political alternatives to elite rule. In the Andean countries the white elite, ever fearful of indigenous rebellion, made sure the vote went only to the literate, thereby excluding the indigenous majority from a say in government (in Peru, illiterates did not get the vote until 1979). Since voting appeared unlikely to change anything, electoral turnout across Latin America actually fell as the nineteenth century wore on. In Mexico and Argentina, despite universal male suffrage, only about 5 percent of the adult male population bothered to vote. The landowners were quite happy to keep it that way.

Bringing out the vote became the specialty of a quintessential Latin American figure, the *cacique*. Originally the name for an indigenous chief, the term

---

Let Them Eat Meat: Vote-Buying in Colombia

The problem was how to find something to eat. We were talking this over when Oscar arrived with the news that over at Don Tiberio's they were giving out roast suckling pig because there were elections on Sunday. We rushed over, and it was true. They were handing out meat and beer on a piece of land at the edge of the village decorated with photos of the candidates and Conservative Party flags. Everyone was very friendly. Most of the people there were relatives, plus a few drunks and others filling their bellies as if they'd never eaten before. We tucked in and promised to vote for the Conservatives.

   Half drunk, we were wandering off when someone told us that, on the other side of the village, that the Liberals were giving out *aguardiente* (cane liquor), so off we went. There was a great party going on, red flags, rockets and booze coming out of our ears! So once again we promised our vote, this time to the great Liberal Party. The comrades of the Patriotic Union also had their stall to hunt votes, but all they gave people were soft drinks and lots of speeches. We left with our heads full of ideology, ready to vote for the new party.

   We ate twice in each political café and in the end we each voted for whoever we liked. Everyone thought we had voted for their party.

—Alfredo Molano, *Aguas Arriba,* Bogotá: El Áncora Editores, 1990 (author's translation)

came to mean a rural boss, an authoritative figure in traditional rural society who proved adept at drumming up support for his *patrón*'s chosen party.

As long as Latin America remained a largely rural society, the *caciques* and other "alchemists" (as vote-riggers are known in Mexico) could ensure that politics stayed in the hands of the elite. But economic growth precipitated the destruction of the cozy, if exclusive, nineteenth-century political arrangement. Convinced by their own racism and their need for skilled labor that European blood was necessary if their countries were to develop, governments in countries such as Argentina, Brazil, and Chile encouraged mass immigration, predominantly from southern Europe. With the immigrants came new and radical political influences, such as the anarchist trade unionists from Italy who founded the Argentine labor movement.

After decades of authoritarian rule, the Mexican elite moved to implement a limited liberal democracy in 1910 and in so doing unleashed a momentous revolution. Seven years before the Bolshevik uprising in Russia, Mexicans overthrew their own dictator, but without an overall leader or fundamental ideology, the rebels soon lost their way. The dictator Díaz had been ousted by a coalition of wealthy liberals and disgruntled peasants, but once in power, the alliance broke down. The peasants, inspired by Emiliano Zapata, occupied lands belonging to local ranchers, only to face renewed constraints imposed by the new government. It was not until the nationwide land reform of the 1930s that the conflict between peasants and landowners began to abate.

Immigration, urbanization, and growth produced an urban working class that proved both more articulate and far harder to control than the peasantry. Society was becoming more complex. The abyss separating the holders of political power from these new social forces grew ever wider. Something had to give, and in the end, as with independence, it took an event thousands of miles away to provide the catalyst for change. The Wall Street Crash of 1929 and ensuing Depression in the industrialized nations proved a major turning point in Latin American history.

The Great Depression of the 1930s destroyed the world market for Latin America's commodity exports, bringing to an end the era of unquestioned dominance by the agro-exporting elite. The initial effect was a rash of military takeovers and a change in economic direction toward building up industry. In the longer run, the new drive to industrialize created growing working and middle classes, laying the basis for a new kind of politics—populism. A new generation of political leaders came to the fore, bringing together workers and industrialists in an alliance that tried to bridge class barriers, often in opposition to the old guard of conservative landowners. Politics left the hacienda forever, to find its new home in the bustling world of the city and the slum.

The Rise and Fall of Populism

Populism was both popular and authoritarian. In the 1930s many of its leaders were military or ex-military men who drew inspiration from Hitler's or Mussolini's rise to power. It was also fiercely nationalistic, condemning Latin America's traditional dependence on outside powers and often nationalizing key foreign-owned industries, such as Mexican oil (1938) or the hugely popular purchase of the Argentine railways from Britain (1948). By bringing together both industrialists and workers in the same alliance, it was bound in the end to generate internal conflicts, although initially these were masked by the personal charisma of its leaders.

The great populists included Mexico's Lázaro Cárdenas, Getúlio Vargas in Brazil, and Carlos Ibáñez in Chile, but the greatest of them all was Juan Domingo Perón, Argentina's beloved father figure. Perón was elected in 1946, and Peronism has dominated Argentine politics ever since, despite Perón's death in 1974. Together with his wife Eva (Evita), he forged a personality cult, portraying himself as the heroic defender of the nation's *descamisados* (shirtless ones), a man of the people who oversaw the growth of industry, redistribution of income, and the development of a welfare state. Evita's star quality allowed Perón to woo another new political constituency—women, who won the right to vote in 1947.

Thirty years after his death, saint-like portraits of Juan and Evita adorn walls in the shantytowns of Buenos Aires. In one of them, Ciudad Oculta, where cooking smells mix with the tang of eucalyptus leaves trampled with the rubbish into the muddy street, a mural of blond, beautiful Evita looks out at the dark-skinned Paraguayan immigrant families. As one hard-bitten local activist, Juan Cymes, recalls: "Evita was a goddess for me when I was a kid. I wrote to ask her to help some poor neighbors and she wrote back to me within a week!" Bearing the slogan "Social Justice will be achieved inexorably, whatever the cost, whoever falls," the freshly painted mural looks like publicity for this year's presidential candidate. Evita died of cancer in 1952, but her cult live on. When the pop star Madonna went to Buenos Aires in 1996 to film the musical of Evita's life, outraged Argentines plastered the walls of the city with graffiti saying "Long live Evita, Madonna go home!"

Perón expounded the doctrine of *justicialismo* (social justice), which he saw as a third way between capitalism and communism in a world gripped by the deepening Cold War. The state replaced the *caudillo* as the all-powerful provider; it mediated in any dispute between different sectors of society, cared for the sick and elderly, and took a commanding role in the economy via a burgeoning network of state-run industries. Perón's support rested on a highly

organized and devoutly Peronist trade union movement, which became virtually an arm of government.

In 1955 Perón's conflicts with the military and the Church led to his overthrow and exile in Madrid. He returned only for a brief and chaotic period
as president in 1973–74. Nonetheless, despite his exile and death, and years
of military prohibition and persecution, Peronism continues to dominate
Argentine politics.

Populism was more prominent in the larger countries, where industrialization could take root. In the smaller, weaker economies of Central America and
the Caribbean, a cruder solution emerged to the problems of economic collapse. In Nicaragua, El Salvador, Cuba, and the Dominican Republic, military
dictators took over in the 1930s. Men such as General Maximiliano Hernández in El Salvador or Nicaragua's Anastasio Somoza were willing to go to
extreme lengths to stamp out unrest. After massacring 30,000 rebellious peasants in the *matanza* (massacre) of 1932, virtually wiping out El Salvador's
indigenous population, General Hernández explained in a radio broadcast,
"It is a greater crime to kill an ant than a man, because a man who dies is rein-
carnated, while an ant dies forever." The Central American and Caribbean
dictators remained in power for decades, stifling political modernization and
sowing the seeds for future upheaval, including revolutions in Cuba (1959)
and Nicaragua (1979) and a bloody guerrilla war in El Salvador in the 1980s.
In the Dominican Republic, a U.S. military intervention in 1965 helped prevent upheaval, installing another quintessential *caudillo*, Joaquín Balaguer,
who proceeded to dominate the country's politics well into the 1990s.

Populist governments saw the state as the means to achieve development,
by kick-starting the industrialization of the economy. From the 1930s onward,
governments created hundreds of semi-independent agencies covering everything from state steel or oil companies to agencies for agrarian reform or water
supply. The state came to dominate the economy, employing a large part of the
middle class and owning much of industry.

In the larger countries, notably Brazil, Argentina, and Mexico, populism
went hand in hand with corporatism—ruling parties set up and then controlled labor unions and other mass organizations, such as those of peasants
and state employees. In return for the government improving wages and working conditions, these organizations had to sacrifice any pretense of independence. The unequal dialogue between state and mass organizations played
the main role in controlling and channeling the demands of the new social
groups, and legitimizing the government in the eyes of the public. Elections
were often marred by fraud or the huge inequality between the state/party
machine and any opposition. Mass organizations worked to turn out the vote
for the ruling party. Any individual or organization that rebelled against this

system could expect to be excluded from the state's bounty, to be hounded by the legal system, and was likely to face physical intimidation.

The strategy worked at first, as state intervention propelled economies into industrial growth. Booming economies and taxes on exports allowed governments to keep everybody happy, and when those were insufficient, governments overspent to buy off opposition at the expense of inflation.

With the exception of Argentina and Mexico, populism's star rose and fell with that of its economic brainchild, import substitution. After notching up huge successes after the Second World War, import substitution started to run out of steam. By the 1960s, Latin American economies were slipping into crisis, and the improbable alliance of industrialist and worker came apart in spectacular fashion. Moreover, economic growth and the rise of the middle class had further increased the number of social groups clamoring for a voice in running the country. When radical elements, such as the student movement, were inspired by the Cuban Revolution of 1959 to seek power through armed struggle, the generals decided that enough was enough. Military coups in Brazil (1964) and Argentina (1966) brought to power governments supported by a business sector determined to stamp out political opposition, crush the unions, reduce wages, and give state-led development a new lease of life. They achieved it in Brazil, which underwent an "economic miracle" in the form of a period of record growth from 1968 to 1975.

The switch from civilian (if authoritarian) rule to military dictatorship was also helped by the international climate. After the Cuban Revolution, the U.S. and Latin American military were determined to prevent revolution from spreading, and Washington was happy to support almost any military government that promised to crack down on leftism. There was also widespread support for military rule within Latin America, especially from the middle classes. Latin America's interwoven traditions of authoritarianism and democracy meant that many people did not see elections as the only legitimate route to power, and were prepared to support a military government if they thought it could impose order or improve their economic situation.

In Mexico, the exceptionally adroit and chameleon-like Institutional Revolutionary Party (PRI) bucked the regional trend to cling, limpet-like, to power for an astonishing seventy-one years. It did so through a process of endless transformation, moving from being the party of the Mexican Revolution to midwife of the North American Free Trade Agreement with the United States and Canada. When all else failed, the PRI was also adept at electoral fraud, sending out teams of ballot-box stuffers and co-opting promising opposition leaders. In 2000, however, it finally succumbed to political mortality, losing power to the PAN, a right-wing pro-business party led by the ineffectual former Coca-Cola executive, Vicente Fox.

When the military fell in Argentina, the Peronists returned from the political wilderness in a baffling range of guises, turning themselves first into a free-market party under Carlos Menem, and then back into a statist party under Néstor Kirchner, following the catastrophic economic crisis in 2001.

Men at Arms: The Generals

General Albano Harguindeguy sat on the sofa in his Buenos Aires flat. Now a retired Latin American patriarch, his genial back-slapping style must once have made him popular with his men. Over a glass of whisky he reflected on his period in office as Argentina's minister of the interior, priding himself on his grasp of world events. While his wife served pizza, he mused over what he would have done differently if he had the chance to be in government all over again. "Not so many disappeared people—we should have used the law instead," he concluded.

The bluff general in his cardigan and slippers was in charge of internal security during the worst years of the military junta that seized power in 1976. During the "dirty war," Harguindeguy's men took thousands of young men and women from their homes, often at night, and drove them away in the sinister unmarked Ford Falcons favored by the security forces. Their relatives and friends never heard from them again, amid rumors of torture cells, concentration camps, and mass graves. After the military regime fell, the rumors proved to be true. The official number of documented disappearances is just under 12,000, but the real number could be twice as many.

Argentina's dark hours of fear and doubt have been repeated up and down Latin America. Aída de Suárez remembers how her son disappeared:

> On 2 December 1977 at four o'clock in the morning, twenty armed men broke into our house with rifles and pistols pointed at us. They were nervous. They opened and closed the cupboards, the fridge. They were looking for things, guns apparently. They took everything of any value they could carry, the few things of value that a working-class family has in their home, sentimental things. But that wasn't important to me. They could have taken everything, but my son, no. He was sitting on the bed, trying to get dressed. One man shouted, "There's one in here!" and then two huge men with guns in their hands told me not to move. They asked only if he was Hugo Héctor Suárez and that he had to go with them.
>
> "Who are you?" I screamed. "We are the security forces." They were in civilian suits but underneath they were wearing army fatigues and boots, and green bullet-proof vests, the color of the army. So it was the army. I said,

"Why? My son has done nothing, he's not a criminal. Why have you come in like this, frightening the children with guns pointed at everyone?"—twenty armed men for a child of 21, an old woman like me, and two young children. "We've come to take him away for questioning." "Why?" I asked and they pushed me and threw me against the wall. They took my son. That was the last time I saw him.

—JO FISHER, *Mothers of the Disappeared*

By the end of 1976 two-thirds of people on the Latin American mainland lived under dictatorial rule. Among the major countries, only Mexico, Venezuela, Colombia, and Costa Rica had no general in the presidential palace. Pinochet, Stroessner, Videla: the continent became synonymous with vicious military dictators in sunglasses and the midnight knock on the door. As the 1980s passed, the generals began to return to the barracks, some in defeat and humiliation, others managing to retain a significant voice in politics. In March 1990, Chile's General Augusto Pinochet became the last of the great Latin American dictators to leave power when he reluctantly handed over the presidency to the elected Christian Democrat leader Patricio Aylwin. In many Latin American countries the military retained considerable influence, and during the 1990s, military rumblings occurred in Haiti, Paraguay, Venezuela, Brazil, and Chile, among others, but by early 2005, the "failed state" of Haiti and Fidel Castro's Cuban regime remained the last unelected governments in the Western Hemisphere. The "old" military found itself with few remaining friends, prey to budget cuts, public contempt, and a profound identity crisis over its role in the post–Cold War world. Furthermore, a rash of prosecutions and overturned amnesties meant that justice could finally be pursued; Generals Pinochet and Harguindeguy found themselves under arrest (albeit the comfortable "house arrest" variety) and facing prosecution for their parts in the murder of thousands of political opponents.

Military History

Unlike the UK or United States, where civilian political control over the armed forces has long been taken for granted, the military in Latin America has always been an independent political force. The nature of the Spanish Conquest, led by soldiers who defeated the Aztec and Inca Empires and were rewarded with land, slaves, and booty, was in marked contrast to the methods and lifestyle of the civilian settlers who emigrated to start a new life in the United States and Canada. When Spanish power collapsed, Latin America won its independence through the exploits of military heroes like Simón

Bolívar (1783–1830) and José de San Martín (1778–1852). Today, the streets of every Latin American capital are littered with statues of heroic military figures on horseback, swords raised, and schoolchildren diligently learn the names of the military fathers of the nation.

Between 1808 and 1826, independence wars raged throughout Spanish America. Armed uprisings turned into liberation armies that marched across the continent in two great arcs: in the south, General José San Martín's Army of the Andes crossed the Pampas from Buenos Aires, marched over the Andes into Chile, and then moved up toward Peru. In the north, Simón Bolívar's followers marched from Venezuela into Colombia and down to liberate Ecuador. The two armies converged on Peru, where they decisively defeated the remaining Spanish forces at the Battle of Ayacucho in 1824. In Mexico, violent social rebellion followed a course of its own. By 1826 Spain had lost everything except Cuba and Puerto Rico. Brazil declared its independence from Portugal in 1822, but in contrast to the republics of Spanish America, the new nation emerged with little violence, ruled by members of the Portuguese royal family.

The independence armies were led by the small *criollo* class fighting to seize power from Spain, but otherwise intent on maintaining Latin America's social structures largely unchanged. "Liberation" brought few benefits for the indigenous population. Black slaves were, however, promised their freedom in exchange for fighting, and formed much of San Martín's Army of the Andes. Indigenous people were press-ganged to fight by both sides. White leaders, whether royalist or republican, feared revolt by the blacks and indigenous people more than they feared one another—when the Spanish viceroy decided to abandon Lima in 1821, the terrified and hitherto royalist citizens asked San Martín for protection against a feared black uprising.

In the first decades after independence, the military often consisted of little more than armed members of the peasantry. Then, from the mid-nineteenth century onward, a process of professionalization took place, transforming the military from an irregular army in the hands of local chieftains into a sophisticated institution, though never erasing its taste for occupying the presidential palace.

Professionalization has involved building a national army with a proper career structure and a separate value system, encouraging its self-image as a caste apart from, and often superior to, the rest of society. Military schools and staff colleges were set up to forge young boys into tomorrow's generals. The schools take boys in their early teens and impose military discipline and values. A high percentage of the intake are sons of officers, which only increases the sense of separation from society. Once the boy has entered the military structure, he will often stay isolated from civilian society until he is a high-ranking officer—his life will revolve around the school and the barracks.

The isolation of the [Argentine] armed forces intensified over the course of the twentieth century. Beginning in the 1920s, special neighborhoods and clubs were constructed for officers and their families. These new institutions included free country clubs or "*círculos*" used for recreation, business functions, and weddings of officers and their children. Paid for out of the military budget, these clubs—like the special apartment complexes erected near major military installations—accentuated the officers' ignorance of civilian values and aspirations. Usually only those with the rank of colonel or above could acquire their own apartments in civilian neighborhoods. The virtual apartheid separating officers from both enlisted soldiers and civilians was epitomized in the rules governing elevators in military buildings: one set of lifts used by officers and another for civilians and lower-ranking soldiers.

—EMILIO MIGNONE, *The Military: What Is to Be Done?*

In the absence of combat experience, most Latin American armies place enormous importance on educational qualifications as the path to promotion. The standard of education in military schools is often higher than in civilian life, reinforcing the officers' sense of innate superiority.

But education has not prevented graft. In Paraguay General Stroessner kept his officers happy by cutting them in on the smuggling trade with Brazil; in Panama General Noriega bought his men's loyalty and silence by involving them in everything from protection rackets to prostitution; in El Salvador local commanders left soldiers killed in action on the battalion's books and pocketed their wages. As one army leader in the Mexican Revolution of 1910 commented, "There is no general who can withstand a bombardment of 50,000 pesos."

From the early days of import substitution, some of the region's most developed armies began to assemble a military-industrial complex that gave them enormous economic muscle. In Brazil and Argentina, military conglomerates came to control everything from arms manufacture to petrochemicals. Brazil came to rival Israel as the Third World's foremost arms exporter, exporting weaponry worth US$1 billion a year during the 1980s. In Chile, the Pinochet regime sang the virtues of privatization, except when it came to the lucrative state copper company, which was still obliged to give 10 percent of its income directly to the armed forces. The military's growing economic power further strengthened its political autonomy from the central government.

The social gulf between officers and men in Latin America's armies is exacerbated by the widespread use of conscription. Many of the young men who shivered in the Argentine trenches during the Falklands/Malvinas war of 1982 were conscripts with little interest in fighting. Non-commissioned officers, or young officers who have not yet acquired the privileges that go with senior rank, are traditionally a source of unrest within the military, often leading uprisings against the military hierarchy.

The Specter of Communism

Following the Second World War, Latin America's military forces increasingly adopted a Cold War ideology. This worldview was refined at the military staff colleges, where high-flying young officers were prepared for the high command. In Brazil, the military set up the Higher War School (*Escola Superior de Guerra*, ESG) in 1949, where young officers studied not only military tactics, but also politics, economics, and sociology. From the outset, the ESG also recruited among the civilian elite—business leaders, top civil servants, politicians, and judges, who by 1966 made up half the graduates. The ESG thus served both to train the future military top brass and to establish firm links between them and Brazil's civilian rulers.

The ESG was instrumental in developing what became known as national security doctrine, an all-embracing viewpoint that saw the military as the guardians of order in the broadest sense, including economic development and the prevention of internal political or social division. The enemy of the continent's social order was the specter of international communism, which was supposedly conducting a stealthy war of internal subversion against pro-Western governments throughout Latin America.

National security doctrine became established as the linchpin of military thinking following the Cuban Revolution of 1959, which the generals saw as proof of the international communist conspiracy. The doctrine provided the intellectual justification for the military to make the defeat of "internal subversion" its top priority. Subversion was defined as anything that threatened the status quo—trade unionism, peasant movements, socialist politics, or student protest. Since this was a "Third World War" against the communist menace, human rights considerations and the rule of law became redundant, clearing the way for the atrocities, disappearances, and bloodshed that followed.

Some of the wilder excesses of national security doctrine had a tragicomic air: in the late 1970s the Argentine junta reportedly burned books on Cubism under the mistaken belief that they expounded the philosophy of Fidel Castro. Junta members were much given to describing themselves as the defenders of Western Christian democracy, despite their aversion to elections. The Argentine military's perception of what constituted a threat to Western Christendom has always been broad; in the 1960s General Onganía defended the sanctity of the family by outlawing miniskirts.

Until the Second World War, U.S. influence was greatest in its traditional backyard of Central America and the Caribbean. In the early years of the twentieth century, Washington regularly sent in the marines to overthrow governments, before setting up client armies such as General Somoza's National Guard in Nicaragua, enabling U.S. forces to retreat to bases in the Panama Canal Zone. Farther south, in Brazil, Chile, and Argentina, the German army had considerable influence in the early professionalization of regular armies.

The Second World War destroyed Germany as a regional influence and established the United States as the supreme foreign power throughout Latin America. U.S. military missions spread across Latin America to supply and train the region's armies, ensuring in the process that future military leaderships would be firmly pro-United States. As the Cold War gathered pace, U.S. influence was crucial in forging national security doctrine.

In addition to sending military missions to the various countries, the United States trained thousands of Latin American officers and future military leaders, either in the the States or at the School of the Americas in the Panama Canal Zone—earning it the name "School of the Dictators." Pupils included Major Roberto d'Aubuisson, godfather of El Salvador's death squads, and the Panamanian dictator, General Manuel Antonio Noriega. In 1996, the Pentagon provoked a scandal when it declassified documents showing that Spanish-language training manuals used at the school in the 1980s recommended to its Latin American trainees using threats, bribery, blackmail, and the torture of guerrillas.

As a result of President Carter's short-lived human rights policy in the late 1970s, brutal military regimes in Latin America found their arms supplies from Washington reduced or cut off. Their response was to look elsewhere for suppliers and develop their own armaments industries. This undermined U.S. supremacy in the region, as arms suppliers from the UK, France, Italy, Germany, the Soviet Union, and Israel broke into the market.

In 1981 President Reagan took office, determined to end Carter's human rights policy, which he blamed for the United States "losing" Nicaragua as a client state through the 1979 revolution. One of the key right-wing think tanks behind Reagan's new policy, the Council for Inter-American Security, painted a lurid, and farcically incorrect, picture of the challenge facing the United States in Latin America: "World War III is almost over. The Soviet Union, operating under the cover of increasing nuclear superiority, is strangling the Western industrialized nations. . . . America is everywhere in retreat. The Caribbean, America's maritime crossroad and petroleum refining center, is becoming a Marxist-Leninist lake."

President Reagan chose to "draw the line against communism" in Central America and the Caribbean. U.S. marines invaded Grenada in 1983 and overthrew its left-wing government, while in Nicaragua and El Salvador U.S. strategists refined Vietnam-style counter-guerrilla tactics into a more general technique known as "low-intensity conflict." This attempted to defeat the guerrilla movement in El Salvador and the Sandinista government in Nicaragua through the use of proxy armies in order to avoid the use of U.S. troops, which might lead to an antiwar backlash at home. In El Salvador the army was encouraged to "win hearts and minds" among the peasantry, but at the same time had the conflicting objective of striking at anyone considered sympathetic to the guerrillas. In the end repression took precedence over reform. In Nicaragua the Contras played a significant part in the downfall of the left-wing Sandinista government by sabotaging the economy and forcing the government to divert scarce resources into defense.

Despite pouring US$6 billion into aid into El Salvador, the war ended in stalemate and a 1992 peace agreement, which effectively removed the military from politics and made way for guerrillas to reenter civilian politics. In Nicaragua, Washington's war of attrition undermined public support for the Sandinistas, who were voted from office in 1990 (but won back power in 2006).

Relief at the end of the fighting was tempered by the problem of what to do with the newly unemployed soldiers from both sides. In El Salvador the UN accused the army of having links to armed robbery and murder; in Guatemala the military is widely believed to be involved in crime rings that steal cars and run the drug trade; in Nicaragua banditry became endemic in the countryside. More generally, the militarization of the 1980s left the legacy of a more violent society, littered with leftover guns. As one former member of an elite Salvadoran anti-guerrilla battalion commented in an unguarded moment: "I need to kill." Having been fired from the army and tormented by nightmares from his years behind guerrilla lines, the man was about to cross the U.S.-Mexican border on his way to join a gang in Los Angeles—one small example of the violence sown by U.S. anti-guerrilla tactics coming back to haunt it.

General Unrest

The quintessentially Latin American phenomenon of the military coup and military government long preceded the invention of national security doctrine, stretching back to the Spanish and Portuguese roots of the region's political systems. Prior to the Second World War, military interventions usually aimed to return power to the military's civilian allies, or took place in response to threats against the military as an institution, such as government attempts to interfere in the promotion system or cut the military budget. However, with national security doctrine came not only the notion that government was a legitimate role for the military, but that squabbling civilian politicians were often less fit to govern than well-educated military men with only their country's interests at heart. When the Brazilian military took power in 1964, even the U.S. ambassador expected it to hand over power to a suitable civilian government within the year. Instead it ruled for two decades.

In most cases, military coups took place with the support of at least a section of the civilian political elite. In Chile Christian Democrat leader Patricio Aylwin openly supported the coup that brought General Pinochet to power in 1973, presumably hoping that once his socialist rival, President Salvador Allende, was removed, the army would then hand power to Aylwin's party before retiring to the barracks. Instead Pinochet kept power for himself and remained in the presidential palace for the next seventeen years, until a chastened Aylwin led the campaign that secured his departure.

The military's willingness to interfere, and civilian leaders' readiness to encourage it, destabilized democratic civilian politics by offering politicians a shortcut to power, which seemed more seductive than the prospect of long years in opposition. Parties no longer needed to succeed by developing sound

A Rich Man's Coup

The evening of that mild spring day, Tuesday 11 September, General Augusto Pinochet had been in power for a few hours. The guests were assembled in the main hall of the Hotel Carrera, a sumptuous room three storys high. . . . The new regime had decreed a curfew. The doors were barred.

People sat around on the sofas or at the little copper-topped tables. They talked animatedly, the suave men and the elegant ladies. They laughed and joked and drank noisily, the sound of their celebration bouncing and echoing off the shiny walls. Every so often there was an expectant hush when the television came up with a *bando*, some new message from the new masters of Chile. When it was ended there were cheers, more champagne corks popped and from ladies' slippers toasts were drunk to Pinochet and his brave companions.

In the corner the service door opened from time to time and groups of waiters peered timidly out. The juxtaposition of the stylish carousers and the apprehensive serving staff was dramatic and served like nothing else to bring home the social impact of the putsch above and beyond the patriotic and martial music that the radio and the television were broadcasting. The waiters and the rest of those below stairs knew what military rule was going to bring and they were afraid.

—Hugh O'Shaughnessy, *Latin Americans*, London: BBC Books, 1988

policies to win more support than their rivals, but could gain power by curry-
ing favor with the high command. The art of conspiracy became the successful politician's chief weapon.

The generals who seized power declared themselves to be "above politics," disparaging all civilian politicians as corrupt incompetents. Instead,
they saw the problems facing the continent as essentially technical, and cast
themselves as "iron surgeons," who would carry out profound restructuring
operations for which few anesthetics were available. In the larger countries,
the military ruled as an institution, seeking to avoid the temptations of *cau-
dillismo* in Argentina by governing by committee—the junta—or in Brazil by
rotating the presidency among the top generals.

The military's low opinion of politics did not include the state itself. It
saw an efficient, well-managed state as essential to the achievement of national
security and development, and if anything, increased the state's intrusion into
every nook and cranny of society: in Argentina even the head of the national
ballet was a military officer. Boosting state arms industries also proved popular with the generals. Only in Chile under General Pinochet, and to a lesser
extent in Argentina after the coup in 1976, did military governments abandon state-led development in favor of a ferocious pursuit of the market. In the
name of free trade and boosting competitiveness, both governments suddenly
removed any protection from local industries, with the inevitable result that
cheap imports flooded in, undercutting and bankrupting much of the industrial base so painstakingly assembled over the previous forty years.

The military's belief in its economic prowess proved seriously mistaken.
Military governments showed themselves to be, if anything, even less competent than their predecessors, running up vast national debts during the
free-spending 1970s, squandering resources on prestige megaprojects such
as dams and nuclear power programs, and neglecting the nuts and bolts of
long-term economic success, such as health and education.

In the longer run, the military's attempt to stamp out politics backfired.
Banning political parties in countries such as Argentina, Chile, and Uruguay
created a political vacuum into which a new generation of grassroots movements grew, led by human rights and neighborhood organizations. These
were the first groups to fight back against military rule, becoming the catalyst
for a broader opposition that brought about the military's eventual downfall.
The new movements brought new sections of the population into politics,
such as women and slum dwellers, creating a richer, more plural spectrum of
social organizations that augured well for the future.

Military rule was at its starkest in the Southern Cone countries of Argentina, Chile, and Uruguay, along with Brazil. The development of the state
elsewhere was more varied. In Venezuela and Mexico, the proceeds from

oil exports helped governments to soften the impact of the crisis of state-led industrialization, preventing the kind of political crisis that could have precipitated a military coup. Colombia pursued a more cautious role for the state, running up fewer debts and avoiding the worst of the collapse that afflicted the others. Paraguay looked more like Central America, as it languished under the rule of General Stroessner for thirty-five years from 1954. In Peru and Bolivia the recalcitrance of the landed elite blocked political change, eventually precipitating a revolution in Bolivia in 1952, and a modernizing military takeover in Peru in 1968, when General Juan Velasco seized power, promising sweeping reforms. Within months his government nationalized the property of the U.S. transnational, International Petroleum Company, and began a radical land reform. These two measures marked the high point of military radicalism in Peru. Soon the government became engulfed in economic crisis and internal divisions, and just before Velasco's death in 1975, a conservative faction within the military seized power. Velasco's reforms, however, left a radically altered rural society, where the feudal powers of the hacienda owners had in many cases been destroyed forever.

In 1992, a section of the Venezuelan military demonstrated a similar strand of left-wing nationalism when Lt.-Col. Hugo Chávez led a military revolt by the Revolutionary Bolivarian Movement. The uprising was swiftly crushed, leaving seventy dead, but not before Chávez's opposition to the government's economic austerity program had turned him into a folk hero, a status that later propelled him to the presidency.

Yet most military regimes have been firmly on the right, following the example of Brazil, whose generals, when they seized power in 1964, attempted to revitalize the economy as import substitution was running out of steam. By cutting real wages (by 35–40 percent in the first four years of the government), opening the economy to foreign investors and transnational companies, and investing massively in state companies and economic infrastructure, they succeeded in temporarily galvanizing the Brazilian economy, before the debt crisis of the 1980s forced the military's long and orderly withdrawal from politics. Direct elections for a civilian president finally took place in 1989.

Costa Rica has succeeded in ridding itself of its military altogether. After a brief civil war in 1948, Costa Rica's rival political parties agreed to abolish the army. Free of the military burden, Costa Rica now has a much higher standard of living than its Central American neighbors. In Bolivia the revolution of 1952 also radically weakened the army, but within four years the government had agreed to reestablish the armed forces as a condition for a vital US$25 million loan from the International Monetary Fund.

By the end of the 1990s, the international political climate had changed. The U.S. government concluded that military governments were both politically destabilizing and economically less competent than civilian ones. Washington showed its new resolve by pressuring the Salvadoran and Guatemalan militaries to accept deep cuts as part of the peace agreements that ended the civil wars in those countries. The United States also effectively abolished the armies of Panama and Haiti following its military occupations of those countries in 1989 and 1994. Military leaders found themselves subject to prosecution, and throughout the 1990s the public mood moved steadily against the idea of military power and embraced such concepts as human rights and democracy.

Transitions to Democracy

Just as the nature of military regimes varied enormously between different Latin American countries, so did the way they handed over power to elected governments. In many cases, the outgoing military government tried to cover its retreat by passing legislation giving its officers immunity from prosecution over human rights violations. Success in achieving immunity depended on the degree of military unity during withdrawal to barracks and the pressure exerted by the civilian opposition. The regimes in Brazil and Uruguay both managed an orderly exit, not only acquiring immunity for crimes committed in government, but retaining considerable political power. It appeared that the accession of left-wing governments in both countries at the turn of the century might threaten the immunity of the retired generals but this did not happen. Elsewhere, investigation and prosecution for past atrocities remains one of the main areas of civilian-military conflict everywhere, from Chile to Honduras.

The Argentine military's humiliation in the Falklands/Malvinas war forced it into a shame faced flight from power, giving the incoming Alfonsín government the chance to waive immunity; in 1985 five military leaders, including President Videla, were found guilty and given long prison sentences. Alfonsín thus achieved a Latin American first—never before had officers of a defeated military dictatorship been brought to trial. The trials were followed by a new law confining military activities solely to defending the nation's frontiers. Nationalist officers responded with a wave of military uprisings between 1987 and 1990, which ended only when incoming president Carlos Menem amnestied the 300 jailed officers, and found new roles for the military in UN peacekeeping forces and "civic action" programs of public improvements. The 2003 election of Néstor Kirchner, a Peronist who had been jailed by the military junta in the 1970s, marked a significant change in Argentina. He strongly supported the Argentine Supreme Court's decision to overturn two amnesty laws and a dozen or so former police officials and army officers received heavy prison sentences. His wife, Cristina Fernández, who followed Kirchner in 2007, continues to press for the conclusion of human rights cases from the past.

The assault on military privilege has also been financial. Under pressure from Washington, the IMF, and the World Bank to reduce spending, governments have cut military budgets and privatized the military industries set up under import substitution. Across the region military spending per head of the population was halved between 1985 and 1994, and has remained at a fairly constant 1.3 percent of GDP since then.

Reviled by the public and former allies, confused over its role, and facing falling wages, the military in many countries has entered a profound crisis of identity and morale. Where guerrilla insurgencies have continued to operate, in Colombia and Peru, joined in 1994 by Mexico following the Zapatista uprising, the military role has been clear, if bloody. Elsewhere, less introspective officers have turned to crime, creating a military mafia involved in drugs, car theft rings, and kidnapping. Many of the army's more talented members have left. The small number of military thinkers that remains has struggled to define a new role that can restore the military's legitimacy with the general public and provide a renewed sense of purpose as an institution.

There have been many suggestions. Some governments have opted for civic action programs to restore the army's reputation, covering everything from traditional road-building to environmental campaigns such as cleaning up piles of rotting garbage in Lima, or soaping down oil-soaked penguins in Argentine Patagonia.

In Venezuela, military engineers have been employed in a civic role, and the line between policeman and soldier has been significantly blurred. Washington has prodded insistently for the military to take a higher profile in the fight against the narcotics trade, but the military leadership fears that entering the "war on drugs" opens the door to corruption, as soldiers on ever lower wages are tempted by the vast sums at the drug traffickers' disposal. Drug-related corruption is already on the increase in several Central American armies, and two former military leaders, Bolivia's General García Meza and Panama's General Manuel Antonio Noriega, are currently serving long prison sentences for drug trafficking.

The Left in Latin America

The Guerrillas

In the 1970s no Western student's dorm room seemed complete without its poster of Che Guevara, with beret and beard, gazing mistily off into the middle distance. Che personified the myth of the guerrilla fighter, caricatured by Peruvian novelist Mario Vargas Llosa in *The Real Life of Alejandro Mayta*:

> His beard had grown, he was thin, in his eyes there was an unconquerable resolve, and his fingers had grown calloused from squeezing the trigger, fighting fuses and throwing dynamite. Any sign of depression he might feel would disappear as soon as he saw how new militants joined every day, how the front widened, and how there, in the cities, the workers, servants, students and poor employees began understanding that the revolution was for them, belonged to them.

Che was heir to a long Latin American tradition. In nineteenth-century Argentina the cowboy Montoneros of the Pampas fought an unsuccessful civil war to free the interior from the stranglehold of Buenos Aires. Elsewhere, irregulars helped to win independence from Spain. As the century wore on, such exotic bands passed into folklore as they were replaced by regular standing armies.

The guerrilla tradition was rediscovered in the 1920s by Augusto César Sandino, the Nicaraguan rebel whose distinctive ten-gallon hat became the symbol of revolutionary Nicaragua. When U.S. marines occupied Sandino's homeland in 1912, Sandino, who as a young man had worked in the Mexican oil fields and been influenced by the anti-Yankee and socialist ideas of the Mexican revolution, returned to Nicaragua. With a band of twenty-nine fighters, he began to harass the U.S. forces. When conventional tactics led to a series of defeats, reducing his company to just six, he developed a new style of fighting that became the blueprint for guerrilla warfare. According to Sandino, guerrillas should:

- Avoid set-piece confrontations where the enemy's superior firepower will give it an advantage.

- Use hit-and-run tactics and surprise rather than defend fixed positions. The objective is not to seize and defend territory, but to make the costs of staying unacceptably high to the enemy.

- Stay in small groups to avoid detection and increase mobility.

- Rely on superior knowledge of the terrain and contacts with local people to outwit the enemy.

Sandino's movement gathered force, giving the Nicaraguan brief fame as a romantic hero at the head of 6,000 fighters. When the Guomintang marched into Beijing in 1928, they named a division after Sandino, and a thriving anti-war movement in the United States sang his praises. For the first time, the United States experienced the frustration of facing an enemy that wouldn't "fight fair." In the words of the writer and former Sandinista vice president Sergio Ramírez: "The well-trained and elegantly uniformed Yankee soldiers could find only one phrase to describe it: 'damned country.' Rains, mosquitoes, swamps, swollen rivers, wild animals, the horror of suddenly falling into an ambush, fevers, an always invisible enemy." The words could just as well describe the U.S. nightmare in Vietnam, and the U.S. forces in Sandino's Nicaragua reacted in much the same way, venting their anger on civilians they suspected of supporting the guerrillas and thereby swelling the numbers of Sandino's supporters.

In 1933 the United States changed tactics, withdrawing from Nicaragua and setting up a National Guard that soon came under the control of Anastasio Somoza. Sandino's fight had always been primarily a nationalist one, so when the marines left he accepted partial disarmament and peace talks. In 1934, as Sandino and his generals were leaving a dinner in the presidential palace, they were ambushed and shot dead by Somoza's men.

The world forgot about Sandino, and the ensuing Somoza dictatorship did its utmost to wipe out his memory in Nicaragua, but his example inspired a group of radical students in the 1960s, who formed a new guerrilla band, the Sandinista National Liberation Front (FSLN), and took to the hills in Sandino's old strongholds. There they found many aging Sandinistas willing to help them. One guerrilla leader, Omar Cabezas, recalls the time when a young Sandinista came for the first time to an old farmer's hut. "see, I knew you'd come back," the campesino said with a grin, "I've got something you left behind last time." He then dug up an Enfield rifle from the time of the marines, buried for fifty years since the days when Sandino roamed the mountains.

Castro, Cuba, and Che

While Sandino's memory smoldered in the Nicaraguan hills, it was the Cuban Revolution of 1959 that marked the start of the modern guerrilla era. Cuba under the Batista dictatorship combined misery in the countryside and urban slums with a millionaire's playground of casinos and brothels for U.S. tourists and organized crime. Cuba's guerrilla war began in 1956 when Fidel Castro and 81 men, including the young Argentine Che Guevara, squeezed on to a motor launch with the unlikely name of *Granma* and set off from Mexico to invade Cuba. The mission was a disaster; Castro's 26 July Movement had already been infiltrated by Batista's secret service, and the Cuban troops were waiting for them. Fewer than twenty survivors fled to the mountains of the Sierra Maestra to lick their wounds and begin a two-year guerrilla war. Batista's ferocity and intransigence fueled peasant support for the guerrillas; in 1957 he attempted to forcibly relocate the rural population of the Sierra Maestra. By 1958 opposition political parties, landowners, and businesses had joined in, while the guerrilla force had grown into a rebel army that was attacking the government forces on three separate fronts and was able to take and hold fixed positions. Castro mounted a nationwide offensive, during which Che Guevara's soldiers succeeded in splitting the country in two. Batista fled to the Dominican Republic in early 1959 and Fidel Castro swept into Havana.

Cuba had a huge impact on the thinking of the Latin American left, convincing it that revolution could be triggered in underdeveloped countries by *focos* (small nuclei) of guerrillas. Previously the Communist Party had dominated the debate, insisting that revolution could be achieved only when the "objective conditions" were present. This entailed the creation of a "bourgeois democracy" and the growth of an industrial proletariat that would then form the vanguard for a predominantly urban revolution.

There followed a wave of unsuccessful attempts to repeat the Cuban experience across Latin America. Many of the young men and women who took to the guerrillas' harsh life in the mountains did so because they had seen all peaceful means for bringing about change blocked by a combination of electoral fraud and physical repression. In El Salvador the military denied electoral victory to a reforming coalition of political parties in the 1972 and 1977 elections, thereby triggering a spiral of frustration and violence that would plunge the country into a decade of horror during the 1980s.

The rise in the guerrilla movement was partly driven by another social change: the extraordinary expansion of higher education in Latin America after 1960. In Mexico and Brazil, the student population increased fifteen-fold by 1980. Universities became centers of political and cultural ferment. The growing gulf between the expectations raised by education and the economy's inability to meet them turned the universities into prime recruiting grounds for future guerrilla leaders.

Guerrilla war, especially *foquismo*, suited student idealism and impatience in its offer of a short-cut to power. A few young heroes with sufficient courage and political clarity could go up into the mountains and lead the people to inevitable victory, it was thought. For the region's angry and disenchanted middle-class youth, this was a far more exciting prospect than years of toil in the trade union and peasant movement.

Young radicals formed guerrilla groups in Brazil, Venezuela, the Dominican Republic, Colombia, Argentina, Peru, Bolivia, Guatemala, and Nicaragua, all of which met with failure or were forced radically to rethink their tactics. A generation of young radicals, poets, students, and peasant leaders lost their lives.

Guevara's own attempt to bring revolution to Bolivia in 1966 showed many of the fatal errors of *foquismo*. Choosing Bolivia because it was the poorest country in Latin America and "ripe for revolution," Guevara set off with a team of sixteen Cubans and headed for a remote southeastern province to set up their *foco*. The obstacles proved insuperable; although the guerrillas managed to recruit a few Bolivians, the leadership was entirely Cuban. As none of them could speak Guaraní, the local indigenous language, local people viewed the outsiders with suspicion. Furthermore, the region they chose was more prosperous than surrounding regions, and was so cut off that it had almost no contact with the capital, La Paz, and therefore no one had suffered directly at the hands of the central government.

With intensive counterinsurgency training from the United States, the Bolivian army soon tracked down and defeated the isolated "freedom fighters," and Guevara was shot. Following his death, *foquismo* came in for severe criticism, as new wars in Vietnam and later Nicaragua provided alternative models for guerrilla war.

The late 1960s and early 1970s saw a new phenomenon—urban guerrilla movements. In Argentina, the Montoneros named themselves after the horseback irregulars of the nineteenth century, and in Uruguay the Tupamaros took their name from Peru's eighteenth-century indigenous rebel leader Tupac Amaru II. Similar movements sprang up in Brazil and Colombia. These groups concentrated on spectacular actions, described as "armed propaganda," intended to win publicity and popular support. Some kidnapped prominent politicians, ambassadors, and businessmen. In Colombia the M-19 guerrilla group showed a keen sense of history by symbolically stealing the sword of independence hero Simón Bolívar. Such actions, however, won little lasting support and frequently led to severe repression at the hands of the military, who aimed far beyond the guerrillas to attack the whole popular movement. In Argentina, 90 percent of the 5,000 Montoneros lost their lives. Such groups have been criticized for their lack of political direction and tendency to use methods little different from terrorism.

After the failure of the *foquistas* and the urban guerrilla movements, the armed left continued to seek the elusive magic formula that would enable them to overthrow the state. Learning from the U.S. defeat at the hands of a guerrilla army in Vietnam, organizations such as the Popular Liberation Forces (FPL) in El Salvador embarked upon a strategy of "prolonged popular war," involving a patient long-term program of political work with the peasantry. As a result, guerrilla organizations became less dominated by students, and instead evolved into genuine peasant armies.

Other experiences enriched guerrilla thinking; the Nicaraguan revolution of 1979 showed the need for unity between different ideological currents on the left and demonstrated how a combination of rural guerrilla warfare and urban insurrection could produce a quick victory. In Peru, the Sendero Luminoso (Shining Path) showed that an authoritarian and violent movement built around a godlike leader in Abimael Guzmán—"President Gonzalo"—could win over the oppressed indigenous communities of the Andes with a combination of intimidation and the promise of unheard-of security. Following Guzmán's capture in 1992, Sendero went into decline as a serious threat to the government, though it has recently reemerged as a player in the cocaine trade.

The left-wing guerrilla group in the region that continues to stimulate revolutionary fervor abroad is Mexico's Zapatista National Liberation Army (EZLN). The Zapatistas burst on the scene in spectacular fashion on New Year's Day 1994, when 1,500 to 2,000 fighters simultaneously occupied four towns in the impoverished southern state of Chiapas. The action stands out as by far the largest inaugural operation by any guerrilla movement in Latin American history. Following the initial weeks of warfare, the Zapatistas holed up in their strongholds in the Lacandón jungle, conducting interminable and frustrating talks with the Mexican government and playing host to endless visits by the great and good of the European and U.S. left, from Danièle Mitterrand to Oliver Stone.

The Zapatistas are governed by a council of representatives from the region's indigenous communities. Their main demands are for the defense of indigenous culture and peasant agriculture. The group seems largely confined to Chiapas, and most of their fighters are indigenous, many speaking

Ernesto "Che" Guevara

The twentieth century's most famous guerrilla fighter was born Ernesto Guevara in Argentina in 1928 to middle-class parents, and qualified as a doctor in 1953. Guevara became a committed communist from the time of the 1954 CIA-instigated overthrow of the reforming Arbenz government in Guatemala. In that sense, he was much more radical than Fidel Castro, who embraced communism only when U.S. hostility forced revolutionary Cuba into the arms of the Soviet Union.

Guevara, a tall asthmatic man, became a Cuban citizen a month after the revolution. Castro made him president of the National Bank and Minister of Industries. Always a hard-liner, he argued that Cuba should seize the Soviet missiles when Krushchev agreed to withdraw them to end the 1962 missile crisis. In 1965 he left Havana on an eight-month tour of revolutionary movements around the world. Itching to return to the guerrilla struggle, he embarked in 1966 on the Bolivian episode that led to his death the following year.

Part of Guevara's legacy to Cuba has been insistence on the need for a "new man," motivated not by profit but by moral commitment to the cause of progress and equality:

"The process is a conscious one. The individual perceives the impact of the new social power and perceives that he is not completely adequate to it. He tries to adjust.… He is educating himself. We can see the new man who begins to emerge in this period of the building of socialism.… The [new men] no longer march in complete solitude along lost roads toward far-off longings. They follow their vanguard, composed of the party, of the most advanced workers, of the advanced men who move along bound to the masses and in close communion with them.… The reward is the new society, where human beings will have different characteristics: the society of communist man.… He will thus achieve total awareness of his social being, which is equivalent to his full realization as a human being, having broken the chains of alienation."

—Ernesto Che Guevara, *Man and Socialism in Cuba*, Havana: Book Institute, 1967

little or no Spanish, but the Zapatistas' most prominent leader is a mestizo, the charismatic "Subcomandante Marcos," a former philosophy professor whose witty and biting communiqués and press interviews have made him a household name and Robin Hood figure in Mexico.

The Zapatistas disavow the guerrilla organizations' traditional aim of seizing state power. Instead, the EZLN explain that they see themselves as only one part of a broad-based effort to make Mexico more democratic. Despite the

The Face of the Zapastista uprising: Subcomandante Insurgente Marcos. (Latinphoto)

idealism and courage of generations of Latin American guerrillas, the only two outright victories they have to show for forty years of fighting and bloodshed are Cuba and Nicaragua. In both instances, the brutality and intransigence of the previous regime had at least as much to do with eventual victory as the guerrillas themselves. In Nicaragua, the Sandinistas were voted out of office in 1990 with the aid of the Contras, themselves midway between a genuine guerrilla group and a band of hired thugs. Fidel Castro, on the other hand, has survived every challenge, from a more than fifty-year economic embargo imposed by the United States to a crippling recession following the collapse of the Soviet Union, from mass defections of sports teams to semi-comic but deadly serious CIA-sponsored assassination attempts. It seemed that the real difficulty for Cuba would come with the inevitable succession of power. But, unintentionally, Fidel himself paved the way: in 2006, he was brought low by a mysterious intestinal illness and forced to hand over the presidency to his brother, Raúl Castro. Although he has become very frail, he has, in 2012, so far survived, making it much harder for Washington to take advantage of the transition. Clearly frustrated, then U.S. president George W. Bush commented in exasperation: "One day the good Lord will take Fidel Castro away." To which Fidel, an atheist and not one to miss a chance for a quip, replied ironically: "Now I understand why I survived Bush's plan and the plans of other presidents to assassinate me: The good Lord protected me."

In Central America the guerrilla wars came to an end in the 1990s with negotiated peace agreements between government and guerrillas in El Salvador (1992) and Guatemala (1996). The Central American wars had been particularly bloody, as brutal counterinsurgency campaigns by the Guatemalan and Salvadoran armies accounted for 100,000 and 70,000 lives, respectively, although such totals are only the roughest of estimates. The FMLN guerrillas' military strength in El Salvador enabled them to achieve greater concessions at the negotiating table, largely demilitarizing the political system. Human rights abusers in the armed forces were purged (though not put on trial), the police were removed from army control, and the military establishment halved in size. Yet the unequal economic system that had prompted the guerrillas' uprising remained largely untouched, and when the FMLN took part in elections in 1994, they lost heavily (although subsequently won a number of local government elections, including in the capital, San Salvador). In Guatemala, the guerrillas were much weaker, and so extracted fewer concessions from the government in return for laying down their arms.

A number of factors account for this dismal record of guerrilla achievement:

- The state and army invariably possess an overwhelming advantage in firepower, troops, and logistical support.

- It is difficult to reconcile military and political work, both of which are needed for eventual victory. Military success requires a small, tightly disciplined group, able to keep mobile, preferably in secret, not defending fixed positions. Political support requires steady contact with the "masses," staying put to build up a relationship, and being able to defend them against any ensuing attack by the army.

- The U.S. has placed enormous importance on preventing first "another Cuba" then "another Nicaragua" in its hemisphere. Since Vietnam, the Pentagon has tried to develop effective counter-guerrilla strategies—"low-intensity conflict." These have combined elements of reform, "winning hearts and minds," with anti-guerrilla military tactics. Counterinsurgency has often involved severe repression of civilians judged sympathetic to the guerrillas, and Washington's readiness to support human rights abusers in El Salvador and Nicaragua has lost it many friends in the region. The relatively successful EZLN has never been challenged by U.S. troops, whose presence in Mexico would not be countenanced by even the most Washington-friendly government.

Nicaragua and Cuba show that military victory only heralds the start of a revolution's problems. Both governments managed to survive a U.S. economic and political siege only by turning to the Soviet Union for oil and other supplies. Radical governments in Bolivia (1952–56) and Chile (1970–73), which did not have Eastern Bloc support, soon fell or caved in to a combination of pressure from the United States and local economic and military elites. Since the collapse of the USSR, Soviet aid is no longer an option.

In Colombia, the Fuerzas Armadas Revolucionarias Colombianas (FARC) has been a key player in the country's internal war, and control much national territory. Rural in origin, the FARC has never been strong in the cities. They are very different from the media-savvy Zapatistas in Mexico, who have expertly publicized their case through a canny use of the Internet. FARC's doctrines, insofar as they exist, are vague. They pay respects to the revolutionary experiences of the Soviet Union, Cuba, and Vietnam, but say that they are blazing their own trail.

From the time they were founded, the FARC sought to control territory, and in doing so to amass funds. In the 1990s drug money began to overtake kidnapping and extortion as a source of funding for the organization. In recent years the FARC has lost much popular support due to widespread disapproval of their authoritarianism, human rights violations, kidnappings and extortion, yet they continue to occupy large areas of the country.

Social Movements

Recent decades have seen an upsurge of social movements in Latin America. Social movements are broad-based coalitions of the powerless who demand access to a political system that often excludes them. They had a key role to play under military dictatorships, for example, when the white headscarves of Argentina's Madres del Plaza de Mayo—the mothers of the disappeared— became an icon for human rights around the world.

In recent years social movements have tended to form around struggles against neoliberalism and the governments that impose it. Contemporary social movements to make headlines in recent years are the coca growers in Bolivia, the Indigenous People's Council (CONAIE) in Ecuador, and the largest social movement in the world, the Movimento Sem Terra, the landless rural workers of Brazil.

While often characterized as resistance movements, social movements do far more than resist: they push forward real social change, and work proactively to expand the range of rights that democracies in Latin America have hitherto often failed to provide for citizens. It is social movements, and not formal politics, that have often given Latin America its political dynamism—although some commentators would call it "instability." It is true that they have played a leading role in destabilizing elected governments, notably in Bolivia, Argentina, and Ecuador at the turn of the century, ousting presidents and calling for constitutional reforms.

The Left in Power

Latin America's left has long had an ambivalent relationship to democracy. In the heyday of revolutionary socialism, left activists derided "bourgeois" democratic structures, portraying them as little more than a confidence trick played by the elite, which did nothing to achieve real participation and empowerment for the region's poor majority. Since the failure of the guerrilla movements and the barbarities of military rule, however, many have changed their views and come to accept the virtues of elections. Activists who suffered repression and exile under military rule decided that formal democracy and the rule of law were not so bad after all, while the fall of the Berlin Wall and the collapse of state socialism in Eastern Europe convinced many doubters of the importance of accountability and democracy in ensuring that politicians remain in touch with the people.

Nicaragua under the Sandinista government (1979–90) encapsulated many of the arguments and dilemmas over the left's attitude to formal democracy. The Sandinistas came to power in 1979 as a small guerrilla organization whose structure and ideas had been forged in the underground war against the Somoza dictatorship. Throughout the period of Sandinista rule, the party itself remained a small, vanguard organization of hand-picked activists who sought to provide leadership to a wider popular movement.

At first the FSLN appeared to disparage electoral democracy, preferring more direct forms of participation. The party's leaders toured the country conducting face-to-face talks with peasants and workers to hear their complaints, and popular organizations such as trade unions, peasants, and women's groups were given seats on a consultative Council of State, established to advise the FSLN in government. The party's cadres were told to act as the eyes and ears of the government, keeping it in touch with ordinary Nicaraguans.

The results were mixed. The emphasis on participation and organization transformed a large part of Nicaraguan society. Many of the poor gained self-confidence as they learned to read and write and became involved in myriad "mass organizations." Since these organizations were largely controlled by the party, however, they were often forced to put party or national interests before those of their members. Participation dropped off as people became exhausted by endless meetings, the growing economic crisis, and the rigors of the war against the U.S.-backed Contra rebels.

In 1984 the FSLN held presidential elections to try to win international recognition as a legitimate government, but failed to convince Washington to stop funding the Contras. From 1984 to 1990, the FSLN ruled Nicaragua in the dual role of a government that had been freely elected and as an extra-parliamentary vanguard party working directly with mass organizations. Over time, its views changed. From being a tactical measure designed to forestall U.S. pressure, elections became more central to Sandinista philosophy.

In February 1990 the FSLN was stunned when it lost the elections to Violeta Chamorro's UNO coalition, but passed the democratic test by accepting the result. The revolutionary vanguard assumed the role of opposition in a party political system. Its credentials were further tested in 1996 when it again lost the elections, this time to right-wing populist Arnoldo Alemán. However, a much-changed Daniel Ortega, who was previously president from 1985 to 1990, led a much-changed FSLN to victory in the elections in 2006. Adopting market economics, albeit with a strong social welfare element, he is set to stand for reelection in autumn 2012.

Many of the same dilemmas faced the Brazilian left as the Workers' Party (PT) grew in strength throughout the 1990s. The PT won the giant city of São Paulo and thirty-five other major towns in November 1988. The PT built up a reputation as a trustworthy and "safe" electoral alternative by governing at municipal, city, and state levels and gaining a good reputation through innovations such as the participatory budget in Porto Alegre, whereby voters were involved to an unprecedented extent in directly deciding how local government should set its spending priorities. This helped pave the way for Lula's success in the 2002 presidential elections. His victory was of great significance for the Latin American left, and heralded a regional realignment toward the left in Argentina, Ecuador, Uruguay, and Paraguay.

In many parts of Latin America the left gained experience for national government by first winning local elections. Whereas in 1997 just 60 million Latin Americans were governed by the left at the municipal level, by 2003 this number had risen to more than 200 million. However, leftist local governments had to work within severe constraints, since their budgets were usually determined by hostile national administrations. Even so, many acquired a reputation for efficiency and honesty and, just as in Brazil, introduced groundbreaking experiments in local democracy and accountability. In 1990 the *Frente Amplio* (Broad Front) broke Uruguay's two-party duopoly to take control of the capital city, Montevideo, and introduced innovative programs to decentralize services and make them more account-

Hugo Chávez,
President of Venezuela

able to residents. This undoubtedly contributed to the successive victory of two Frente Amplio candidates, first Tabaré Vázquez (2004) and then José Mujica, a former guerrilla fighter (2009). In 2011 seven Latin American countries—Argentina, Bolivia, Brazil, Ecuador, Nicaragua, Paraguay, and Venezuela—had left-of-center governments.

The ideology of the "New Left" is far from revolutionary; instead it combines a desire for social justice with a commitment to a measure of economic liberalism and an adherence to the existing geopolitical "rules of the game." By reaching out to unions and social movements, Lula in Brazil and Néstor Kirchner in Argentina sought to combine political stability, economic growth, and a degree of economic justice through increased spending on social services and some success at tackling extreme inequality.

Venezuela has undergone a unique leftward shift of its own. Hugo Chávez, a paratrooper who in 1992 led a failed insurrection against the corrupt party system, reinvented himself as a populist civilian politician. His daring promise to break the control over the country by *"los escuálidos"* (the squalid ones, referring to rich and largely white elites) excited millions of poor, largely black, excluded Venezuelans and he stormed to a landslide victory in the 1998 presidential election. He soon implemented far-reaching constitutional and social legislation, funded by a timely flood of oil revenues. Predictably, his regime faced a conservative backlash, including charges of cronyism and a disregard for legal procedures. In 2002, Chávez was briefly deposed in a coup organized by media and business leaders with close links to the old parties that had been swept away by Chávez's "revolution" and to the United States. But to the consternation of the plotters, the army remained largely loyal to the elected government, and amid much confusion and rioting, Chávez was reinstalled as president.

While most left-wing governments in Latin America did not break with the neoliberal model but attempted to "humanize" it, so it brought more benefits for the poor, Chávez said in 2005 that he was seeking to build "socialism of the twenty-first century" (although he did not specify at the time—and has not done since—what this actually means). And in many ways in his years in power Chávez has delivered on this promise, for he has undoubtedly shaken up the political and social system. More Venezuelans, largely from the poorest sectors, have been registered as voters and political participation has increased, with an impressive 69 percent of the population voting in elections in 2006. More than 30,000 communal councils have been created to increase participation at a local level. Unemployment has dropped dramatically, from 14.5 percent of the workforce in 1999 to 7 percent in 2010. At the same time, there has been an even more impressive decline in poverty, from 21 percent of households in 1998 to 6 percent in 2009. Almost three times as many young people attend university. These are real advances and help explain why Chávez continues to enjoy the support of about half of the population.

Yet there have also been limitations to what Chávez has achieved. At a macroeconomic level, his administration has failed to deliver the transformation he promised and there has been little socialism, if this means the state taking over key areas of the economy. It is true that the state has regained control over the oil industry, which was previously run as a quasi-independent company in the interests of private enterprise, but PDVSA, the state-owned oil company, is still run on fairly traditional capitalist lines, without much involvement of workers in management. In other sectors workers have taken over a few factories but no large and important companies are involved. Chávez has also failed to diversify the economy, which was one of the few specific targets he set himself. Some 90 percent of export earnings still come from oil and the government is heavily dependent on this revenue. Venezuela is still clearly run as a market economy. What has changed is that much of the government's revenue is now used to fund social programs. Indeed, Chávez has spent a great deal on these programs and has run up an alarming level of public debt. As a result, Venezuela was unable to fund countercyclical measures and was hit more severely by the world recession in 2008 than most other countries in Latin America. Other shortcomings include a severe housing shortage, a rise in crime (though it still runs below the Latin American average), and an undoubted increase in the inefficiency of the public administration, with many people resorting to bribery in order to expedite simple procedures like obtaining a passport.

What is, paradoxically, both the greatest strength and the greatest weakness of *Chavismo* is Chávez himself. He is extraordinarily charismatic and his capacity to chat amusingly for hours on television in his *Aló Presidente* show is remarkable. He comes across as friendly and accessible, almost a member of the family. Yet Chávez does not hide the fact hat he is also the boss. Perhaps because he was trained as a military officer and is head of the armed forces (something he is very proud of), he has a very hierarchical style of management, which, in practice, clashes with his oft-repeated commitment to a more open and participatory form of government. Indeed, perhaps the best way of seeing him is as a modern-day *caudillo*. But, when *caudillos* die or are forced out of office, their fiefdom collapses overnight. And this is a grave risk for *Chavismo*, something that became embarrassingly apparent in June 2011, when the government lurched to a virtual standstill after it was announced that Chávez was receiving treatment for cancer in Cuba. Even the opposition parties, who harbor a visceral hatred of Chávez, were hoping for his speedy recovery because of the chaos that would occur if he died in office. Much better, they said, to vote him out of government.

By 2011 democracy was thriving in the whole of South America. The only anomaly is Colombia where, despite elections broadly seen as fair, a guerrilla movement is still active, controlling significant areas of the country. This gives the impression that Colombia is somehow frozen in the 1980s. Indeed, in the mid-1980s the armed left attempted to enter electoral politics, as happened in other South American countries, but the endeavor failed. Within a few years of its creation, the Unión Patriótica, a political party set up by the FARC guerrilla group, had over 3,000 leaders assassinated by paramilitaries. The victims included mayors, governors, and two very capable presidential candidates. Not surprisingly, this attempt to move into the formal political arena was eventually abandoned and armed conflict continued to dominate Colombian politics.

North of the Panama Canal democracy feels more fragile. In Mexico a groundbreaking advance was made in 2000 when the old corrupt PRI (Institutional Revolutionary Party) lost office for the first time in seventy years. But the progress was more apparent than real. Because the two rival parties— the right-of-center PAN and the leftish PRD—were both too fragmented to develop their own networks to challenge the PRI's system of patronage, they were forced to work with PRI power brokers to get their legislation approved. As a result, they have been corrupted by the very system they once vowed to

Porto Alegre: The Dynamism of the Organized

When Tarso Genro assumed, for the second time, the *prefeitura* (mayoralty) of Porto Alegre in January 2001, the city became home to the first four-term *Partido dos Trabalhadores* (PT, Worker's Party) administration in Brazil, and one of the longest-running leftist city governments in Latin America:

"The city of Porto Alegre stands at the center of a metropolitan area of almost three million people. Literacy rates of over 90 percent are among the highest in the country for a large city, as is its life expectancy (72 years). But Porto Alegre is also a highly socially segregated city. Almost a third of its population lives in irregular housing, such as slums or 'invaded' areas. By the time the PT administration was voted into office in 1989, the city had experienced, like much of Brazil, an exacerbation in urban poverty and a decline in service provision throughout the 1980s. The Participatory Budget revolves around the OP (Orçamento Participativo) meetings, which alone drew over 20,000 people in 2000. Budget meetings provide the bulk of citizen participation and have been in place since the PT's second year in government. Over the years they have evolved into a structure of councils where citizens deliberate all year round and decide on both district-specific projects and broad municipal investment priorities. The city has recently achieved a sort of 'global status' for this participatory scheme, being recognized by activists, international organizations and policy makers from North and South alike. Most recently, as host city for the World Social Forum, Porto Alegre has continued to attract attention from progressives around the world."

—Gianpaolo Baiocchi in Daniel Chávez and Benjamin Goldfrank, eds., *The Left in the City: Participatory Local Governments in Latin America*, London: LAB, 2004

change. Along with a dysfunctional political system, Mexico has a growing problem of crime, much of it linked to drug trafficking. Although the problem may be exaggerated by the media (Mexico had 22 homicides per 100,000 in 2010, compared with 78 in Honduras, 48 in Venezuela, and 25 in Brazil), violence is growing at a rapid rate, which is very alarming for the local population. Democracy in Mexico feels shallow and brittle.

Democratization

Despite massive recessions, economic crises, and corruption scandals, which in earlier decades would have had the generals champing at the bit, the military has mostly stayed in the barracks in recent decades. Isolated bouts of saber rattling, when commanders have sent tanks on to the streets of Lima or Santiago, have been easily seen off, not least because U.S. support for military interference in politics largely ended with the fall of the Berlin Wall. As a result the last thirty years has been a period of unprecedented political stability under civilian governments. When Argentina's Raúl Alfonsín handed over the presidency to Carlos Menem in 1989, it was the first constitutional transfer between Argentine presidents of rival parties in the twentieth century. Until the 1990s, most presidents had struggled to finish even one term in office without being forcibly ejected from the presidential palace. The growing stability has led ambitious politicians to demand a change in the rules. A series of constitutional amendments have been passed to allow presidents such as Carlos Menem (Argentina), Fernando Henrique Cardoso (Brazil), and Alberto Fujimori (Peru) to run for a second (in the case of Fujimori, a third) term in office.

In recent years, Latin American leaders have shown a newfound vulnerability to public opinion. Corruption scandals have seen national parliaments and public pressure combine to oust Brazil's Fernando Collor in 1992, Venezuela's Carlos Andrés Pérez in 1993, and Peru's Alberto Fujimori in 2000. Ecuador gets through presidents at regular intervals, either through legal avenues or street protests. Argentina famously had five presidents in two weeks during the economic collapse of December 2001. What were once highly centralized presidential systems have become significantly more accountable to public and political pressure.

Optimists see all this as evidence of a lasting transition to democracy. It is true that the systems of governance are flawed. Many presidents are authoritarian. Corruption is prevalent. Legal systems fail to uphold the law. Party political systems are fragile and volatile. New parties rise and sink without trace at an increasing rate, while parliamentary politics are often chaotic and corrupt. Brazil has probably the most unstable party system in the region. During one term in office in the 1990s, 170 out of 513 members of the lower house switched parties, some of them more than once—one defected seven times. Party loyalty is almost nonexistent, a nightmare for any president and an almost certain guarantee of pork-barrel politics, as political managers seek to buy the votes of deputies on key issues.

Pessimists stress the lack of true citizenship, believing that real democracy is impossible when inequality, crumbling social services, the crime wave, and police intimidation and immunity from prosecution are so widespread. A functioning democracy relies on a degree of social consensus; people have to accept the legitimacy of the system. Yet, according to Brazilian political scientist Paulo Sérgio Pinheiro, "In almost all Latin American countries, the poor see the law as an instrument of oppression at the service of the wealthy and powerful." According to Brazil's Pastoral Land Commission, 1,465 land reform activists and peasants, including dozens of children, were killed in dif-

Evo Morales, Bolivia's
first indigenous president.
(Latinphoto)

ferent rural conflicts between 1985 and 2006. Only 8 percent of the cases
were ever brought to trial, and only twenty of the landlords who hired the
gunmen to execute such crimes have been convicted. In Venezuela, 18,800 of
the country's 25,000 prisoners have not been sentenced, while 92 percent of
Venezuelans say that justice does not apply equally to rich and poor, and 51
percent say people should take the law into their own hands.

This is hardly the basis for a functioning democracy, where disputes and
conflicts are settled through a judicial system that everyone believes in or at
least accepts as in some sense legitimate. Yet, for all that, democracy seems
alive and well in Latin America. Partly because of the rise of left-of-center governments, the living standards of the poorer sectors of society have improved
in recent decades. It seems likely that while this continues the mass of the
population will continue to support, if only halfheartedly, a system of government that is giving results.

The Future

Latin America has to some extent achieved democracy by default. The Cold War has ended and for the time being Washington and foreign investors see democratic regimes as the best route to political stability (though they are happy to turn a blind eye to undemocratic practices in strategically important countries such as Mexico). The military has withdrawn to the barracks to lick its wounds after disastrous performances in government. There are now enough leftist governments in the region to declare a resurgence.

Winning a presidency was itself an epic achievement for the Latin American left, but in many cases it marked only the beginning of a difficult road. Once in office, left-wing presidents of even large countries such as Brazil or Chile have swiftly found that their options are severely constrained. With economies deeply integrated into international capital markets, any move that "unsettles the markets"—too high an inflation figure, a spat with the IMF, or a decision to shelve privatization plans—can lead to a sudden exodus of capital, precipitating a run on the currency and economic collapse, as happened in Mexico in 1994 and Argentina in 2001. It is possible for governments to implement reforms but the pace must be slow and cautious.

Commentators have always imagined that the latest Latin American trend was going to last for ever: in the 1950s the modernizers claimed that Latin America had finally made it on to the road to industrial development; in the 1960s the future was revolutionary after Cuba; in the 1970s and early 1980s, Latin America would forever remain grimly authoritarian. Each prediction was promptly disproved by events. Now foreign pundits and politicians alike once again rashly affirm that Latin America is irreversibly democratic. If history is any guide, it is more probable that the future will see the twin threads of authoritarianism and democracy once more combine to create a more complex and quintessentially Latin American brand of politics.

Even so, one probably lasting trend is emerging: the weakening of U.S. influence in the region. Embroiled in unpopular wars in the Middle East and losing ground to the new world powers, the United States is no longer in a position to intervene militarily in South America. Brazil, South America's emerging regional power, would react strongly to heavy-handed meddling by the United States in the countries within its sphere of influence. South of Panama, Uncle Sam's undisputed reign may be ending, particularly as this region largely resisted the U.S. attempt in the first decade of the twenty-first century to extend NAFTA into one giant Free Trade Area of the Americas (FTAA).

The situation is somewhat different in Mexico, Central America, and the Caribbean. This region is still dominated by the United States, with trade agreements binding the countries closely to Washington. The exception, of course, is Cuba, which over fifty years ago broke away from U.S. dominance, thanks to intervention by the USSR, and is still a thorn in Washington's side. Washington has no intention of ever allowing another nation in this region to gain comparable independence. The big challenge is Mexico, which is just too close to the United States for Washington to relinquish its role as final arbiter. In a report in 2008 the U.S. Joint Forces Command said that Mexico was vulnerable to "a rapid and sudden collapse." It went on: "The government, its politicians, police and judicial infrastructure are all under sustained assault and pressure by criminal gangs and drug cartels. How that internal conflict turns out over the next several years will have a major impact on the stability of the Mexican state. Any descent by Mexico into chaos would demand an American response based on the serious implications for homeland security alone." Put bluntly, Washington is not ruling out military or police intervention, should law and order be deemed to be under threat.

3.
Land, the City,
and Environment

Promised Land: Landownership, Power, and Conflict

The priest is holding an open-air Mass for the indigenous coffee pickers. Women in their bright traditional costumes listen on rough benches under the hot sun; the men sit on the ground, hats in hands. Round about are their tents, made of transparent plastic sheets stretched over sticks. Maize grinders, essential for the staple food, tortillas, are mounted on branches stuck into the earth. A few possessions are hung from other branches, clear of the pigs.

In Guatemala such scenes are reenacted every December, as the coffee harvest starts and indigenous villagers are trucked down from their tiny plots of land in the highlands of Chimaltenango to camp out and pick coffee for several months. The wages are US$3–$4 a day, the food is worm-ridden and insufficient, but they come every year because they have no choice. Their land does not grow enough food to keep them going all year round, so they must pick coffee.

As the priest says Mass, the owner of the coffee plantation, Loren, opens a beer on the veranda of his estate house. He has driven out in his jeep from his town house in Guatemala City to visit his farm, a crumbling but still beautiful building with whitewashed walls, palm trees and a stagnant swimming pool full of tadpoles. Green fields of coffee bushes cloak the hillsides.

Loren is white, owns a great deal of land, speaks French, English, and Spanish, and is very rich. Back in Guatemala City, he plays the international coffee market by computer. His Indians inhabit a different world; they own minute plots of land, are mostly illiterate, speak Kekchi and broken Spanish, and will probably never see either a computer or Guatemala City. Loren makes his excuses: "I can't give them meat and vegetables on top of everything else or I'd go bankrupt. Anyway, those people are not used to it—they don't want it." Outside, the priest exhorts the coffee pickers to "work hard and be humble."

Life on a Sugar Plantation

I saw many horrific punishments in slavery. That's why I hated that life. In the boilerhouse were the stocks, which were the most cruel. There were stocks that made you lie down, and others that kept you on your feet. They were made from wide boards with holes where they forced the slaves to put their feet, hands and head. They kept them stuck like that for two or three months, for any unimportant misdemeanor. They used to whip pregnant women as well, but lying face down with a hole in the earth to protect their bellies. They used to really give them a good beating! They took care not to damage the child because they wanted them unharmed.

The rowdiest days on the plantations were the Sundays. I don't know how the slaves had so much energy. That's when slavery's biggest fiestas took place. On some plantations the drums started at midday. The hubbub started as soon as the sun rose, and the kids started to run around and get underfoot. The slave quarters were throbbing from early on, it felt like the end of the world! And to think that after all that work, people woke up happy.

—Miguel Barnet, *Biografía de un cimarrón* (author's translation), Havana, Instituto de Etnología y Folklore 1966,

Guatemala is an extreme example of the abyss that separates peasant from large landowner in most of rural Latin America. In this essentially apartheid system, the struggle for land and the other farming essentials such as water, credit, and roads has been a source of political conflict and instability for many years, producing revolutions, massacres, and innumerable simmering disputes. The wave of market reforms in the region in the 1990s further exacerbated such tensions.

The continent had vast underused areas of cultivable land, climates, and soils to suit every crop, and good water resources, yet in 1998 44 percent of the rural population lived in poverty (that is, on less than US$2 a day) and 26 percent in extreme poverty (less than US$1.25 a day). At least six million children were malnourished, a million of them severely so. Rural children were three times as likely to live in extreme poverty as their counterparts in towns and cities. Since then, the situation has improved. By 2008 only 20 percent of the rural population lived in poverty and 7 percent in extreme poverty. People are not doing better because they are earning more from the crops they grow. Instead, they have learned how to earn money from elsewhere: today only a fraction of agricultural households live on what they produce on the farm. Most have at least one family member employed outside the farm and many receive money from relatives in towns, which is where about 80 percent of the population lives today. Families that don't have these systems of support tend to be very poor, with poverty concentrated among landless farmers, indigenous peoples, and women and children.

Latin American countries, particularly large nations like Brazil and Argentina, are big agricultural exporters, mainly of crops like soya, sugarcane and coffee, which are grown on plantations. Yet many Latin Americans ask whether this type of rural development, which brings big profits to the large farmers but exclusion and poverty to the mass of the rural population, is the best way of using their vast natural resources. The roots of this kind of development, in which opulence coexists with hunger, are to be found in the patterns of unequal landownership established from the first days of the Spanish Conquest.

Before the conquistadores came, most land was communally owned and largely used for arable crops. The most advanced civilization, the Incas in Peru, had large-scale irrigation systems, crop terracing whose remnants can still be seen today, and a sophisticated storage and distribution system. The Spanish and Portuguese introduced cows, sheep, horses, wheat, and sugarcane, and raised them alongside traditional crops like maize, beans, tobacco, and potatoes. Both Spanish and Portuguese monarchs rewarded their troops and settlers with grants of land and indigenous slaves. Under the *encomienda* system in the Andes, conquistadores had the right to exact forced labor from specified indigenous communities. In return they had to send a percentage of the proceeds to Madrid and, in theory, convert the natives to Catholicism.

From these massive land grants, three main forms of landownership became established during the colonial period:

PLANTATIONS: these were large farms geared to exports, often using foreign capital and slave labor (the first slaves were brought from Africa to Brazil in 1538). They were mainly in areas where the indigenous population was less advanced and soon wiped out by the European conquerors. The first great plantation crop was sugar in northeastern Brazil, coastal Peru, parts of Colombia, and the Caribbean. On the plantations African slaves worked in gangs, often in the harshest of conditions, watched over by armed guards. Plantation owners were businessmen, motivated by profit, and their farms were usually both efficient and brutal.

HACIENDAS: These produced for the domestic market, rather than export (known as *fazendas* in Brazil). They grew food crops for pack animals and raised cattle to feed the Spanish armies and mine workers. The haciendas were mainly in regions with advanced indigenous civilizations at the time of the Conquest, such as Peru, Ecuador, and Mexico. Rather than profits, haci-

Life on the Hacienda

On the haciendas of Bolivia, prior to the revolution of 1952, *pongos* were peasant farmers who did three or four days of unpaid work a month for the owner in exchange for the right to farm a small piece of often substandard land:

The pongo must bring his own food, even though he has a right to the leftovers from the master's table. So when he goes to fulfill his obligation, he takes with him an earthenware or copper cooking pot, quite covered in soot, a faggot of kindling wood and a sack of llama turds for fuel, and some supplies of food.

The pongo is given a spot in the great house for his quarters, some alleyway near the mangers and pigsties, and here he builds a fire to prepare his soup, boil up his corn-grits or toast his corn. But like a watchdog he must sleep in the lobby ready to open the door for the master's children and for the master himself if he is a night bird and likes to spend his time at the club or in a tavern.

His work occupies him from dawn until far into the night, amongst his labors are the following: to help in the kitchen, to look after the harness and mind the poultry. He must sweep out the rooms, the courtyards, clean the stables and pigsties and do the garden. The traditional colonial estate house is a little world, a kind of Noah's ark with every kind of animal in it. The pongo is builder, messenger, nanny and brewer of *chicha* (corn beer). He fills in the gaps in the phalanx of servants during the day. And at night he has other tasks to complete the dark rosary of his obligations: spinning, weaving, husking corn, *mukeo* (chewing corn for chicha, fermented with saliva) and of course, minding the doorway.

—Rafael Reyeros, *El Pongueaje*, La Paz, 1949

enda owners valued the power and status conferred by land ownership; they more closely resembled aristocrats than businessmen and their farms were frequently underused and inefficient. The workers on the hacienda had a feudal relationship with the landlord, renting land in return for either a share of their crop (sharecropping) or for cash, or more often paying by working on the landowner's estate for a certain number of days a year. Hacienda owners controlled every aspect of their lives—some even ran their own local police and jails. The hacienda was a closed world where the owner was the main channel for contact with the outside.

SMALLHOLDER COMMUNITIES: Residual indigenous communities in inaccessible areas tried to carry on as before, despite the heavy tribute and labor payments exacted by the colonial authorities. The indigenous farmers retained many pre-Columbian practices, such as communal ownership of land, a strong spiritual bond with the soil, and the use of simple technology such as hoes and digging sticks. As time went by, their numbers were swelled by poor *mestizo* (mixed blood) farmers, many of whom spoke Spanish.

A typical peasant family today still lives in a one- or two-room shack made of wood or adobe. They own a few animals and hand tools, and plow by hand or rented oxen from a better-off local family. Families are large, sons helping from an early age in the fields, while daughters work both on the land and in the home. They usually grow traditional food crops such as beans, maize, or potatoes. In recent decades, such households have depended on income from labor on neighboring large farms and from family members migrating in search of work.

Unbridgeable Gulf

The legacy of the colonial system has been an extreme and growing concentration of land, wealth, and power in the hands of big landowners, who are a tiny minority, while the vast majority of rural people have insufficient or no land, and are poor, hungry, and excluded from the political system. In Mexico at the start of the twentieth century 1 percent of farmers owned an extraordinary 97 percent of the land, while even as late as 1962, 1 percent of Peruvian farmers owned 80 percent of the land. These dry statistics hardly convey

---

"We Too Are Falling"

In the black community of Vertente, in the Brazilian northeast, 60 families live crowded onto five hectares of drought-stricken land. It is April, and six months since the last rain fell. The only water supply is a trickle of a stream, where it can take four hours to fill a bucket. Dusk is falling and a shining green hummingbird hovers in front of an enormous purple bud on one of the few banana trees that keep the community going. As it grows dark, sounds seem louder: children's voices, birdsong, the rustle of banana leaves. "The banana trees are falling, because they only have one leg," says one old man. "A man has two legs to support him, but now we too are falling." The potbellied children gather round to dance, as the adults talk of their endless struggle for farms big enough to feed their families. At the moment they are sharecropping, so a large portion of whatever pitiful crop they harvest must go to the landlord. There is good soil lying idle nearby, but they dare not farm it for fear of reprisals. A greater proportion of Vertente's children die than anywhere else in northeastern Brazil.

A Green Prison

In the midst of a dense undergrowth of brambles, reeds and tall grasses that choked the abandoned banana fields, the clearers made their machetes whistle through the air as, bent double and breathing noisily like cattle, they hacked their way through the tangle. Clouds of thistledown flew up and settled again, sticking into their reddened, sweaty skin as they plodded along like sleepwalkers, heavy with weariness and enervation. And, amidst all this confusion of laborers and banana trees, sun and pestilence, sweat and machines, creeks and malaria, rang out the cocky shouts of the foremen, the whistling of the overseers, and the arrogant, all-powerful gringo slang.

So it went on all day long. The peasants' exhausting toil stretched out until nightfall when, their legs buckling under them with weariness, they quit the green prison of the banana plantations only to be engulfed in the dispiriting prison of their soulless, barrack-like quarters.

—Ramón Amaya Amador, *Prisión Verde*, trans. Nick Caistor, Mexico, 1950

the almost unbridgeable cultural and economic gulf that still divides the rich elites from peasant farmers. After independence, and especially in the second half of the nineteenth century, Latin America became increasingly bound to the world economy. Foreign investment from the new industrial powers such as Britain and the United States started to arrive, turning the old plantations into modern capitalist farms. Wage labor replaced slavery, which was abolished everywhere in Latin America by the end of the nineteenth century, and farmers began to invest more capital in machinery and fertilizers. This model proved extremely profitable, and grew at the expense of the traditional but inefficient hacienda system. As each new crop was introduced, the plantation system and the power of the plantation owners grew.

At the end of the nineteenth century, U.S. companies started to buy up land themselves, rather than work through local farmers. The pioneers were the multinational banana companies, like United Fruit, which set up banana enclaves in Central America and the Caribbean. On these enclaves workers lived in barracks, permanently in debt to the company store, while the multinational company built its own railroads to take the bananas to ports and its waiting ships. The system brought scant benefit to the host country, which usually received very little tax income from the banana trade.

The concentration of land in very few hands, which grew as capitalist agriculture expanded, made Latin America the most unequal continent in the world. Big farmers, whether local or foreign, became rich and used their influence to ensure government policies favored their interests. Governments duly encouraged exports, kept taxes low on the luxury imports the elites desired, and made sure that the big farmers received the lion's share of state spending through bank loans, investment in roads and railways, and training and technical advice for their administrators. As they grew richer, the big farmers bought more land, whereas the peasant farmers were deprived of state help, credit, and social services like health care and education. The gap between rich and poor grew ever wider. In her autobiography, the Guatemalan indigenous leader and Nobel Peace Prize–winner Rigoberta Menchú recalls how her parents lost their land to incoming Ladinos (Spanish-speaking Guatemalans of mixed race):

Land Inequalities in Honduras

Standing on a hillside above the melon farm in southern Honduras, I am surrounded by foot-high maize plants that belong to Samuel, a local farmer. The valley below is criss-crossed with neat green lines of honey melons. Although it is only 6:30 in the morning, the large farm is a hive of activity, with workers applying water and pesticides to the fruit destined for export to Europe and the United States.

The slopes around me are a mosaic of maize plots and remnants of the dry forest that used to stretch in a continuous band along the Pacific coast from Mexico to Panama. Once farmers clear the forest to grow crops, the soil loses its protective cover and, on exposure to the intense rains, the result is soil erosion. As the land degrades, production falls. Some farmers will clear more patches of forest or eke out a living on the original plot; others will migrate to the cities to find work.

The melon farm exemplifies the type of agriculture that emerged during the Green Revolution, an agricultural system that relies on large and expensive technical inputs such as irrigation, pesticides, herbicides and fertilizer to restore and maintain soil productivity. The Green Revolution has undoubtedly led to a substantial increase in production, but it has also bypassed millions and millions of farmers, such as Samuel, who simply cannot afford the costly inputs.

Inequalities in land distribution in countries such as Honduras mean that resource-poor farmers have few alternatives but to cultivate marginal agricultural areas such as hillsides. Driven off prime land in the valley floors, small farmers in small, densely populated areas have been forced to cultivate steep slopes, leading to soil erosion.

—Jon Hellin, ed., *Better Land Husbandry: From Soil Conservation to Holistic Land Management*, Oxford: Oxford Brookes University Press, 2006

Canned Imperialism in Mexico

When Del Monte first sent its technicians to look at the Bajío [valley in Mexico] in 1959, they found a region ill-suited to the needs of the world's largest canner of fruits and vegetables. Grain production predominated, with corn and beans serving as the mainstays of the local diet. In Del Monte's own words, "Vegetable production was small and limited to a few crops grown exclusively for the local fresh market." The Bajío's land tenure system was also incompatible with Del Monte's needs. Due to the valley's population density, and the breakup of the large landed estates under Mexico's agrarian reform laws, the average land holding was small—10–20 acres. Some of the land was held in *ejidos*, large state-owned farms that are subdivided into many small plots and worked by peasants. Mexican law prohibited the sale of these lands, and it also placed restrictions on land ownership by foreign corporations. For a company used to owning plantations and working with U.S. growers who own hundreds or even thousands of acres, the conditions in the Bajio did not appear auspicious.

But Del Monte found the perfect tool for changing the valley's agriculture: contract farming. Under the contract system, the farmer or grower agrees to plant a set number of acres of a particular crop, and the company in return provides financial assistance, which usually includes seeds and special machinery, as well as cash outlays for purchasing fertilizers and hiring farm labor. All these costs are discounted from the farmer's income when the crop is delivered to the cannery. In a country like Mexico, where agricultural credit is limited or nonexistent, contract farming is a powerful instrument. Del Monte revealed just how influential its crop financing was when it noted that "in the early 1960s Productos Del Monte was practically the only source that many of its growers could turn to for short-term crop loans." By skillfully using its financial leverage, Del Monte affected the valley in several ways: it introduced crops that had never been grown there, favored the development of the larger growers at the expense of the smaller more marginal producers, and gained operating control over large tracts of land.

—"Canned Imperialism," *NACLA Report on the Americas,* New York, September 1976

They weren't exactly evicted but the Ladinos just gradually took over. My parents spent everything they earned and they incurred so many debts with these people that they had to leave the house to pay them. The rich are always like that. When people owe them some money they take a bit of land or some of their belongings and slowly end up with everything.

As the rural population grew, families had to subdivide their land among their children. Broken up, their small plots proved unable to sustain a family, and both adults and children were forced to seek work on the plantations at harvest time. Millions more abandoned the countryside for the shantytowns that were springing up around the major cities. The combination of peasant farming and seasonal labor, known as semi-proletarianization, has become the norm in much of the countryside. In Central America, 70 percent of the rural population are seasonal migrants, joining the coffee pickers of Guatemala in their annual trek to the plantations at harvest time. For the plantation owners, this system provides a cheap labor force at harvest time, with no need to pay year-round wages to regular employees.

Factory Farms

After the Second World War many politicians and economists saw further modernization as the solution to Latin America's inadequate agricultural system. This meant increasing productivity and making Latin America's farms more like the capital-intensive farms of the United States and Canada. From the 1960s, a new wave of state and foreign investment transformed Latin American agriculture. In Colombia, state spending on agriculture increased fifty-fold between 1950 and 1972. Most of the money went toward grandiose schemes favoring large-scale export agriculture; for example, the Mexican government irrigated the arid northwest of the country, which subsequently became a major producer of fruit and vegetables for the U.S. market.

> Driving through the rich Cauca valley of Colombia, one passes through mile after mile of lush new sugar and sorghum fields, punctuated by billboards advertising the latest in tractors and pesticides. In Mexico's Northwest, the fast-growing fruit and vegetable industry has transformed the fertile river valleys into a vast patchwork of irrigated fields and packing sheds resembling those of California's Imperial Valley. In southern Brazil, more than a dozen multimillion-dollar soybean processing plants owned by U.S. multinationals are scattered through the region, surrounded by large-scale mechanized soybean farms, none of which existed two decades ago. While a few countries such as Brazil, Colombia, Mexico and Argentina are clearly in the forefront of the agricultural revolution, no part of the countryside has been left untouched by capitalist development.
>
> —ROGER BURBACH AND PATRICIA FLYNN,
> *Agribusiness in the Americas*

Following the military coup of 1964, Brazil provided the most dramatic example of government involvement in boosting agro-exports. Through lending, tax concessions, state investment, and a guaranteed minimum price for farmers growing export crops, southern Brazil was transformed into one of the most modern agricultural regions in the hemisphere and a leading global exporter of crops such as soybeans. Although a few Brazilian families grew very rich in the process, they remained heavily dependent on foreign banks and multinationals to finance and buy their crops. For the mass of the population, the new crops meant yet another round of land concentration, increasing inequality of wealth and growing malnutrition as food crops were once again squeezed out by commodity exports. Rather than abolishing hunger in the countryside, modernization often made it worse.

In some cases foreign investors bought and farmed land, but in the late twentieth century transnational companies largely drew back from the direct control that had made them so unpopular in the past, leading to extensive nationalization of their operations in the 1960s and 1970s. Instead, they preferred to sign contracts with local farmers, under which the companies provide credit and agricultural inputs such as fertilizers and equipment in return for buying the farmers' crops at a guaranteed price. This left the transnational in control of the profitable processing and marketing of a product, while the local farmers had to deal with the local labor force and run the risk of a failed harvest. The transnationals lost little through this arrangement: in 2003, of each US$1 earned by bananas in the marketplace, only 10 cents found its way back to the producer country, and just 1.5 cents went to the workers on the banana plantations.

In 2010 and 2011 government fears of losing control of prime farmland intensified, largely as the result of Chinese interest in buying up land in Latin America on which to grow food crops to send back home. Both Argentina and Brazil introduced legislation to make it harder for foreigners to purchase land.

In today's Latin America, high-tech farms coexist with traditional peasant agriculture. The two worlds are intimately connected: peasant farms provide seasonal labor and often sell their produce to local agribusinesses. But power lies firmly in the hands of the big farms, with their near-monopoly on capital, credit, state support, and access to world markets.

In some countries, farming has to some extent moved on from the triple stereotype of plantation, hacienda, and impoverished smallholder. In parts of Colombia, Central America, and Brazil, for example, some small farmers have absorbed technology and have gained limited access to credit, notably to produce horticultural products for the growing urban markets, or even for export. In other cases, cooperatives have helped smallholders to gain access to credit and markets. But most regions of Latin America still manifest the threefold structure. Some recent changes have made life harder for small farmers. Increasingly, the farm trade in Latin America, like that in the United States and Europe, is dominated by large supermarket chains that use their market

clout to drive down prices and impose ever higher standards of uniform quality that are particularly hard for small, low-tech farmers to meet.

Fighting for Land

Plantations, haciendas, and peasant farms have competed for land, and the
expansion of one form at the expense of the others has generated conflict, land
seizures, political unrest, and even war.

As commercial agriculture has spread on to lands traditionally farmed by
peasant families, the big landowners have forced them out through a combination of money, legal trickery (for example, over the deeds to the land), and
brute force. In the Brazilian Amazon, landowners commonly hire gunmen to
expel peasant farmers from land they want to turn over to cattle. Peasants have
responded by seizing land left idle by the landowners and organizing political
movements to demand agrarian reform and access to social services.

On the plantations, disputes have been over wages and conditions, rather
than demands for land and credit. Since plantation owners are determined
to keep wages as low as possible, these disputes have frequently been bloody,
often involving the army and police on the side of the owners. One of the
worst-hit areas has been Colombia's banana-growing Urabá region:

> A typical incident was the arrest by members of the [local army] battalion
> of 19 banana plantation workers in the municipality of Apartadó in March
> 1989. They were taken to the battalion headquarters in Carepa and twelve
> were later released. Four others were released after several days during which
> they were tortured, and three needed hospital treatment for their injuries. The
> bodies, or rather the remains, of two other workers were found on 4 April.
> They had been killed by having charges of dynamite attached to their bodies
> and exploded.
>
> —JENNY PEARCE, *Colombia: Inside the Labyrinth*

In many cases, when local disputes were met with repression, they have
escalated into national political protest movements. In El Salvador in the
1970s frustrated peasant activists decided they could not improve conditions in the countryside without a radical change of government. As a result,
many joined new guerrilla movements, fighting in a bloody civil war in which
over 70,000 people died, mostly at the hands of the army and their associated
death squads.

Since the mid-twentieth century, governments have tried to alleviate pressure on the land through colonization programs. These have consisted largely

of irrigation projects to reclaim arid land in countries such as Mexico and Peru, and the deforestation and occupation of the Amazon basin in Brazil and the neighboring Andean nations of Bolivia, Peru, Ecuador, and Colombia. Governments have often seen these programs as an alternative to agrarian reform, since they can ease pressure on the land by sending landless peasants off to colonize new areas. Unfortunately, rain forest land being colonized has often been unsuitable for sustained agriculture and has been in remote areas, making it expensive or impossible for small farmers to get their produce to market. Colonization programs have often been chaotic and violent, as in Brazil, where large landowners have moved in to throw peasants off the land, once they have cleared it for farming. In her autobiography, *Mi Despertar* (My Awakening), Ana María Condori, a Bolivian indigenous woman, describes the colonization program of the 1950s:

> My father went there because our farm at home was all divided up and wasn't producing enough for all the children. Going on the colonization seemed like a solution to him, because the government at that time promised people heaven and earth. They gave out publicity at the fairs in the Altiplano [the high plateau region of the Andes where most Bolivians live] trying to get people to sign up—leaflets, posters, adverts on the radio—offering ready-made houses, a hectare of land already cleared, schools, hospitals, paved roads, technical assistance, and credit for the farm. But once people got to the colonization zone, they found nothing of all that; the government handed out food to make sure people didn't actually starve to death, but apart from that they were left to their fate.
>
> —ANA MARÍA CONDORI, *Mi Despertar* (author's translation)

The conflicts generated by growing inequality in the countryside have made agrarian reform one of the hottest issues in Latin American politics. For both rich and poor, land is literally a matter of life and death.

The first and greatest Latin American agrarian reform followed the Mexican revolution of 1910–17. Over the ensuing decades, especially during the radical presidency of Lázaro Cárdenas (1934–40), Mexico's vast haciendas were broken up and given out to 1.5 million families in the form of *ejidos,* communally owned land administered by indigenous communities along traditional lines. The reform consolidated the ruling party's grip on the countryside, laying the foundations for fifty years of one-party rule.

The Mexican government gave out land, but failed to back up the program with a reform of credit and investment to benefit the peasants. Credit is the financial oxygen for farmers because of the cyclical nature of agriculture. Every year a farmer has to borrow cash to buy seeds and fertilizer, pay

Peasants harvesting coca leaves, the primary ingredient in cocaine, on a Colombian hillside. (Latinphoto)

employees, and hire or buy equipment before the harvest brings in the money to pay off debts and maintain the farmer's family until the next harvest. Even after the agrarian reform in Mexico, big farmers have continued to receive most of the credits, and government spending on roads and irrigation has benefited their farms most. Agrarian reform provided the security that goes with owning a piece of land, but did little to improve the living standards of Mexico's peasantry.

The Bolivian Revolution of 1952 also led to a radical reform of its almost feudal rural society, directly benefiting three-quarters of the country's peasantry. Large estates were divided up among the sharecroppers, who had previously been forced to give the landowner a large proportion of their crop in exchange for farming the land. Titles were established for indigenous communities, and the worst forms of labor exploitation were made illegal. In Guatemala a similarly radical land reform after 1952 came to an abrupt end when the Arbenz government was overthrown by a U.S.-backed military coup.

Agrarian reform at a continental level took off in the 1960s. Following the Cuban Revolution in 1959, the U.S. government decided that it had to end social unrest in the countryside of Latin America if it was to preempt further revolutions. In 1961 President John F. Kennedy launched the Alliance for Progress, a joint Latin American–U.S. initiative under which the United

States gave money and advice for agrarian reform programs in countries such as Chile, Colombia, and Venezuela.

Agrarian reform as understood by Washington, however, had two often incompatible aims: it sought to increase productivity by modernizing agriculture along capitalist lines, and at the same time redistribute land and wealth to the rural poor. In practice, modernization came first, often causing further land expulsions and impoverishment for the peasantry. Landlords successfully resisted U.S. pressure to reduce their influence, and instead benefited from the drive for modernization. Landlord opposition and government incompetence meant that even when apparently progressive reform laws were passed, they were seldom implemented. Such laws became a focus of discontent, as peasants in countries such as Honduras and Brazil occupied idle lands to force the government to enact its own laws, expropriating the lands and distributing them among landless peasants.

There were high hopes that when Lula became president of Brazil in January 2003 the situation would change and he would keep his electoral promise of carrying out a radical program of agrarian reform. Hundreds of thousands of landless peasants squatted on the edge of highways, hoping to be the first to benefit when land was distributed. However, Lula soon dashed these hopes. The economy was riding high on the commodity boom of the 2000s, with a huge increase in soybeans, sugarcane, and eucalyptus plantations, and Lula was keen to keep the dollars rolling in from agricultural exports. Brazil's Landless Peasant Movement (Movimento Sem Terra, MST), a large and powerful social movement, mobilized to force the government to keep its promise. But to little avail: at the end of his eight years in government, Lula had dis-

---

Peasant Life in the 1960s

In the early 1960s I visited Peruvian haciendas where corporal punishment was still arbitrarily administered by estate owners and managers for minor infractions of rules. On some estates, indigenous tenant workers were expected to kneel and kiss the *patrón's* poncho as a symbol of submission and respect. Even in Chile, many large estate owners in 1960 strictly regulated who could enter or leave the property, and used an iron hand to maintain control over the goods and printed information available to debt-ridden residents through the estate's commissary. Until 1956, Chilean estate owners could effectively direct the votes of their tenants, workers, and other clients to the candidate and party of their choice. Union organization of agricultural workers was for all practical purposes prohibited by law until 1967.

—Solon Barraclough, *NACLA Report on the Americas,* New York, November 1994 tributed less land to the landless than his neoliberal predecessor, Fernando Henrique Cardoso. And three-quarters of the land that was distributed was in the remote—and often ecologically fragile—Amazon basin. Moreover, rural violence, particularly the assassination of rural peasant leaders, continued to be a serious problem. Lula's main achievement—and this is, by no means, insignificant—was to improve the flow of subsidized credit going to small-scale farmers, including many who had obtained their land through the agrarian reform programs. This helped to stem the rural exodus and has meant that small-scale farmers have been able to keep on supplying most of Brazil's staple foods, particularly *feijão* (beans), maize, and cassava.

Where agrarian reforms have worked to the advantage of the rural poor, they have generally been associated either with revolution (Mexico, Bolivia 1952; Cuba 1959; Nicaragua 1979) or with an elected left-wing government (Chile 1970–73; Guatemala 1950–54). In both Chile and Guatemala, the governments were overthrown by military coups, in part because of the hostility of the landed elite to agrarian reform. In Peru, one of Latin America's few radical military governments, the regime of General Velasco (1968–75), also transformed the country's semifeudal land system with a radical reform.

In the 1990s agriculture was deeply affected by the wave of neoliberal reforms that opened up the Latin American economy to market forces. As part of the drive to encourage private investment in agriculture, especially in nontraditional agro-export crops, governments in countries such as Peru, Mexico, Ecuador, and Nicaragua put past reform processes into reverse in a new wave of "modernization" that had disastrous implications for many peasants. Credits were cut back and private buyers began to acquire the land, causing outbreaks of violence such as the "First National Indigenous Uprising" in Ecuador in 1990. In 1991, the earlier gains of the Mexican peasantry were eroded by President Carlos Salinas, whose constitutional reforms allowed for the breakup and privatization of the communal *ejidos*. Since then, *ejidatarios* have been able to sell their land or go into joint ventures with private companies. The reform, coupled with the structural requirements of NAFTA, has placed great pressure on millions of peasant families, pressure that in part contributed to the Zapatista uprising of 1994.

In Venezuela, just 5 percent of the population have historically owned three-quarters of farmland, with the vast majority owning no land at all. The landslide election of Hugo Chávez in 1997 was due in part to his promises of land reform, and within months the Chavista parliament introduced legislation to hand out land. By 2010 the state had taken control of four million hectares of privately owned land and turned it over to either small farmers or state farms. The process has been fraught with difficulties, partly because of long legal battles, but real progress has been made.

The Movimento Sem Terra (MST)

Testimony of Maria Joaquina de Nascimento (Nazinha)

I'm 57 years old. I was born on Agua Branca in Ceará. My father had a small plot of land. We were lucky because it had a spring, so we always had water. I was the only girl, but I had five brothers. I went to school for a short while. I had to get up, cook lunch for my parents and then walk the four kilometers to school. I really only learned to sign my name. When I was 22 years old, I married. My husband didn't have land of his own so he worked with my father.

We all left Ceará because my father got ill. One of my brothers lived in Petrolina, so we went there. We found it difficult living in a town. We had to buy everything, even gas for cooking. Before that we'd always used wood from the countryside. It was difficult. I went hungry for the first time in my life in Petrolina. My husband got a job on a building site. I had seven children, but three died. But the other four—three girls and a boy—survived.

We were living in Petrolina with all these problems when some lads came to the door and invited us to a meeting. They said they were from the MST and they could help us win land. We were so pleased! So we all took part in the occupation of Safra estate. It was six years ago—August 7, 1995. I felt so happy when we arrived. I had two of my daughters with me. I left the other one in Petrolina because she was completing her last year at school. We had to take everything—black polythene, mattresses, bedclothes, hammocks, pots, food. It was difficult because we didn't have much protection from the wind and the rain. But we didn't care. In the town you suffer without hope, but here we were suffering with hope. That makes all the difference.

We spent five months in this camp. But there wasn't enough land in Safra for all the families. So on January 5, 1996, we went with 105 other families to occupy Ouro Verde estate and that's where we won land. We were evicted once from here. The police came and it was really frightening. But we reoccupied again and in the end we won the land. Everything is fine now. I've got a nice house, with a veranda. It was my dream, to have a house like this. My parents had a house with a veranda. It was better than the one I've got, but I'm going to make this one as good as theirs one day. It looks like a real home.

We can grow all our food now. That's so much better. The only bill we have to pay is for the electricity, for the house and for the water pump for the grapes. We only have two crops to sell on the market—grapes and *açerola* [a tropical fruit]. They don't really bring in enough money. We still suffer, but life is so much better.

—Sue Branford and Jan Rocha, *Cutting the Wire: The Story of the Landless Movement in Brazil*, London: LAB, 2002

Although the growing urbanization of the continent has reduced the relevance of rural questions to many Latin Americans, a fifth of the region's people still live in the countryside, where they suffer the consequences of unequal land distribution and a system that invariably favors the rich farmers over the peasants. The modernization of agriculture seems only to exacerbate the situation, while halfhearted colonization programs and agrarian reforms have done little to change the system, and in some cases may have made matters worse. Experience shows that initiatives such as agrarian reform can work only when carried out democratically, in consultation with their supposed beneficiaries, and when government is willing to challenge the power of the big landowners. Even then, the change must be locked into the constitution, protected against future government policy, otherwise the gains may be lost, as in Mexico or Nicaragua. Only if such reforms take place is there hope that a more just society can grow in rural Latin America, one that does not perpetuate poverty, hunger, sickness, and an endless flight to the cities.

Mean Streets:
Migration and Life in the City

The tourist hotels along Ipanema Beach in Rio de Janeiro are some of the most expensive real estate in the world. Luxury tower blocks, their balconies bursting with foliage, overlook beaches strewn with perfect brown bodies sporting skimpy bikinis known locally as "dental floss." Far above the beach, dozens of hang-gliders circle lazily down from one of Rio's extraordinary bare-rock mountains, to which clings the Rocinha *favela*, a shantytown that is home to 350,000 of Rio's poor. Shimmering in the heat haze, Rocinha looks down on the beaches like a bad conscience.

Although the rate of migration has slowed, shantytowns surround most Latin American cities, bulging with migrants from the economically stagnant countryside or with young people fleeing the overcrowded tenements of the inner city in search of a house of their own. In Peru the poor have built their settlements on the barren desert around Lima. In Ecuador, 60 percent of Guayaquil's population have built shacks over the muddy and polluted water of the swamps, their houses suspended on stilts. Some homes are a forty minute walk along rickety boardwalks to dry land.

For many decades, the cities acted as a magnet to the rural poor, particularly when family members came back with tales of city life. For instance, this Aymara indigenous woman in Bolivia recalls:

> At that time I was nine years old, and was already seeing the older girls coming back from working as servants saying: "I"m happy in the city. Life is great there." To me they seemed physically happier; they talked beautifully, they had lovely clothes with embroidered shawls, with luxurious skirts. Pretty Indian girls, they looked. So I said "Ah! I'm going too."
>
> —ANA MARÍA CONDORI, *Mi Despertar* (author's translation),

Favela overlooking downtown Rio de Janeiro. (South American Pictures)

Unless driven by war or natural disaster, migration was usually a carefully planned operation; for example, a family would send an eldest daughter on ahead to find work and establish a base before other family members follow. Since they were mainly young people, migrants then had their children in the city, further boosting urban population growth.

The growth of the cities was astounding. In 1930, Latin America's total urban population was 20 million, out of a total population of around 100 million. Now around 470 million Latin Americans live in cities, out of a total of 590 million. Since the 1930s, millions of peasant families have left their farms and villages and joined the great trek to the cities. The driving forces behind this human tide include war, famine, shortage of land, and the often illusory glitter of the city, with its promise of jobs, education and excitement. By the early twenty-first century, much of Latin America was more urbanized than the United States, and if present trends continue South America will be among the world's most urbanized regions by 2030. Already the majority of people live in towns and cities in all but one nation in the region—the troubled state of Haiti, battered by earthquakes and manmade disasters.

Contrary to the common image of poor, desperate peasants trailing into the cities, most migrants are literate young adults, frustrated with the lack of opportunity in the countryside. In Latin America, unlike Asia and Africa, women migrants outnumber men, reflecting women's lesser role in agriculture compared to the other continents. Catastrophes like war and famine, however,

Portrait of a Migrant

Sergio, 19, is from Guadalajara. A stocky, scruffy youth in black jeans and T-shirt with a skimpy moustache, he is excited about his planned "jump" this afternoon and cannot stop talking. When the "migra"—the U.S. immigration patrol—changes shift at 2:30 p.m., Sergio, along with hundreds of other Mexican youths, will jump the chain-link fence that separates the United States from Mexico in the border town of Tijuana. If he can make it across a stretch of waste ground to the burger bars on the far side, he can pay for a ride to Los Angeles in the trunk of a car waiting on the U.S. side of the border. Tijuana is the main crossing point into the United States. The San Diego border patrol say they make 500,000 captures a year, and reckon that for every person they catch, two or three get through. They say 85 percent are men, and nearly all are Mexican.

Sergio has just been home to visit his family, and is now on his way back to work. Since he first crossed over three years ago, he has worked loading vans and serving coffee in San Bernardino, California. He works all hours and earns US$350 a week. In Guadalajara, where he worked in a cobbler's workshop, he was earning about US$20 a week. He lives cheaply, sharing an apartment with six other Mexican men, and wires his savings to his family from the local Western Union office. He calculates that in four or five years he can save the US$6–7,000 he needs to open his own shoe workshop or clothes shop back in Guadalajara.

change the pattern, as then people of all ages and educational backgrounds flee to the cities en masse.

The way people migrate has been affected by changes in public transport. As roads and bus and truck services have improved, migration has become a less daunting prospect. Not only has it made it easier for people to move to big cities from once remote rural villages, but better transport now means that the move need no longer be a definitive break with the past. Increasing numbers of poor Latin Americans now divide their time between town and country, visiting the family farm at weekends. The distinctions between urban and rural lifestyles are becoming blurred. As the rural population has declined in relative terms, the driving force for growth in urban areas has increasingly come from residents having children and moving between towns, rather than traditional rural-urban migration.

The growth of the cities was a consequence of Latin America's drive for industrialization. As industry grew from the 1930s onward, the prospect of jobs pulled in the rural population. In addition, as commercial agriculture spread farther into the countryside, peasants were forced off the land and left with the choice of seasonal labor on the plantations or moving to the city in search of a better life. Although many migrants never found regular employment, they often lived better in urban squalor than in rural poverty. Their children were more likely to get some schooling, and there was more chance of winning eventual access to basic services like water and electricity. At a national level, wealth in Latin American countries is disproportionately concentrated in the urban areas, especially the capital cities. However, one of the consequences of the debt crisis of the 1980s was a sharp rise in urban poverty, which tarnished the glitter of the cities and reduced migratory pressures in many countries.

Even though it is generally easier and cheaper to provide health, education, and water to people clustered in towns, rather than dispersed across the countryside, the speed of urbanization has been a serious headache for Latin America's planners, swamping existing services, and stretching such resources as water and food dangerously thin. In recent years pollution and congestion have added to their problems. Governments' attempts to check urban growth have had little impact, however, since they have failed to question the logic of the development model that was fueling migration. The only exception has been Cuba, where the Castro government used its central planning of jobs, housing, and food distribution to dissuade would-be migrants to Havana, while investing in other, smaller cities and rural improvements. As a result, it managed to reverse the growth in Havana's share of the population. In some giant cities like Buenos Aires, congestion and pollution have started to make life so difficult that some companies are relocating to nearby cities.

Crossing the Border

Many migrants, especially those from Mexico, Central America, the Caribbean, and Colombia, decide to leave their country altogether. Their usual destination is *El Norte*, the promised land of the United States, where they work illegally in factories, on farms, or in restaurants in the hope of one day acquiring the coveted green card, or work permit. The route to the United States is uncertain and dangerous, and involves running the gauntlet of unscrupulous *coyotes*, or guides, as well as U.S. Immigration Service patrols. Migrants caught at the border are swiftly returned to their home country, often to begin another attempt to head north and find safety in the anonymity of the Hispanic quarters of major U.S. cities.

The influx has changed U.S. society. By 2010 an estimated 16 percent of the U.S. population—some 49 million people—were "Hispanics," over two-thirds of them hailing originally from Mexico. Hispanics are concentrated in a few states, notably California, Texas, and New Mexico, where by 2009 they made up almost half (47 percent) of the population. Successive immigration amnesties have swelled the number who hold green cards to prove legal citizenship and the right to vote, and Hispanics are finally beginning to have an impact on national politics. The latest member of the Bush dynasty, George P. Bush, campaigned on behalf of his uncle, George W. Bush, using his Mexican heritage (his mother, Columba, was born in Mexico) to reach out to the increasingly important Latino electorate. After reelection in 2004, Bush nominated two Hispanics to his cabinet—Cuban-born Carlos Gutierrez to Commerce, and Alberto Gonzales (the Texan-born son of Mexican immigrants) as attorney general—and President Barack Obama appointed an unprecedented 60 Hispanics to positions within his administration. Perhaps the most senior is Cecilia Muñoz, who became director of intergovernmental affairs in the Executive Office of the President. However, while Cuban émigrés dominate political life in Florida and high-profile Hispanic mayors have governed major cities such as Los Angeles, the Hispanic community has not found a united voice or national leaders to match Jesse Jackson's role in galvanizing black voters. Part of the reason is that the Hispanic community is fragmented—Puerto Ricans and Dominicans dominate in New York, whereas Mexicans and Central Americans are the main groups in Los Angeles.

Within the United States, attitudes to Hispanic immigrants have depended on the state of the economy. After the Second World War, when U.S. agriculture was suffering a labor shortage, Mexicans were encouraged to migrate on the *bracero* farm-worker program. In recent years, however, a rising tide of anti-immigrant feeling has prompted discrimination and attacks against Hispanics. In a largely unreported sideshow to George W. Bush's reelection in 2004, voters in Arizona approved Proposition 200. This required Arizonans to prove citizenship when seeking public benefits or when registering to vote and was targeted at the state's estimated 300,000 to 350,000 undocumented immigrants who, Latino leaders fear, are being forced further underground.

Politicians have been swift to capitalize on the issue. In March 2005, Representative Steve King, a Republican from Iowa, and 57 additional members of Congress introduced the English Language Unity Act of 2005, which would make English the sole official language of the U.S. government. The bill, which is controversial, had still not been approved by 2011 but it had been reintroduced by two Republican members of Congress.

For those who have stayed behind in Latin America, money sent by relatives from abroad has become vital to the survival of many rural communities. One study of Mixteca communities in Mexico showed that remittances from family members working in New York now pay for everything from a new drinking-water system to the religious festivals that bind the villages together.

The numbers are huge and, until recently, were growing rapidly. In 2008, total remittances from the estimated 25 million Latin Americans living overseas came to US$69 billion, which in many countries was more than overseas aid and foreign investment combined. Mexico took a third, followed by Brazil and Colombia, but proportionally the impact is often greatest in small economies in the Caribbean and Central America, where remittances often exceed total export income. Because of the global recession and because today there are more employment opportunities in the region itself, remittances fell in 2009 and have remained lower than in earlier years. They were estimated to have been about US$59 billion in 2011.

Builders and Squatters

Migrants recently arrived in Latin America's cities frequently stay with friends and relatives until they get used to their new surroundings and find some way of earning a living. With space at a premium, however, they soon come under pressure to find a place of their own. Choices are limited. They can rent a tiny room in an overcrowded inner-city tenement, but the development of bus and other mass urban transport networks in the last fifty years has given them another option—joining the increasing number of squatters in the shantytowns on the outskirts of the cities.

Shantytowns have transformed Latin America's urban landscape. In Rio de Janeiro the first were recorded in 1920. Today they house over a third of the city's inhabitants. In Caracas that figure is nearer two-thirds. Each country has a different word for them—in Brazil they are *favelas*, in Argentina the evocative term is *villas miseria* (towns of poverty), in Peru the progressive military regime that came to power in 1968 insisted on the more dignified *pueblos jovenes* (young towns). In Chile they are simply *callampas* (mushrooms), springing up overnight on the outskirts of Santiago.

Shantytown homes are built by their residents and are nearly always illegal, either because the squatters do not own the land, or because they have no planning permission to build. Many squatter settlements begin with a "land invasion"; a group of the urban poor, often including recent migrants, invades a piece of ground at night and hastily raises temporary shacks. If they succeed in fending off initial attempts by the authorities or the landlord to evict them, the temporary homes stand a chance of becoming permanent.

As time goes by and the settlement's prospects improve, residents start the long struggle to improve their homes. The improvements take up much of their spare time and money. The first cardboard and plastic shacks are replaced by planks or corrugated iron. Over the years brick houses start to appear, some even acquiring a second story. Eventually they come to resemble other parts of the city, and become absorbed into the city's economy as increasing numbers

Building a Self-Help Home

Alfonso and Izabel Rodríguez live with their three children in a low-income settlement in the south of Valencia, a Venezuelan city with around 800,000 inhabitants. The population has grown rapidly as manufacturing plants have moved to the city in preference to the crowded conditions found in Caracas. Alfonso works in the Ford plant. He was born in the mountain state of Mérida and arrived in Valencia in 1975 after an uncle told him that work was available. He stayed with his uncle for a while in a consolidated self-help house in the south of the city and then moved into rental accommodation nearer the center. He met Isabel, who had been born in Valencia, six months later. They rented a new home together and stayed there for 18 months. Two years later, he managed to obtain a plot of land through an invasion. The invasion was organized by an employee of the local authority who was trying to win support for a councillor who was hoping to be reelected that year.

One hundred and twenty families established rudimentary shacks early one Sunday morning. Because of the protection given by the councillor there was little trouble with the police and the settlers soon began to improve their accommodation. Since Alfonso had a reasonably well-paid job, he could afford to buy cement and bricks with which to improve the house. In addition, he sold half of the 20- by 35-meter plot he had obtained to two other families; this was sufficient to buy the rest of the materials he needed. He could also employ, on an occasional basis, a friend who worked in the construction industry. Progress on the house was slow but steady. Since he had to work at his paid job during the week, he could do little except on weekends. Even then there were interruptions, family visits, the occasional fiesta, demands by the children to go out. Isabel helped with some of the lighter jobs when she could, but three rapid pregnancies and a miscarriage limited her participation in the actual building.

By 1985, five years later, the house had three rooms. It was not pretty to look at, but it was solidly built and the roof kept out the rain. It had electricity, stolen from the mains by a neighbor who worked for the electricity board. Water had been provided by the government during the last election campaign, but sewerage was still lacking. There was a school in the next settlement, and the eldest child would start to attend it in a couple of years' time.

—Alan Gilbert, *The Latin American City*, London: LAB, 1990

of the houses are sold or rented out by their original inhabitants.

Squatter settlements face enormous initial problems. Often the land they have occupied was empty precisely because it was unsuitable for building. In Rio the poor cling to sheer hillsides, risking landslides every time it rains. In El Salvador's capital, San Salvador, shantytowns are strung terrifyingly close

to railway lines or huddled into ravines, often side by side with the local garbage dump. In Lima the *pueblos jovenes* are built into the desert, leaving the
new arrivals at the mercy of private water suppliers. Typically, the most urgent
problems are water and sanitation. In São Paulo, over a third of the city's
houses, mainly in the peripheral shantytowns, have no sewer connections or
cesspools. People use open holes or dry latrines, which often contaminate the
shallow wells that provide their only water supply.

The key to improving living standards is organization, and squatter settlements have produced some of Latin America's best-organized and most vocal
neighborhood organizations. The list of demands is dispiritingly long: roads,
drinking water, sewers, electricity, schools, garbage collection, health clin-
ics, and bus routes. Another major battlefield concerns their illegality, since
without proper legal title to the land, the inhabitants will never be secure in
their homes. Once a settlement is established it can grow rapidly. In Lima 500
people organized a land invasion in 1960 and founded the Cuevas settlement.
By 1970, 12,000 people lived there.

The authorities may respond to land invasions with violent attempts at
eviction, but in the long term many recognize that illegal settlement and self-
built housing are the only solution to the shortage of accommodation. In cities
like Lima and Mexico City, local politicians support squatters in exchange for
votes, while political parties frequently try to co-opt the neighborhood organizations' leaders. In Argentina, on the other hand, the military government
bulldozed the *villas miseria* while cleaning up the city for the World Cup in
1978. Bolivian and Paraguayan migrants were beaten up, then herded onto
trains and trucks for deportation. Often, however, the settlements' successes
produce a spirit of optimism and self-confidence that is lacking in the gloomy
tenements of the city center.

The only alternative to the current uneasy coexistence between authorities
and squatters is serious urban land reform. There are many parallels between
the rural land crisis and that in the cities. Like agrarian reform, urban land
reform requires far more than mere distribution of land if it is to succeed.
Settlers also need access to credit to enable them to buy building materials,
physical infrastructure such as roads and electricity, and technical advice
on building. Just as in the countryside, the big urban landowners resist any
attempt to challenge their control, and are usually successful in their efforts.

Visitors to Latin America may see little of life in the shantytowns and tenements, since tourists' hotels and friends or contacts are usually in the wealth-
ier areas, either pleasant suburbs or modern city centers. In the middle-class
areas, families lead a relatively comfortable existence, aided by servants and
access to household appliances. As a proportion of the total population the
middle class in Latin America is far smaller than in Europe or the United

States, and a vast gulf separates it from the poor masses of the slums. The middle-class enclaves are often little more than islands of "modernity" in vast surrounding expanses of poverty. Along the main road north out of Recife, in northeastern Brazil, car drivers are even spared the sight of the long lines of cardboard and wooden shacks. A municipal billboard hundreds of yards long apologizes for the "inconvenience caused by temporary housing." The bill-board can hide the houses from view, but not the hot stench of the canal pass-ing through the encampment. Scrawny children swim in the polluted waters. In places the canal banks are made up entirely of garbage.

Scraping a Living

New Year's Eve on the road to Mexico City's airport: when the cars pull up at the traffic lights, a fire-breather steps out in front of the queue. A jet of flame lances across the night, lighting up a shiny face, glazed eyes, and a hand clutching a bottle of gasoline. After the show, the ragged performer goes up the line of car windows, hand outstretched. On New Year's Eve the drivers are in a good mood and he does well.

Although many migrants come to the city looking for regular paid jobs in industry, few find them. Although Latin America has industrialized, most of the investment has been in capital-intensive industry where machines do the work instead of people. Consequently, manufacturing employment has failed to keep up with the demand for jobs. In most Latin American nations, social security provisions apply only to those in regular employment for the state or big companies—unemployment and maternity benefits or pensions are not available to the majority. Without the safety net of a welfare state, migrants unable to find a way of earning an income face starvation, and most of the inhabitants of the shantytowns are forced to find work in what has become known as the "informal sector" of the economy.

The informal sector is the umbrella term for a mass of different tasks including street selling, domestic service, odd jobs, day laborers in construc-tion, small-scale industry—recycling tires into sandals, for example—picking through garbage for tin cans and paper, or even fire breathing at traffic lights.

Such work is in stark contrast to the formal sector of waged jobs more familiar to those in the industrialized nations. Formal-sector jobs are pro-vided by large private and state-owned businesses, subsidiaries of multina-tional companies, and the public sector. Such jobs generally take place in the Westernized centers of the cities, with their office blocks, government depart-ments, and shops, while economic life in the poor fringes of the city operates through the networks of the informal sector. Perhaps the clearest distinction between the two is over the level of protection: if someone in the informal sector is injured or sacked, they are on their own. Increasingly, the deregulation of workplaces and spread of activities such as subcontracting to sweatshops by textile companies means that the informal sector is encroaching on what were formal sector occupations.

To the visitor, the street traders are the most striking members of the informal economy. In La Paz, the Avenida Buenos Aires and adjoining streets are the site of the capital's biggest street market. Young men dressed in denim sell the latest line in microwaves or mobile phones smuggled in from Brazil while,

---

Shantytown Women in Peru

At the settlement Márquez del Callao, hundreds of children line up in front of the dining hall. They begin two hours before noon, every day, plate and spoon in hand. They beg and shout in hopes of getting a free portion from the mothers who organized this communal kitchen. Forty mothers cook 400 portions a day, half for member families and half for the hungry children.

These organizations depend on donations of oil, oatmeal and flour, and on their own purchases. In their search for better prices, the women will frequently contact the producers directly. This form of organizing has proven so successful that, by 1986, 800 *comedores* (communal canteens) were represented by a National Commission of Comedores. Some are independent while others may be funded by the Church, the state, political parties or development agencies.

Rosario de Meléndez, recently laid off from a stocking factory, is a new member of the Glass of Milk committee of the neighborhood of El Carcamo. When it is her turn, she gets up at five in the morning, turns on the stove and begins to heat a huge pot of milk, oatmeal, some sugar, cloves, and cinnamon. She knows that at seven the children will begin lining up at the door of her house waiting for the hot milk. Each member of her committee contributes less than 10 cents a week for the purchase of kerosene, cocoa and cloves.

By working together, these women come to see their oppression as a social ill and open up new horizons for themselves. The voice of the women, before silent, is making itself heard. Formerly taboo subjects are now discussed. The mere fact that they are no longer shut up in their houses cooking for their husbands transforms relationships within the home. The women like to talk about the time one leader arrived at a meeting barefoot because her husband had hidden her shoes to keep her from going.

—Carolina Carlessi, "The Reconquest," *NACLA Report on the Americas,* New York, November 1989

An Informal Sector Success Story

At a busy traffic intersection in the Honduran capital of Tegucigalpa, Don Alfonso is an example of the informal sector in operation. Now a grizzled patriarch of 68, Don Alfonso has spent 15 years steering his family through the rapids of the Central American economy. He sits on the pavement next to stacks of today's newspapers, as six of his sons and daughters weave through the choking traffic. When the lights turn to red, the children move up and down the lines of cars in search of customers. Periodically they return to Don Alfonso to exchange their haul of grubby notes for a new supply of papers. The family makes a profit of about eight cents on each paper sold, and business is brisk.

When the time comes, Don Alfonso packs his various children off to school, scattered across the morning and afternoon shifts of the creaking Honduran education system. Franklin, 15, goes to night school from 6 p.m. to 8.30 p.m., even though he has to be up and on the streets by 5.30 the next morning for another seven-hour stint at the traffic lights.

Fifteen years ago, Don Alfonso abandoned his barren farm and headed for the city. By working together with his family, he can keep a firm eye on his children, and has succeeded in keeping the family united when many others have collapsed. With the proceeds of 15 years at the traffic lights, he has steadily upgraded his shantytown hut into a solid house, with a new tin roof, cement floor and electricity. The walls are hung with family photos and their children's diplomas. Don Alfonso is proudest of his eldest son, who trained as a mechanic and now has a prized regular job in a factory.

—Duncan Green, *Hidden Lives: Voices of Children in Latin America and the Caribbean,*
London: LAB, Cassell and SCF, 1997

one street along, indigenous women sit patiently in their bowler hats and ponchos, selling dried llama fetuses which are buried under the foundations of most new houses in Bolivia to bring good luck. Herbal remedies, BMX bicycles, imported disposable diapers, toiletries, and pots and pans—the list of available goods is endless.

As the numbers of the urban poor grew, so did the informal sector. During the recession of the 1980s and the subsequent neoliberal reforms, the informal sector acted as a gigantic sponge, soaking up those who had been laid off or who were entering the workforce for the first time. The comparison between formal and informal sectors has led some economists to talk of two parallel circuits existing within the urban economy. The first circuit is a formal, Western-style world of banks, factories, and supermarkets, existing alongside a second circuit of street traders, moneylenders, and day laborers.

The two worlds are linked, however, since the informal sector provides low-cost services that often benefit the formal economy. The system resembles agriculture, where modern capital-intensive commercial agriculture exists alongside traditional labor-intensive peasant farming, which supplies cheap labor at harvest time.

As Latin America's streets became clogged with vendors desperately seeking customers, income inequality increased, with the income of those in the formal sector growing far more quickly than those in the informal sector. The informal sector tends to be higher in poorer nations, being responsible for over half of the country's economic output in Bolivia, Panama, and Guatemala, but even in the more developed countries of Brazil and Mexico the share of the informal sector is estimated at 40 percent and 30 percent, respectively.

In La Paz, where 60 percent of the workforce is now in the informal sector, there is one street trader for every three families—there are just not enough buyers to go around. Informal sector work impacts heavily on women, especially single mothers or those without family support; long hours spent traveling to work mean that some single mothers have no choice but to leave even young children locked up at home alone. In an equally wasteful middle-class variant, the informal sector also absorbs Latin America's surplus lawyers, doctors, and architects into its fleet of overqualified taxi drivers.

In the first decade of the twenty-first century, Latin America recovered from the recession, with economic output growing by 3.5 percent a year from 2000 to 2008. Even so, many people cannot find jobs in the formal sector. For instance, when the Argentine economy bounced back from a deep crisis in 2001–2, economic output returned to pre-crisis levels, but the nature of employment had shifted radically away from waged jobs toward the informal sector.

Future Cities

Latin America is now an urban continent, and will remain so. In many ways, its cities have been remarkably successful, absorbing nearly 400 million new inhabitants over a seventy-year period. The fact that more keep arriving is proof that, whatever the difficulties of city life, for many it is still preferable to the struggle for existence in the countryside.

Yet if a better future for the region is to be forged in the cities, much has to change. The energy and dynamism of the self-help housing movement must be channeled into community development; governments must help rather than hinder the process by passing urban land reform laws, providing support for the informal sector, and ensuring that the next generation gets adequate

education and health care. The ability of city authorities and national governments to provide such a future for their citizens is largely determined by the
performance of the economy and the role of the state. The millions who have
moved to Latin America's cities in search of a steady income will find work
only if economic stability, jobs, and effective welfare systems can be developed
in tandem. There are causes for hope, such as the spread of public participation in setting local government budgets; what began as an experiment in a
left-wing administration in Porto Alegre in southern Brazil has been repli-
cated in numerous towns and cities across the continent. Yet such efforts still
swim against an economic tide of instability and deep-rooted inequality.

A Land in Flames:
The Environment

The burning season starts in June in the Brazilian Amazon. The sky turns a dirty ochre, as a pall of smoke closes local airports and cuts off whole towns from the outside world. Each year the flames engulf a vast and irreplaceable area of virgin rainforest. By 2010, a fifth of the forest—an area twice the size of France—had been felled. Even though governments are increasingly trying to stem the destruction, they are finding it difficult to monitor such a huge area. In some remote areas of the Brazilian Amazon, cattle farmers are still using defoliants, similar to the Agent Orange that the Americans used against the Vietnamese during the Vietnam War, to clear virgin forest so that they can plant pasture.

Although many people in the industrialized nations see environmental questions in Latin America as synonymous with the Amazon rain forest, the damage stretches to every corner of the continent, blighting cities and countryside alike.

In Costa Rica, resort developers have filled in and built upon the fragile mangrove swamps that form a buffer against the wind and waves. Furthermore, shrimping is poorly regulated and intense aquaculture is not prohibited under Costa Rican law, meaning that those areas of mangrove swamp unaffected by construction and development have found themselves open to overfishing and degradation. In 2000, a landmark ruling ordered a company to repair the environmental damage it had caused during a construction project, but little has been done to prevent further breaches.

The economically booming border zone where Mexico meets Texas has been blighted by pollution and disease on both sides of the border, although U.S. settlements are in a far better position to deal with these problems. Tuberculosis and dysentery are particularly problematic for residents of the *maquiladora* towns on the Mexican side of the border, while ozone pollution has made the air in large towns unsafe. Another critical issue is hazardous waste, which is supposed to return to its country of origin, which for *maquila* goods would be the United States. It is estimated, however, that less than one-third of waste is actually transported, while less than 12 percent is treated in accordance with environmental agreements.

In Ecuador, the rain forest region has been polluted by oil companies. The area known as *El Oriente* is one of the most biologically diverse in the world, but also provides the oil that furnishes Ecuador with 40 percent of its export earnings. Around 5 million gallons of untreated toxic waste are dumped into this fragile environment every year, while the temptation to cut corners in the extraction process causes an average of two large oil spills each week.

The Conquest of Nature

The Conquest of the Americas lessened one kind of environmental pressure, but introduced many new ones. Recent archaeological evidence suggests that indigenous agriculture in Mexico and the Andes was in a state of crisis when the Spaniards arrived, as population pressure and soil erosion combined to produce a food crisis that may have been an important factor in enabling the Spaniards to win against the odds. The ensuing collapse of the indigenous population, through disease and forced labor, did much to ease the immediate pressure on the ecosystem. The population of Latin America did not return to pre-Conquest levels until the nineteenth century.

However, the subsistence economies of the great indigenous civilizations were replaced by a colonial gold-rush mentality that aimed to plunder Latin America's resources, whether mineral or agricultural, as quickly as possible and send them abroad. When one resource was exhausted, another was found, with no attempt to build long-term sustainability. The philosophy was even applied to people: when indigenous laborers began to die out on Brazil's sugar plantations, the plantation owners chose to ship in Africans to do the job, rather than try to reduce the death rate among the indigenous population. As the centuries have passed, and Latin America has become ever more enmeshed in the world economy, natural resources have been raided to pay for imports of manufactured goods.

In the twentieth century, an urban environmental crisis took off following the aggressive industrialization programs introduced in the 1930s and 1940s. As cities sprang up, sucking the rural poor into shantytowns with few facilities, unregulated industry has poured effluents into the air and water, and millions of dilapidated cars have choked the cities with carbon monoxide.

Big Is Beautiful

Since the Second World War, governments and international lenders have added to the damage done to Latin America's environment through their predilection for "pharaonic" projects. Especially attractive to military governments, giant dams, huge road-building programs, nuclear power, and vast mining complexes have wrought enormous human and environmental damage on the continent.

Roads are the kiss of death for the rain forest. Amazonian roads can be seen from the air to be bordered by a corridor of deforested land, spanning roughly a day's walk either side, the result of forest clearance largely carried out by the peasant farmers who move in as soon as a road is built and start hacking back the forest.

Dams were originally hailed as a clean and renewable energy source—every environmentalist's dream. Small-scale dam projects, such as those of Costa Rica, which relies on hydro-schemes for 99 percent of its energy, are indeed environment-friendly. They affect a small area and do not create the social, economic, or environmental disruption caused by the great dams. Elsewhere, notably in Brazil and Argentina, governments have built gigantic constructions, flooding vast areas of the countryside, displacing indigenous peoples and local farmers, and contributing to climate change.

On the border between Brazil and Paraguay, the Itaipú dam has been described as "a monument built of raw superlatives." For five years Brazilian construction companies poured enough concrete every day to build a 350-story building. The construction contract alone weighed 220 pounds. The dam began operation in 1984, straddling the giant Paraná River, which flows out to sea as the River Plate between Argentina and Uruguay.

Itaipú produces as much electricity as ten average nuclear power stations. Dams on this scale carry costs not associated with smaller projects. The initial investment adds enormously to the country's debt burden—Itaipú cost Brazil US$20 billion, roughly 20 percent of its entire foreign debt at that time. Dams are usually accompanied by other developments, such as industries using cheap energy. Since they are often built in relatively untouched parts of the country, this can cause great environmental damage. A prime example is the Grande Carajás project, for which Brazil built the Tucuruí dam, 50 percent larger in area than Itaipú. Furthermore, flooding leads to a massive loss of forest and kills wildlife. The Tucuruí dam flooded 216,000 hectares in 1984, killing 2.8 million trees that were first sprayed with chemical defoliants. In populated areas the valleys flooded by dam projects are often the most fertile farmland. In some regions, the sudden increase in standing water has led to epidemics of parasitic diseases such as malaria, and can even substantially alter the local climate. Finally, deforestation upstream can increase siltation rates, shortening the dam's life span and turning it into a huge loss-maker, even before environmental costs are included in the balance sheet.

Extractive Industries

Latin America is now the recipient of the world's largest share of mining investment. At the start of the 1990s, the region attracted 12 percent of worldwide investment in mining. But by the early 2000s this amount had nearly tripled to 33 percent. The main mining countries, such as Chile, Peru, and Brazil, have seen their exports boom to an all-time high. Price rises, Chinese demand, and the tax breaks and relaxed labor laws approved in the 1990s as part of structural adjustment programs have driven the new boom, which has shifted the continent back toward its traditional role as a producer of raw materials for the world's industries. The environmental threat posed by such a boom is serious. Mining in forest areas leads to deforestation, while the tailings and other waste products of mineral extraction pollute rivers and farmland downstream from the mines.

Massive foreign mining projects are not the only environmental villains. Following a steep rise in the price of gold in 1979, 500,000 impoverished gold prospectors (*garimpeiros*) poured onto lands occupied by the Yanomami people on Brazil's northern border. The Yanomami were previously one of the largest and most isolated of Brazil's indigenous groups. The miners brought guns, diseases such as malaria and TB, and mercury, which they used in a crude process to separate gold dust from mud. According to Survival International, 1,500 of the 9,000 Yanomami died over a two-year period, while in settlements near the mining camps there were almost no children under the age of two.

Fight for the Forest

Deforestation has galvanized the green movement outside Latin America. Public opinion has been horrified at the spectacle of vast tracts of rain forest falling under the chainsaw, and the possible implications for the global climate. Latin America contains 62 percent of the world's remaining tropical rain forest, chiefly in the Amazon basin countries of Brazil, Peru, Colombia, Venezuela, and the Guianas. There are also smaller areas in Mexico and Central America, where the process of deforestation is both more rapid and much more advanced.

Slash-and-burn, the destructive method of clearing rain forest for pastureland in the Amazon. (South American Pictures)

In the Amazon, forests are burned in order to turn the land over to pasture for cattle. The huge, inefficient cattle ranches have been encouraged by the Brazilian government with a variety of tax concessions and other incentives as part of its scheme for colonizing the Amazon. One study in the 1970s showed that each ton of beef received US$4,000 in subsidies, yet earned only US$1,000 on the international market. Although the farms made little commercial sense, they were seen as an inflation-proof investment by companies or individuals living in the industrialized south.

The forest is also hacked down by poor peasant colonizers using "slash-and-burn" methods. The precise division of blame between peasants and cattle barons is controversial. Up until 1980, cattle ranching is believed to have accounted for about 70 percent of the deforestation. Since then, however, hundreds of thousands of peasants have marched in along the new roads like an army of leaf-cutter ants, while some of the tax incentives for cattle ranching have been removed in response to international pressure. Many of the peasant colonizers are themselves environmental refugees from soil erosion elsewhere or have lost their land to the onward march of soybeans and other agribusi-

Fight for the Forest: Chico Mendes

The fight by local people to defend the Amazon gained worldwide attention when Chico Mendes, the leader of the Brazilian rubber tappers, was assassinated by a landowner in 1988. Mendes pioneered the idea of "extractive reserves," using the forest sustainably to produce fruit, rubber and nuts:

"We realized that in order to guarantee the future of the Amazon we had to find a way to preserve the forest while at the same time developing the region's economy. So what were our thoughts originally? We accepted that the Amazon could not be turned into some kind of sanctuary that nobody could touch. On the other hand, we knew it was important to stop the deforestation that is threatening the Amazon and all human life on the planet. We felt our alternative should involve preserving the forest, but it should also include a plan to develop the economy. So we came up with the idea of extractive reserves.

"What do we mean by an extractive reserve? We mean the land is under public ownership but the rubber tappers and other workers that live on that land should have the right to live and work there. I say 'other workers' because there are not only rubber tappers in the forest. In our area, rubber tappers also harvest Brazil nuts, but in other parts of the Amazon there are people who earn a living solely from harvesting nuts, while there are others who harvest babaçu and jute."

— Chico Mendes, *Fight for the Forest*, London: LAB, 1989

ness in the south. Frequently they migrate following government advice to seek their fortunes as pioneers in the Amazon. What the government fails to tell them is that rain forest soil is unsuitable for sustained agriculture. Stripped of its trees, the fragile ecosystem rapidly collapses, nutrients are washed out of the soil, and within two or three years declining fertility forces the peasant farmer to move on and cut down more forest. Most recently, Brazil's development of new strains of soya suitable for more tropical climates has led to a new wave of deforestation, this time to make way for giant agribusiness producers of soybeans destined for animal feed.

The destruction of the Amazon has reached a critical point. In 2005 and 2010 the Amazon basin recorded very severe droughts, of the kind that are only expected to occur once every 100 years. Several districts were declared disaster areas and the army brought in emergency supplies to towns and villages. Scientists are beginning to fear that, largely as the result of global warming, the region's climate may be permanently changing. Although deforestation may not be the main cause of the droughts, a forest weakened by felling is much less resilient to drought. Public concern is growing, yet, so many years after the murder of peasant leader Chico Mendes, environmentalism can still carry a heavy price tag in Brazil: in February 2005 an American nun who had lived and worked on social and environmental issues in the Amazon basin for twenty years, Dorothy Stang, was shot by gunmen sent by local landowners. In Central America the hamburger, epitome of U.S. consumerism, is the driving force behind the breakneck pace of deforestation. Unlike their Brazilian counterparts, whose meat is destined largely for domestic consumption, cattle ranches in countries like Costa Rica are supplying the U.S. fast-food market. As in the Amazon, peasant farmers enter the forests and do the work of clearing the land for agriculture but are soon squeezed out by declining fertility and pressure from cattle ranchers coming in behind them. Under cattle, the soil deteriorates further over 7–10 years, leaving an increasingly barren scrubland supporting fewer and fewer animals per hectare. By one calculation, Costa Rica loses 2.5 tons of topsoil for every kilogram of beef exported.

The Cost of Deforestation

- Deforested land is quickly eroded, and tons of topsoil are washed into watercourses, silting up streams and rivers, clogging hydroelectric installations, and disrupting marine ecosystems along the coast. In Panama, deforestation has increased soil erosion, threatening to silt up the Panama Canal.

- Deforestation disrupts the local climate, since the trees regulate the storage and release of rainwater. By returning water vapor to the atmosphere, trees also encourage further rainfall. The loss of forests therefore makes both drought and flooding as well as mudslides more likely.

- Many of Latin America's poor rely on firewood for fuel. As the forests become depleted, they must travel farther afield to scavenge for supplies, and in the towns the price rises reflect wood's increasing scarcity.

- Indigenous peoples who live in harmony with the forest have little hope of surviving sustained contact with incoming settlers, although some indigenous groups have successfully mobilized to gain rights over their land.

- The rain forest is a repository of plant and animal species that, besides their intrinsic value, are a vital source of new genetic material—a quarter of all pharmaceutical products are derived from rain forest products, even though only 1 percent of all Amazon plants have been intensively investigated for medicinal properties. Tropical forest plants have provided treatments for leukemia, Hodgkin's disease, breast, cervical, and testicular cancer and are currently being used in AIDS research.

• A number of investigations show that the commercial potential of the forest is far greater than that of the pasture that replaces it. In addition the forest can be farmed in a sustainable way, yielding rubber, brazil nuts, and many kinds of fruit.

• Most Western attention has centered on the issue of global warming. The burning itself releases greenhouse gases (especially carbon dioxide, which accounts for half the global warming effect) into the atmosphere, and the forests that absorb carbon dioxide through photosynthesis are shrinking.. However, developing countries point out that 75 percent of the world's carbon dioxide emissions come from the factories and cars of the industrialized nations, who long ago destroyed their own forest environments. They say the north has not yet put its own house in order, and therefore has little moral authority to tell Latin America what to do with its rain forest.

Soil Erosion

Overintensive agriculture can produce just as much soil erosion as deforestation. In Central America 40 percent of all lands suffer a degree of erosion that undermines their productivity. The worst case is El Salvador, where an estimated 77 percent of arable land is eroded. Ravaged by years of civil war, this tiny country is the most densely populated in Latin America and has an extremely unequal system of land distribution. In the Salvadoran countryside peasant farmers hand-tend tiny plots of maize and beans on steep hillsides, while down below on the fertile valley floor the rich landowners' tractors prepare the land for cotton or sugar.

The El Niño weather pattern has increased the frequency of hurricanes and floods in recent decades, with catastrophic results. The effects of these natural disasters have been magnified by both deforestation and overintensive farming, leading to enormous landslides in parts of Central America and the Caribbean. Now, without the stabilizing root systems of forest trees, rural settlements can be washed away in an instant. Downstream the silt, often laden with pesticides, devastates the marine environment. Siltation, pollution, and

Biopiracy: The Battle for the Yellow Bean

The term "biopiracy" was coined in 1992, and has since gained wide usage in the controversy over scientists and businesses that simply take biological material from developing countries and patent it back home. With his red beard and swashbuckling manner, Colorado bean broker Larry Proctor even looks like the stereotype of the old-fashioned pirate, and has spurred a cross-border turf war in the long fight against biopiracy. The little yellow bean he claims to have invented has become emblematic of the inequities between the north and the south in an age that measures riches not in buried treasure but in the multidigit patents that form what the biotech industry likes to call its "intellectual property estate."

Proctor's use of patent laws to take over an emerging U.S. market for Mexican yellow beans highlights both the inequities and the injustices in the current intellectual property regime. In this case the victims are not poor farmers but a well-organized group of modern Mexican producers seeking to take commercial advantage of NAFTA's opening of cross-border trade.

In 1994, Larry Proctor bought a bag of bean seeds in Sonora, Mexico, and took them home to sow. He began to breed a yellow bean, and in 1996 he applied for a patent from the U.S. Patent and Trademark Office. Patent number 5894079, issued on April 13, 1999, gives his company, Pod-ners, L.L.C , exclusive monopoly rights to market what he calls the "Enola" bean—after his wife's middle name.

Meanwhile in the northwestern state of Sinaloa, Mexico, the farmers who have been producing the yellow bean for generations learned that it was no longer theirs: Proctor's patent bars them from what had become a lucrative market for the beans in southern California. But the powerful Rio Fuerte Growers Association (RFGA) of Los Mochis, Sinaloa, has vowed to fight back.

Policymakers and dealmakers view the yellow bean patent as a precedent-setting case within the murky realm of international biotech protection. Across borders, lawyers, scientists, farmers, activists, trade officials, and now even the United Nations, have all taken up arms in the battle of the bean.

—Timothy A. Wise, Hilda Salazar, and Laura Carlsen, eds., *Confronting Globalization*, Bloomfield, CT: Kumarian Press, 2003

wood-cutting have reduced El Salvador's 300,000 acres of mangrove estuary to a pitiful remnant. The loss is also an economic one: mangroves provide a rich breeding ground for marine life, and one square kilometer of mangrove estuary is worth US$100,000 a year in fish and shellfish. Siltation has also greatly reduced the life span of a number of hydroelectric dams in the region by clogging up the lakes that feed the generators.

Despite efforts to show poor farmers the virtues of terracing, crop rotation, and tree-planting, hard-pressed families are likely to continue to plow hillsides or cut down trees unless serious land reform gives them better land elsewhere.

Pesticide Poisons

All over rural Latin America glossy roadside billboards peddle the wares of the big agrochemical multinationals. Names like Bayer, Ciba-Geigy, Shell, Monsanto, and DuPont adorn ads promising farmers prosperity if they administer just one more dose of chemicals to their crops. In jeeps and village bars, the plantation owners sport brand names such as Tordon or Gramoxone on their T-shirts and baseball caps. The pesticide companies claim to sell their wares in philanthropic pursuit of an end to world hunger: in the words of one Bayer annual report, "Emotional attacks against conscientious agrochemicals research are attacks against humanity."

In fact, nearly all pesticides are used on export crops, not food for local people, and the cotton and banana plantations of Central America provide some of the worst examples of pesticide abuse in the world. In the 1970s Central America consumed 40 percent of all U.S. pesticide exports. Chemicals like DDT, which is illegal in the United States, were routinely exported and

---

Pesticide Contamination among Farm Workers

An early morning bus ride through the cotton-growing area of Central America provides a stinging glimpse of everyday reality. As the bus passes plantations, its windows film over. Most of the passengers, knowing what to expect, close their eyes, slow their breathing, and cover their nose and mouth with a scarf. Those riders caught unaware feel their eyes begin to smart, their lungs involuntarily contract, and a bitter chemical smell starts to clog their noses.

Visitors to the area will likely rush off the bus to change clothes and to wash their stinging skin with soap and water. The local population is not so fortunate; their exposure to agricultural chemicals for the day has only begun. They will toil long hours in the fields, drenched with chemicals that crop dusters sprayed earlier that morning. Three out of four farm workers have no running water in their homes to wash off the day's accumulation of pesticides. Many bathe in irrigation canals or streams contaminated with still more agrochemicals, or try to wash off with water stored in a discarded pesticide drum.

—Tom Barry, *Roots of Rebellion*, Boston: South End Press, 1987 sold in the region, where about 75 percent of the pesticides used are either banned, restricted, or unregistered in the United States. In 1990 the U.S. Congress finally took action and passed laws preventing the "dumping" of banned pesticides on Third World markets. Over the next decade, however, Central American pesticide imports more than doubled. By the turn of the century, the Pan American Health Organization estimated that 400,000 cases of pesticide poisoning were occurring in Central America every year.

Pesticide pollution even finds an echo in the cocaine boom, as aerial spraying of anti-coca herbicides funded by the U.S. Drug Enforcement Agency has led to serious health concerns in rural Colombia and Ecuador.

Lost Volcanoes

The cities of Latin America are losing their volcanoes. In Santiago, Chile, people recall the days when the snow-capped Andes loomed over the city. Now they rarely break through a dense blanket of smog. The Chilean government has even proposed blasting a hole through the mountain chain to allow the wind through to clear away the murk. "They think it's easier to move mountains than to control the bus drivers," explained a resident.

In Mexico, the two great volcanoes of the Aztecs, Popocatépetl and Ixtaccihuatl, have similarly been lost to sight. Average visibility has dropped from 12 kilometers to just 3. Air pollution exceeds internationally acceptable levels in São Paulo, Buenos Aires, Santiago, Caracas, and Mexico City. Mexico is probably the worst, as any visitor will agree who has had the misfortune to be there on one of the 225 days of the year when a thermal inversion prevents the city's filth from escaping. Pedestrians weep as they walk through the streets in air that does as much damage as smoking forty cigarettes a day. Mexico is uniquely damned by geography—it lies in a natural bowl where pollution collects, and at its high altitude of 7,400 feet car engines produce twice their sea-level amount of carbon monoxide. For the inhabitants of such cities, air pollution is far more than an irritant. Seventy percent of all babies are born with unacceptable levels of lead in their bloodstreams. Following the Great Depression of the 1930s, all of the larger Latin American nations embarked on a program of industrialization aimed at reducing their dependence on commodity exports and manufactured imports. The consequence was a sudden surge in unchecked industrial growth and a chaotic exodus of impoverished farmers from the countryside to the cities. Latin America's cities rapidly became some of the biggest in the world—Mexico City had about 20 million inhabitants by 2003.

Three-quarters of Mexico City's pollution comes from millions of cars and the city's huge and filthy industrial complex. "If the [U.S.] Environmental Protection Agency standards were applied to this country," comments one U.S. embassy official, "Mexico would surpass the highest tolerable levels for sulphur dioxide, cadmium, lead, zinc, copper, and particulate matter." What he omits to mention is that many U.S. and other multinational companies have been quick to relocate some of their dirtiest factories to Latin American countries precisely to avoid those EPA standards and the increased costs they imply.

The growth of the cities seems inexorable, but could be slowed if governments undertook serious agrarian reform in the countryside and used regional planning to decentralize the economy. In the towns, the environmental damage could be reduced if factories and vehicles were regulated, and there have been some encouraging signs in recent years, with the Brazilian city of Curitiba offering some impressive lessons to city planners around the world. City schemes to encourage lead-free petrol and make people leave their cars at home for one working day a week have helped to cut air pollution in Santiago, Mexico City, and São Paulo.

Climate Change

Latin America is already suffering the effects of global warming. In the Andes, many glaciers are rapidly retreating, as they melt faster than new snowfalls can replenish the ice. Huge chunks of the Antarctic ice shelf are breaking off and floating out to sea. But scientific studies predict that worse is to come. Farther north of the Andes, semi-arid areas could be turned into deserts, destroying the livelihoods of already vulnerable smallholder farmers in places such as northeast Brazil. Perhaps the most immediate overall threat is an increase in the catastrophic weather cycles known as El Niño and La Niña, periods of warm- and cold-water currents off the shores of the Americas that produce severe droughts and floods. These are becoming much more frequent as a result of climate change, and, as with many other so-called natural disasters, the disruptions they cause are much more likely to harm poor and vulnerable communities.

Exports

The squeeze on the environment accelerated with the debt crisis, as governments stepped up exports to meet escalating repayments to the Western banks. As time went on, the broader processes of "structural adjustment," which pursued an "export-or-die" approach to development, further increased pressure on the ecosystem.

Governments desperate to find new sources of hard currency showed little interest in longer-term issues such as environmental protection. In Guyana largely untouched forests came under the hammer as part of an adjustment program agreed to with the International Monetary Fund (IMF) in the late 1980s. The country duly parceled out its forests and rivers to an unholy alliance of Canadian, Brazilian, and Asian mining and logging companies. In return for a 50-year license on a 4.13-million-acre concession, the notorious Sarawak-based logger Samling Timbers promised to export 1.2 million cubic feet of Guyanese timber a year (compared to national exports of just 94,000 cubic feet in 1989). One of the growth areas was "non-traditional exports" of higher-value agricultural products such as cut flowers or fresh fruit. These require enormous doses of pesticide and fungicide in order to reach supermarkets in the north in pristine condition.

In the twenty-first century, the economic crisis has eased but pressure on the environment has not: governments today are investing heavily in huge, integrated systems of roads, waterways, and hydropower schemes to boost exports of minerals, oil, and agricultural commodities, and in doing so they are carrying on with the destruction of precious ecosystems. In particular, Brazil, anxious to establish itself as an emerging world power, is expanding into neighboring countries and helping them to exploit their natural resources, with scant concern for the impact of these activities on the environment.

The Cost of Exports

In the Chilean port of Puerto Montt, a rich sweet smell of fermenting wood emanates from several huge mounds of wood chip, silhouetted against the dockside floodlights. Dwarfing the wooden houses and shops of the town, the mounds steam gently as they await loading onto the Japanese ship which rides at anchor in the bay. Each pile contains the remnants of a different species of Chilean tree, hauled from the country's dwindling native forest.

Along the Chilean coast, the wire-mesh tanks of innumerable salmon farms dot the picturesque fjords and inlets. On the beaches, the black strings of pelillo seaweed lie drying before being sent to Japan for processing into food preservative. In the ports, the fishmeal factories grind mackerel into animal fodder. All these products will be shipped overseas as part of the Chilean export boom, a vast enterprise which has turned the country into the fastest-growing economy in Latin America and the flagship of the new market-led economic model which has taken the region's governments by storm.

—Duncan Green, *Silent Revolution: The Rise and Crisis of Market Economics in Latin America*, London: LAB, 2003

Genetically modified (GM) crops, involving gene splicing across species rather than traditional forms of selective breeding, have spread in several Latin American countries, particularly Brazil and Argentina, where, as early as 1998, 90 percent of all soybeans were GM. GM has proved controversial in many consumer countries, especially in Europe, which has largely shunned them. However, as in America, GM crops have been largely welcomed by farmers, as they enable them to bring down labor costs through the "no-till" farming technique. Initially, GM soybeans also allowed the farmers to use fewer herbicides, but recently usage has rebounded, as "super weeds" resistant to the chemicals have developed. There is also concern that the widespread adoption of GM will displace local species (genetic erosion) and leave peasant farmers increasingly dependent on the seeds and linked chemical inputs controlled by large multinationals like Monsanto.

Green Guerrillas

In recent years, the environmental movement has taken off in Latin America and has already achieved some notable successes. Environmental groups were initially largely urban and middle-class, taking their cue from the burgeoning green movement in Europe and North America. They were also boosted by the 1992 UN "Earth Summit," held in Rio de Janeiro, which by explicitly linking the two concepts of environment and development, gained general acceptance of the importance of "sustainable development." The work of the middle-class environmentalists and the international green lobby can clearly be seen in the increased media coverage for green issues within the region and the "greening" of political debate. Even ranchers and loggers now feel obliged to dress up their language in green rhetoric. Pressure from the urban environmental movement has also been instrumental in forcing the region's cities to begin to try to control air pollution. In some cases, governments and the private sector have found that environmentalism can also be good for business. One of the most successful green industries is ecotourism, which in Costa Rica was bringing in over US$1 billion by 2000, as northern vacationers were lured by a combination of beaches and spectacular national parks.

Another wing of Latin American environmental activism comes from the grassroots, involving those directly affected, usually poor communities such as those championed by Chico Mendes. Often led by the region's burgeoning indigenous revival, these groups have led campaigns against polluting oil industries in Mexico and Ecuador and have taken up numerous other causes.

Such developments offer hope for the future, but there are also ample grounds for gloom. The greed and shortsightedness of both local and foreign

Dirty Industry

Apart from raw materials, the other growth area in Latin American exports are the *maquiladoras*. These are assembly plants run by transnational companies in Mexico, Central America, and the Caribbean that take advantage of low wages and lax environmental laws to produce goods for re-export to the U.S. market:

"Twelve years ago we came to live here," says Maurilio Sánchez Pachuca, the stout president of the local residents' committee in a dingy *colonia* just outside Tijuana, Mexico. "We thought we'd be in glory because it was an ecological reserve—lots of vegetation, animals, birds. Two years later the *maquiladoras* started to arrive up there." A fat thumb gestures up at the plateau overlooking the colonia, with its clean blue and white *maquiladora* assembly plants. "Now many of us have skin problems—rashes, hair falling out, we get eye pains, fevers. My kids' legs are really bad—all the kids have nervous problems and on the way to school the dust and streams are all polluted. We've tried to stop them playing in the streams, but kids are kids." He flicks despairingly through a treasured folder full of blurred photocopies of the hand-typed letters he has written to the authorities and their replies, a nine-year exercise in Kafkaesque futility. "The first thing [the *maquiladoras*] do is buy the local officials. There are too many vested interests—dark interests, dollars. I have so many lovely letters from the government—but they aren't real."

Up on the plateau, huge container trucks are at the loading bays, gorging themselves on the products of the 189 factories—Maxell cassettes, a crisp new Sanyo plant, Tabuchi Electric de México. A security guard ushers unwelcome visitors from the site. A black and pink slag-heap of battery casings is piled up by the fence surrounding the factories, where truckloads of old batteries from the U.S. are broken up to recycle the lead and acid. By law, the remnants should be returned to the U.S., but they are just dumped here on the edge of the plateau.

—Duncan Green, *Silent Revolution: The Rise and Crisis of Market Economics in Latin America*, London: LAB, 2003

interests have changed little since the Conquest—they still mistakenly treat the New World and its people as an inexhaustible and indestructible source of riches. Since the 1980s, the region's uncritical adoption of a development model based on the unregulated market and ever more rapacious exploitation of its ecosystem has worked against attempts to improve the environment, forcing grassroots campaigners to swim against the prevailing economic tide. When, as part of its commitment to opening up the economy, the Brazilian government removed the tariffs that had protected domestic rubber producers, cheap Malaysian rubber flooded in. The price of latex in Brazil fell from

US$1.80 per kilogram in 1980 to under 40 cents in 1992, and Amazon-grown rubber saw its market share slide from 85 percent to just 28 percent. The first to suffer were the rubber tappers, who in the wake of Chico Mendes's murder had pressured the government into establishing "extractive reserves" covering millions of hectares. Their joy turned sour as they watched prices slump, and thousands of families were forced to leave the new reserves in search of a living wage in the cities, or join the ranks of the *garimpeiros* in the ecologically

---

Ecotourism, Greenwashing, and Ecotourism Lite

Ecotourism in Latin America, as elsewhere, has become big business, both as a label applied to a vast range of tourism destinations, products and experiences and as the focus of vigorous debate. Many examples of ecotourism focus exclusively on tourism that offers encounters with nature. Another definition, this one by the International Ecotourism Society, calls it "responsible travel to natural areas that conserves the environment and improves the well-being of local people."

The liberal and often unjustified claims for ecotourism have brought widespread accusations that many tourism operators and destinations are guilty of "greenwashing," a kind of deceitful public relations message suggesting that a business acts in a more environmentally responsible way than it actually does. Martha Honey, in her article "Giving a Grade to Costa Rica's Green Tourism," in NACLA's *Report on the Americas* in May/June 2003, offers a nicely skeptical viewpoint based on her close acquaintance with the evolution of Costa Rica's highly publicized ecotourism industry:

"Today, everything in Costa Rica seems to carry 'eco' in its name. There is, for instance, 'Eco-Playa' (a typical beach indistinguishable from other gray/black sand beaches), 'Ecological Rent-a-Car' (which rents the same vehicles as Hertz, Budget or Avis), 'eco-gas' (super unleaded), 'eco-musica' (songs with environmental themes), and innumerable ecolodges, ecosafaris and ecological cruises. Many of these tourism enterprises can be categorized as ecotourism 'lite,' meaning that the company's green rhetoric far outstrips the reality of its adherence to sound ecotourism principles. The classic example of this in Costa Rica as elsewhere is the growing number of major hotel chains that offer guests the 'eco-option' of not having their sheets and towels laundered every day. Such sensible but relatively minor environmental innovations are advertised with claims such as 'Keep your towels and help save the world!' The reality is that it is the hotels that are saving sizeable sums on their laundry bills."

—Martin Mowforth and Ian Munt, *Tourism and Responsibility: Perspectives from Latin America and the Caribbean*, London: Routledge, 2007 disastrous gold rush. The blind forces of economics have turned them from defenders of the environment into its destroyers.

Tourism

Travel and tourism to Latin American countries has increased steadily over the last twenty years: Costa Rica, Peru, Brazil, and Mexico are now favored long-haul travel destinations from the UK and Europe. The 1990s saw tourism climb steadily up the list of foreign-exchange earners for many countries; in the case of Costa Rica it had replaced bananas and coffee by the end of the decade as the top earner of foreign cash. Much, but not all, of this tourism is centered around adventure, nature, or ecotourism. Latin America's many pleasures and assets—a rich natural environment, diverse cultures, history, and heritage—suggest that this trend will only grow.

For many countries in Latin America, tourism creates jobs, generates foreign exchange, and raises tax revenues. But it also brings ills such as environmental mismanagement and waste, cultural "pollution" such as travelers bringing unwanted habits like drug-taking, and in some cases it exacerbates already entrenched social inequalities. From the tourists' point of view, many Latin American countries are often seen as high-security risks, with tourist-related crime rampant in some areas. In a sense, much tourism in Latin America produces a more acute version of the abrupt collision between the haves and the have-nots that already takes place among the domestic population.

4.
Identity and Rights

Race and Ethnicity

Latin America has moved on from its colonial days, when a tiny white elite ruled over an indigenous majority. *Mestizaje*, or racial mixing, describes the intermingled nature of the majority of the continent's population today. Whites mixed with indigenous peoples created a *mestizo* race, whereas whites with black African-descended peoples produced *mulattos*. Black and indigenous mixes were often termed *zambo*, or "black indian."

While most studies of race still concentrate on the indigenous experience, increasing attention is being given to the history, culture, and everyday lives of the continent's Afro-Latin Americans. There are significant populations of descendants of Africans in Cuba, the Dominican Republic, Central America—especially Nicaragua, Costa Rica, and Panama—Colombia, Peru, and Brazil. But there are also smaller numbers of Afro-Argentines, and Afro-Venezuelans.

Race—especially "blackness"—is now seen as much a social and cultural construction as a matter of genetic inheritance. In today's Latin America, race, social and economic position, and gender are inevitably intertwined.

Indigenous Peoples

Cape Sunday (Cabo Domingo) is a lonely place. Low, dark hills under an enormous sky sink toward the ocean at the southern tip of the Americas. At this spot one Sunday in the 1920s a German landowner held a banquet for the local Yaganes people. When they were drunk, his hidden henchmen opened fire with a machine gun. The Yaganes died because, unaccustomed to the concept of private property, they had killed and eaten the landowner's sheep. The indigenous people of Tierra del Fuego were an almost Stone Age people dressed in skins and using flint hand tools. When the whites started to colonize the region in the 1880s, the tribes soon succumbed to disease and slaughter. Today only a few old folk remain of the people whose permanent campfires gave Tierra del Fuego (Land of Fire) its name.

Several thousand miles north, in February 2005, Ecuador came to a grinding halt as the Confederation of Indigenous Nationalities of Ecuador (CONAIE) initiated national protests against the government of Lucio Gutiérrez, a president they had helped to elect after a similar uprising in 1999 had ousted the previous president. Gutiérrez had alienated his erstwhile indigenous allies by agreeing to a structural adjustment program with the IMF, initiating military cooperation with the United States, and opening up indigenous regions to oil exploration, and was duly forced from office. In Ecuador, the indigenous people now decide the fate of presidents.

The Ecuadorean movement's dynamism belies the conventional Western image of fatalistic indigenous communities calmly awaiting extinction. Latin America's history is full of the uprisings and resistance of peoples whose civilizations were in many ways far in advance of Europe's at the time of the Conquest.

Modern Indigenous Life

The continent's indigenous survivors now make up 5 percent of its total population and fall into two distinct groups. The first, and by far the largest, is that of the highland indigenous people, descendants of the Inca, Aztec, and Mayan empires. The second are the lowland indigenous groups, largely confined to the Amazon basin and Central America. In both Guatemala and Bolivia, over half the population is indigenous, and the largest number of indigenous people live in Peru and Mexico. Although highland indigenous people number some 22 million, lowlanders do not exceed 1 million, of whom about a quarter live in Brazil, with smaller numbers in the other countries of the Amazon basin: Venezuela, Colombia, Ecuador, Peru, Bolivia, and the Guianas. Isolated lowland groups also survive in the Central American countries of Panama, Nicaragua, and Honduras.

When not tied to the *haciendas* of the big landowners, highland communities farm the land in much the same way as they did five centuries ago. They grow the traditional crops—maize, beans, and squash in Mexico, potatoes and maize in the Andes—using mainly the simple technology of the digging stick and hoe. Communities are tightly knit, and members are encouraged not to sell land to outsiders and to marry within the village. Although their lifestyles are often romanticized by outsiders, indigenous farming communities lead harsh lives, suffering the high levels of infant mortality and insecurity common to all peasant farmers.

Where they have managed to retain a level of independence, such communities frequently enjoy a rich cultural life. In Guatemala, each highland

Ecuadorians protest against the criminalization of social protests and "in defense of water, life, and the dignity of communities."

village has its own distinctive costume, with unique designs passed on from mother to daughter for generations. Many traditional practices have survived the efforts of the colonial authorities. Faith healers combine herbal medicine and magic, and the religion of the European invaders has been fused with its predecessors into an original form of "folk Catholicism." Communities attach great importance to ritual cycles involving saints' days, feast days, and ceremonies such as baptism, marriage, and funerals. In the course of the twentieth century modern influences gradually encroached upon this traditional pattern. Improved roads have increased trading and involvement in the money economy; improved education and contact with the outside world mean that most indigenous people now speak Spanish; satellite television and the Internet have found their way into the most remote villages; and growing numbers of Protestant missionaries have both converted indigenous groups and persuaded them to abandon their traditional customs. The old ways persist most stubbornly in Guatemala, where many speakers of the country's twenty-one indigenous languages still know no more than a few words of Spanish. In most areas men are assimilated into non-indigenous ways faster than women, who have become the custodians of traditional culture. Men have more contact with the money economy through wage labor, and women less frequently go to school, where Spanish is often the only permitted language.

Another major cause of what is known as "acculturation," the loss of traditional culture, is urbanization. The exodus to the cities brings contact with poor mestizos and indigenous people from other communities, and Spanish frequently becomes the common language. The disruption of the move can leave few vestiges of traditional culture intact.

War and repression also accelerate the process. Since the early 1980s in Guatemala, a ferocious army counterinsurgency campaign in the indigenous highlands has left 40,000 dead and over 400 indigenous villages destroyed. Many more fled their villages to seek refuge in the cities, where they sought anonymity by abandoning their traditional dress and customs. Over a million people were displaced from their homes in what bordered on a race war. In the mid-1980s one Guatemalan president warned, "We must get rid of the words 'indigenous' and 'Indian.'" Peru's civil war between the Sendero Luminoso guerrillas and the army also drove many indigenous families into the swelling shantytowns around Lima. The economic difficulties of the 1990s pushed many smallholders in Bolivia, Ecuador, and Mexico away from farming, with its unpredictable returns, to the grim certainty of urban life.

Violent racism persists in most countries with a significant indigenous population. In Guatemala the enormous divide between poor, non-Spanish-speaking indigenous people and wealthy white landowners and entrepreneurs closely resembles apartheid. When indigenous activist Rigoberta Menchú won the Nobel Peace Prize in 1992, "ethnic dolls" in indigenous dress speedily went on to the market in the United States. Wealthy Guatemalans were torn between national pride and class hatred, and were heard to joke that at last Barbie had found a maid.

Lowland Indigenous People

> No one sells his own son or his mother, because he loves them. In the same way, it is an absurd idea for an Indian to sell his land. We can't change our feelings for our land, which is where our ancestors are buried.
>
> —Speaker for Taxáua people, Brazil

In contrast to the highlanders' stable agriculture based on herding and crop rotation, lowland indigenous groups have traditionally practiced mobile slash-and-burn forms of farming, combined with fishing and hunting. Both groups, however, share an overwhelming and mystical bond with the land. Lowlanders, like the highlanders, have strong religious traditions in which worship of aspects of the natural world is mediated through shamans who speak to deities in a trance.

Indigenous Identity

Our parents tell us: "Children, the earth is the mother of man, because she gives him food." This is especially true for us whose life is based on the crops we grow. Our people eat maize, beans and plants. We can't eat ham, or cheese, or things made by machines. So we think of the earth as the mother of man, and our parents teach us to respect the earth. We must only harm the earth when we are in need. This is why, before we sow our maize, we have to ask the earth's permission. By accepting the Catholic religion, we didn't accept a condition, or abandon our culture. It was more like another way of expressing ourselves. It's like expressing ourselves through a tree, for example; we believe that a tree is a being, a part of nature, and that a tree has its image, its representation, its *nahual,* to channel our feelings to the one God. That is the way we Indians conceive it. Catholic Action is like another element which can merge with the elements which already exist within Indian culture. And it confirms our belief that, yes, there is a God, and, yes, there is a father for all of us. And yet it is something we think of as being only for what happens up there. As far as the earth is concerned, we must go on worshipping through our own intermediaries, just as we have always done, through all the elements found in nature.

When we evoke the color of the sun, it's like evoking all the elements which go to make up our life. The sun, as the channel to the one God, receives the plea from his children that they should never violate the rights of all the other beings which surround them. This is how we renew our prayer which says that men, the children of the one God, must respect the life of the trees, the birds, the animals around us. We must respect the life of every single one of them. We must respect the life, the purity, the sacredness, which is water. We must respect the one God, the heart of the sky, which is the sun. We must not do evil while the sun shines upon his children. This is a promise.

—Rigoberta Menchú, *I, Rigoberta Menchú*, ed. Elizabeth Burgos Debray, trans. Ann Wright, London: Verso, 1984

Lowland groups traditionally live more communally than highlanders, often in communal houses known as *malocas*, which can hold several hundred people. *Malocas* have been criticized by Protestant missionaries for encouraging promiscuity and in many cases have been abandoned in favor of family houses. Many hundreds of different language groups exist, some comprising only a few dozen speakers.

Whereas highland communities have been in contact with whites virtually since the first days of the Conquest, lowland peoples have frequently lived in inaccessible areas, especially those in the Amazon basin, which outsiders have only recently penetrated. There are still believed to be a few groups, numbering perhaps a few thousand, of "uncontacted" indigenous people in the area. When contact does occur, it is frequently as disastrous as it was in the sixteenth century, leading to epidemics of disease and violent confrontations with settlers, such as those that befell the Yanomami people in the 1980s.

Lowland peoples have suffered the same "curse of wealth" as their highland relatives. In the rubber boom at the end of the nineteenth century, unscrupulous rubber companies trapped and enslaved large numbers of indigenous people as latex collectors. In the Putumayo region of Colombia, 40,000 were killed by these rubber barons between 1886 and 1919. After rubber came African palm, cattle, and oil, each new commodity penetrating fresh areas of the forest and absorbing or driving out the local indigenous groups. Since the 1990s, indigenous groups in the Ecuadorean Amazon have started to fight back against the oil companies whose drilling is destroying their forest ecosystem. In 2003, after years of legal struggles in U.S. courts had come to naught, they filed a billion-dollar lawsuit in Quito against the U.S. oil giant Chevron-Texaco, accusing the company of destroying large

---

Debt Bondage in Colombia

We called all the Indians together, along with their families, in a ravine or at the mouth of a river and there, in the presence of the Indian authorities, we advanced them: one shirt, one machete, some knives to make the cuts [in the rubber trees], a belt so that they didn't fall out of the trees, and of course, any goods they wanted. Throughout the year, we advanced them anything they, or their women, asked for. The women were their ruin and our business, because they fancied everything. Vanity does not respect color, nor age, nor sex. They wanted combs, perfumes, mirrors and colored beads, cloth and more cloth, high-heeled shoes and ribbons for their hair. The men asked for drink, Italian sweets and German radios. They liked music and partying.

Every day around 4 p.m. the line of Indians would arrive with the rubber, which was weighed on scales and then each Indian's amount was entered in a book. The scales didn't measure the true weight, and the amount we wrote in the book wasn't the amount on the scales. The [German missionary] did a lot of damage because she taught the "cousins" figures and they began to cause trouble the whole time. When they got unhappy, they'd run away. So we had to invent the pass—no boss would give them an advance if the Indians couldn't show a pass signed by their previous boss to prove that they had paid off their debts. Some Indians managed to pay off their debts, and even earned some money on top, but others didn't. Everything depended on their boss. Some bosses fiddled with the books so they never managed to pay it off. But others were very humane and only wrote down what the Indian asked for.

areas of rain forest and contaminating local land and rivers. They also alleged that the company's activities had led to an increased risk of cancer among the local population. Although Chevron-Texaco repeatedly lobbied the U.S. government to take trade reprisals against Ecuador because of the lawsuit, the Ecuadorean judge ruled against the company in early 2011, ordering it to pay billions of dollars in damages. Chevron-Texaco has appealed. In the Peruvian Amazon, fears of the impact of oil exploration have also galvanized lowland indigenous activism.

The other main source of encroachment on indigenous lands has been the colonization programs, either spontaneous or government-run, through which landless peasants have moved into the forest, cutting down the trees to make way for food crops. This has provoked frequent armed conflict between peasants and indigenous communities.

Government attitudes to the lowland indigenous groups have alternated between cynical disregard and a desire to "integrate" them into national life, a process anthropologists condemn as ethnocide. Several decades ago a Brazilian government official proudly described his policy to a visiting journalist:

> We resettle them as quickly as possible in new villages and then remove the children and begin to educate them. We give them the benefit of our medicine and our education, and, once they are completely integrated citizens like you and me and the Minister here, we let them go out into the world.

Once out in the world, "integrated Indians" often end up on the social scrap heap, surviving as beggars or prostitutes on the fringes of the frontier boomtowns of the Amazon. Sometimes the ethnocide was more deliberate. In Brazil in the early 1960s, a government inquiry found that corrupt officials of its own indigenous agency had connived with local landowners to massacre entire tribes using dynamite, machine guns, and poisoned sugar. Other investigations showed that tribes in Mato Grosso had been deliberately infected with smallpox, influenza, tuberculosis, and measles.

Rebellion and Resistance

The slow genocide of the indigenous nations provoked fierce resistance. In some cases, as in the Caribbean or Brazil, indigenous groups opted for mass suicide rather than bow to the dictates of the whites. Many others retreated into the most inaccessible areas of the continent to escape the burden of constant tributes and forced labor. Some took up arms against the Spanish authorities, the most famous being Peru's Túpac Amaru II, the most persistent being the dogged resistance of Chile's Mapuche people, who kept the outsiders at bay until the late nineteenth century, the most recent being the Zapatista uprising in southern Mexico. Yet neither indigenous revolts nor independence succeeded in reestablishing indigenous self-rule. In the endless cycle of revolt and defeat, the rebels learned the wisdom of the advice given by Quintín Lame (1880–1967), a Colombian indigenous revolutionary leader: "Do not believe in the friendship of the white man or the mestizo; distrust gifts and flattery; never consult a white lawyer; do not allow yourself to be hoodwinked by the chattering politicians of any party."

Elsewhere, indigenous resistance to oppression was more subtle, but no less stubborn.

The key battleground has been over culture, in particular religion and language, which are central to indigenous identity. "Religion is a Spanish word. For us, the Mayan priests pass down culture, not religion," explains Justina, a Guatemalan indigenous activist. Through the centuries, Latin America's indigenous peoples have proved extraordinarily able to adapt to outside pressure while safeguarding the essential aspects of their cultural identity. This stubborn, silent refusal to give in explains the reputation for passivity that they acquired in the eyes of outsiders, and goes back to the earliest days of the Conquest. In 1534 Mancu Inca Yupanki, an Inca leader, told his followers:

> Give the outward appearance of complying with their demands. Give them a little tribute, because if you don't give it they will take it from you by force. . . . I know that some day, by force or deceit, they will make you worship what they worship, and when that happens, when you can resist no longer, do it in front of them, but do not forget your ceremonies . . . reveal just what you have to and keep the rest hidden.
>
> —LYMAN L. JOHNSON, *Death, Dismemberment, and Memory:*
> *Body Politics in Latin America*

Through this combination of both passive and violent resistance, Latin America's indigenous peoples have achieved their most remarkable victory— survival. In the face of five centuries of a military, epidemic, cultural, and economic onslaught, they have survived, and are now increasing in numbers. However, most remain outsiders in their own lands, condemned to poverty, racism, and persecution. The last thirty-five years have seen attempts to build a politics based on the indigenous peoples' growing sense of identity and self-confidence, producing an upsurge in indigenous resistance. Among highland groups, indigenous activists have organized peasant associations and taken up arms to become involved in civil wars in Mexico, Guatemala, and Peru, while in Ecuador and Bolivia indigenous peasant groups have risen to dominate

---

The Last Inca: Túpac Amaru II

In 1781 Túpac Amaru laid siege to Cusco. This mestizo chief, a direct descendant of the Inca emperors, headed the broadest of messianic revolutionary movements. The rebellion broke out in Tinta province, which had been almost depopulated by enforced service in the Cerro Rico mines. Mounted on his white horse, Túpac Amaru entered the plaza of Tungasuca and announced to the sound of drums and *pututus* [conch-shell trumpets] that he had condemned the royal *corregidor* Antonio Juan de Arriaga to the gallows and put an end to the Potosí *mita.* A few days later Túpac issued a decree liberating the slaves. He abolished all taxes and forced labor in all forms. The Indians rallied by the thousands to the forces of the "father of all the poor and all the wretched and helpless." He moved against Cusco at the head of his *guerrilleros,* promising that all who died while under his orders in this war would return to life to enjoy the happiness and wealth the invaders had wrested from them. Victories and defeat followed; in the end, betrayed and captured by one of his own chiefs, Túpac was handed over in chains to the royalists. The Examiner Areche entered his cell to demand, in exchange for promises, the names of his rebel accomplices. Túpac Amaru replied scornfully, "There are no accomplices here except you and I. You as oppressor, I as liberator, deserve to die."

Túpac was tortured, along with his wife, his children and his chief aides, in Cusco's Plaza del Wacaypata. His tongue was cut out; his arms and legs were tied to four horses with the intention of quartering him, but his body would not break; he was finally beheaded at the foot of the gallows. His head was sent to Tinta, one arm to Tungasuca and the other to Carabaya, one leg to Santa Rosa and the other to Livitaca.

—Eduardo Galeano, *Open Veins of Latin America,* trans. Cedric Belfrage, New York: Monthly Review Press, 1973

---

national politics. In the lowland areas a plethora of indigenous organizations has sprung up, demanding land and help from the government, and defending themselves against the invasions of agribusiness, mining companies, and poor peasant colonizers. Lowland indigenous movements have achieved a political impact out of all proportion to their numbers: "Five centuries of contact has produced only marginalization, exploitation and misery for our highland colleagues. We're not volunteering for the same," says Evaristo Nugkuag, an Aguaruna leader from lowland Peru.

Mario Juruna, the first indigenous person to become a deputy in Brazil's parliament, made his people's demands quite clear:

Indian wealth lies in customs and communal traditions and land which is sacred. Indians can and want to choose their own road, and this road is not civilization made by whites. . . . Indian civilization is more human. We do not want paternalistic protection from whites. Indians today . . . want political power.

Indigenous organizations typically rely on individual communities as their basic building blocks. Federations of communities then grow to cover an area, in some cases combining to form regional and even national confederations. Crossborder cooperation took off in the indigenous campaign over the 500th anniversary of Columbus's first voyage to the Americas in 1992. The anti-Columbus campaign reached its peak in October 1991, when 500 indigenous delegates from every corner of the Americas met in Guatemala. A year later their campaign received international recognition when Rigoberta Menchú of Guatemala received the Nobel Peace Prize. Many observers now see the Columbus campaign as a watershed for the indigenous movement, a view that seemed to be confirmed when the indigenous peoples of southern Mexico and Ecuador rose in revolt in 1994.

Several problems have dogged these attempts at organization. The first has been the difficulty of building alliances between different indigenous groups and between highlanders and lowlanders. But even more thorny has been the problem of the relationship between indigenous and non-indigenous organizations. Indigenous organizations are often rightly suspicious of non-indigenous political parties and peasant organizations, fearing that they see the world purely in terms of class divisions, and fail to recognize and respect the indigenous peoples' right to be culturally distinct. Conflicts between indigenous communities and poor colonists can further sour the relationship. In Bolivia, one indigenous woman gave voice to the extreme "indigenist" position: "To the Indian, the Spaniard is only a tenant. And we have to hit him, complain about him and tell him to leave, because we are the owners and we are going to return."

Despite these obstacles, the political strength of indigenous organization has grown steadily in recent years, forcing parties, social movements, and governments alike to take their demands seriously. Besides Ecuador, where the indigenous movement routinely makes or breaks presidents, some of the greatest recent advances have been in Bolivia, where Evo Morales of the Movement Toward Socialism (MAS), made up of coca growers and other peasant allies, became president in 2006 after playing heavily upon his Aymara heritage and promising a series of reforms designed to benefit the indigenous poor.

In Brazil and Colombia new constitutions now enshrine a number of indigenous rights. In Mexico, the Zapatistas signed an indigenous rights accord

---

Hair Straightening in the Dominican Republic

In the Dominican Republic, a white woman's hair is described as blonde. Whether it is curly or straight, black or brown, it is said that she is blonde. About the "others," it is said that they have "bad hair."

   "When I quit straightening," Chaki said, a man told me: "You look like you don't have a husband. You will see the beating your husband is going to give you!" Another person asked me: "Where are you going to work, as a cook or a washerwoman?" "Straightening" does not whiten a woman, straightening is about self-denial. Being black in the Dominican Republic has never meant anything else. Accepting oneself as black means recognizing oneself as oppressed and exploited. The construction of a creative and free identity evolves from a double denial: to recognize oneself in the act of "not being" and to affirm it.

   A 45-year-old woman who recently decided to quit straightening commented: "When you quit you feel free, you break the chain that you used to carry in your head before." To quit is an affirmation, a symbolic act of going over to the other faction—the faction of the maroons [runaway slaves who established independent communities]. That is why it is interpreted as an act of rebelliousness and, in the case of women, it is double rebelliousness, because these two oppressions go together. Many women confess that they anxiously wait for the day to have their hair straightened, because they will then be beautiful and will be able to enjoy, for a few days, what they feel has been denied to them. At the same time they recognize themselves as non-whites who can be exposed at any time, when the roots begin to grow and be noticed, when it rains and they get wet.

—Casandra Badilo, "Only My Hairdresser Knows for Sure: Stories of Race, Hair and Gender in the Dominican Republic," NACLA Report on the Americas, 2001

---

with the government that recognizes the "autonomy" of Mexico's ten million indigenous people, and their rights to multilingual education and "adequate" political representation. But the accord did not touch on the economic issues at the heart of the Zapatista uprising, such as land redistribution and control of natural resources. In Guatemala the government signed a similar accord with the Guatemalan National Revolutionary Unity (URNG) guerrillas prior to the peace agreement of 1996. Such paper guarantees do not always translate into real improvements on the ground, but they provide a rallying point for the indigenous movement.

   For optimists, the indigenous people are on the way back. Many in the Andes are convinced that the *pachakut'i*, literally the "balance upheaval" that legends and oral history have prophesied for centuries, has finally arrived, heralding an indigenous cultural and political renaissance that will transform

Latin America. They point to the resurgence in indigenous identity and organization as evidence.

Pessimists see the tide moving in the other direction and blame the region's
obsession with structural adjustment. With its focus on individualism and the
market, neoliberalism stands diametrically opposed to the indigenous traditions of community, subsistence agriculture, and reciprocal aid.

In the long term, the pessimists may be proved wrong. Latin America's
indigenous peoples have shown extraordinary tenacity in surviving five centuries of cultural, political, and economic assault by outsiders. The recent resurgence of indigenous organization faces enormous obstacles, but may indeed
herald a future where indigenous and non-indigenous learn to live in mutual
respect, and different cultures can flourish side by side.

Black Latin America

In recent years, "blackness" in many Latin American countries has gone from
being solely about social exclusion to become a powerful marker of identity,
and has also provided the impetus for a new political consciousness and for
social movements, especially in Colombia. Some nations, notably Cuba and
Brazil, have actively pursued racial integration and a notion of harmony—
"racial democracy." Many Cubans and Brazilians are uncomfortable discuss-
ing race and its implied counterpart, racism. Racism may be acknowledged,
but often only as an ill inherited from a past marred by colonialism and slavery; allegations of racism are seen to undermine national unity. But race, and
notions of race, influence relations among ordinary people in many ways.
Recently Brazil has adopted its own form of affirmative action, creating quotas
for black people in universities and government jobs.

Multicultural Latin America?

> For us race is not a biological concept. For us, it is something spiritual. It constitutes
> a sum of the imponderables that make us what we are and impel us to be what we
> should be, through our origins and through our destiny. It is what dissuades us from
> falling into the imitation of other communities whose natures are foreign to us. For
> us, race constitutes our personal seal, indefinable and irrefutable.
>
> —JUAN DOMINGO PERÓN, 1947

Latin America is a multiethnic region—besides indigenous ethnicities and the
black populations there are also significant Chinese populations, descendants

Youth, Class, and Racism:
Interviews with Peruvian Teenagers in Lima

The boys are fifteen: Lucas and Yuri. Violeta, still in the little blue uniform of her English-style girls' school, is sixteen, but fast developing into a woman. They are full of curiosity and bubbling with life.

They tell me that Lima is going to the dogs and that they come to LarcoMar because it is the only place they can get away from the *cholos*. They refer not to the trading *cholos*, but the comical variation who make a living by dressing up in fishnet stockings and plastic boobs, stuffing cushions down their bums, and then stomp around the streets in stilettos spanking men to get a few *soles* from drivers at the traffic lights. "Ambulant comics" they are called.

"So what is a *cholo* supposed to be like?" I ask, feeling strange just saying the word, as if it were like saying "nigger" or "paki."

"My maid," blurts out Violeta instinctively. They look at each other and giggle. "I don't want more equality," says Violeta. "If we had more equality, we would have to share more and work harder to stay where we are. In Peru there is not enough wealth for everyone. You have to keep what you've got."

She complains that the newly rich *cholos* even turn up at their discotheques. "We go to a place and make it really happening. Then the *cholos* turn up and you think ugh, and you have to start going somewhere else and then they turn up there. It's impossible."

It seems that Violeta and her gang spend the whole time escaping from the *cholos* as if they carried the plague, a quest that strikes me as slightly futile, since the large majority of the Peruvian population is of indigenous descent. They would have to run very, very far before they were rid of the *cholo* face, and even when they reached the U.S. they'd find them here, in baseball caps and Levi's jeans.

—Amaranta Wright, *Ripped and Torn: Levi's, Latin America and the Blue Jean Dream*, London: Ebury Press, 2005

of indentured laborers brought to Latin America in the nineteenth century, as well as a later wave of Japanese immigrants, who mostly settled in Brazil and Peru. In Mexico, European planters held vast tracts of land, while in the Southern Cone, and especially in Argentina, European laborers have left significant cultural legacies—one in two Argentines is descended from an Italian.

However, the coexistence of so many ethnicities and cultures is far from harmonious. The economic downturn in Argentina in 2001 brought to the surface tensions between the urban unemployed and Bolivian immigrant workers. Throughout the 1990s Bolivians were encouraged to travel to Argentine cities to work for less than locals would accept. The scarcity of employment after the crash, however, meant that the immigrants were now accused of "stealing Argentine jobs." The statistics tell a different story. The number of Bolivians in Argentina has remained between 2 and 3 percent since the 1860s, though in hard times the migrant laborers have tended to move into urban areas in search of work.

Tension also exists between the close communities of Central America and the Caribbean. The Haitians who have managed to cross into the Dominican Republic have been ghettoized. They are poorer than their Dominican neighbors and speak a different language, but the most common divide between the two communities concerns self-perception—while Haiti is a self-consciously "black" republic, the Dominican Republic has chosen to emphasize its Hispanic identity. Similarly, Guatemalans working in Mexico often choose to hide their indigenous heritage the better to fit in with the northward-looking Mexican national elite. At the same time, *mestizaje* is being celebrated, at least within official and academic circles. There is a new willingness at government level to recognize and support multiculturalism and the rights that ethnicity confers on groups. Within nations a search is under way to harness the social and political power of competing "identities."

Skeptics, however, are suspicious that the new recognition bestowed on ethnicities by national governments—"neoliberal multiculturalism" is the term coined by U.S. academic Charles Hale—is merely a nod to the official multiculturalism of many countries in the north, while seeking to neutralize the power of social movements based on ethnic identity.

Race and Politics

Racial identity has always been an issue in Latin American politics. Haiti declared itself a "black republic" after rebel slaves achieved independence in 1804, and Ecuador and Bolivia are often described (and describe themselves) as "Indian republics." At the other extreme, Brazil prides itself on a rather false notion of racial harmony, and Cuba sought the eradication of racism after the 1959 revolution and has done more than perhaps any other nation to end social stratification based on skin color. Official proclamations of equality have, however, frequently masked an enduring racism.

In Peru, the checkered career of Japanese-descended Alberto Fujimori reveals some of the ways in which race has been hijacked by opportunistic politicians. In 1990, he played upon his "outsider" image in an attempt to forge an alliance between immigrants and indigenous peoples against the white elite. This approach was tailored to neutralize the popularity of his opponent, the author Mario Vargas Llosa, who represented urban, white conservatives. However, in 2000, the now-disgraced Fujimori was pilloried by supporters of the indigenous Alejandro Toledo, who chanted, "*Cholo* yes, *chino* no." The *Nikkei*, or Japanese Peruvians, have been tarnished by association with Fujimori's corruption—where once they were admired for economic success, they are now viewed as a stereotypically exploitative class. Throughout the Andean region it has become politically expedient for leaders such as Toledo to proclaim their *cholo* credentials, reclaiming the formerly disparaging word for people of indigenous descent.

Gender and Politics

Penha is an imposing figure, a big confident woman who has risen to become president of the Alagoa Grande Rural Workers' Union in Brazil's drought-prone and poverty-ridden northeast. She recounts her life story, the words half lost in the drumming of a sudden downpour which turns the street into a river bearing garbage from the nearby market. A broken home, starting work at age seven, a mother who died from TB when Penha was twelve, early marriage and struggling to feed her six children—hers is the story of countless poor Latin American women. Then came transformation when she joined the union, inspired by a charismatic leader named Margarida Maria Alves. When Margarida was assassinated, probably by local landowners, Penha took over.

Earlier, out on her rounds, Pehna was trying to persuade an impoverished farming community to join the union. Potbellied children with skinny arms played at the feet of men and women as the banter and serious talk rolled easily along. Penha guided the conversation with a blend of authority, humor, and kindness, letting others speak and enjoying the jokes, as the impromptu discussion developed into a full-blown community meeting about the causes of poverty in Brazil. As dusk fell, the meeting turned into music and dance, in honor of the visitors. There are thousands of women like Penha up and down Latin America, inspirational grassroots activists breathing new vigor into the region's social and political life. Although generalizations are always danger-ous in a continent with such a variety of cultures and lifestyles, there has been an undeniable transformation in women's lives over the last forty years. In the past, descriptions of Latin American society have either ignored its women altogether or portrayed them as the submissive victims of a male-dominated order perpetuated by the Catholic Church. Women were shown as helpless figures, condemned to endless pregnancies that destroy their health and con-fine them to the house, subject to the burden of child care and dependent on unreliable and often violent men. In the title of one book, they were "the slaves of slaves." But in recent years, as more women have gone out to do paid work, some, like Penha, have fought for recognition in male-dominated trade

Growing Up in the Countryside

I learnt early on what suffering meant. My father thought that women and girls were nothing. He used to say "*mulher não gente*" (women aren't people). At home I was locked up. I wasn't allowed to have friends either, not even woman friends, and I was often beaten. I hated having been born a girl and envied my brothers like crazy.

Then there was the poverty. We often went hungry. My father had to sell our little plot of land, so we were tenants on a big landowner's *fazenda* (estate). Half of the harvest had to be handed over to the owner as rent. What was left wasn't enough for all of us. Two of the children didn't survive. Hunger and death are everyday occurrences for most of the families in our area.

I thought school was great fun, but after four years my father stopped me going any more. Sending girls to school was like casting pearls before swine, he said.

At 16 I thought I could escape from my father by getting married, so I married the first man who came along. But what I'd let myself in for was worse than I could ever have imagined. It was hell. You see, my husband was an oppressor too. He made me the slave he'd always wanted. I had one child after another, and I was either shut up at home with the babies or had to slog out in the fields.

I had my children, who I had to feed, on one side and a husband who only gave orders on the other. How I suffered!

The worst thing was when he used to hit the children and I wasn't allowed to intervene. He never once hit me, but the endless mental beatings that I had were far harder. If ever I wanted to cry on my mother's shoulder, she used to say, "Take it easy, daughter, don't get worked up about it. Women are born to suffer. And they have to obey their husbands—*mulher não gente!*"

—Caipora Organization, *Women in Brazil*, London: LAB, 1993

unions. Others have built a new form of politics through the social movements, bypassing traditional political parties.

Women's lives and expectations may have changed, but so far there is little evidence of parallel developments among Latin American men. A dictionary translation of the Spanish word *macho* captures the essence of Latin American masculinity. Besides male and masculine, the word means tough, strong, stupid, big, huge, splendid, and terrific, and doubles as a slang term for a sledgehammer. *Machismo* is an extreme form of patriarchy, the social system of male dominance that exists throughout much of the world. The Latin American

Marketplace in Chichicastenango, Guatemala. (Ben Smyth/Grand Opening)

variety has its roots in Iberian culture and the Catholic Church's contorted attitude toward women. As Virgin and Mother, Mary combines impossible and contradictory ideals of Latin American womanhood. Machismo stresses the opposition between male and female; men are fearless, authoritarian, aggressive and promiscuous, and women are naturally submissive, dependent, quiet, and devoted to the family and home. Machismo is often greater among the mestizo population, although indigenous communities have their fair share of domestic violence, often linked to the men's prodigious consumption of alcohol, as an indigenous woman from Chiapas in Mexico recalls:

> Before, when I was poor, my first husband had to go away to work on the hacienda. I went with him, and stayed there for a few nights, but the men always got drunk because the *patrón* gave them money for booze. When he got drunk, he beat me a lot. I thought I would die from the blows. It was horrible. I would go back to our farm with my face all swollen, all beaten up. And I still had to look after the sheep, clean the house, go and cut wood, work on the maize patch, bring in the harvest. If I finished that, I had to sew, spin wool, weave.

Like that, see, lots of work. Still, I was happy when I went home, because there were no more beatings. He gave me no food—no beans or meat. Just beatings. My life was very sad with the husband who went to the hacienda.

—GUIOMAR ROVIRA, *Women of Maize*, London: LAB 2000

Women have their second-class status drummed into them from birth: in rural Peru the midwife receives a sheep for delivering a baby boy, while a girl merits only two chickens. Under the ideological barrage, women often internalize these ideas of femininity and submissiveness, giving rise to a female counterpart to machismo, known as *marianismo*, after the Virgin Mary. In some countries these traditional stereotypes have been overlaid by more modern versions of what constitutes the "perfect woman." In Argentina, girls as young as six or seven show signs of anorexia, part of a nationwide obsession with thinness and the "supermodel" look, resulting in extraordinary levels of cosmetic surgery and eating disorders.

Latin America's most famous women have often filled these submissive and maternal roles. Evita Perón, a gifted politician and the darling of the Argentine masses, described her relationship with her husband as "He the figure, I the shadow," while Violeta Chamorro became president of Nicaragua in 1990 by playing on her position as the widow of a national hero and presenting herself as the healing mother of the nation who could reconcile her divided children. Venezuela's obsession with beauty contests spilt over into politics in the person of Irene Sáez, a former Miss Universe who was reelected as mayor of the country's wealthiest suburb with an impressive 96 percent of the vote. Sáez, who studied political science at the University of Central Venezuela, was widely considered the most popular politician in Venezuela, until she lost against Hugo Chávez in the presidential election of 1998.

Family Ties

Traditionally, girls are groomed from the cradle for their future role as wife and mother. Bolivian parents call their baby daughters "*mamita*" (little mother), and within a few years they can be seen hauling their baby brothers and sisters on their backs around the villages of the Andes. In rural Latin America, families usually have numerous children so that enough will survive high child death rates to work the family farm and to look after their parents in old age. For women this has led to the health problems associated with frequent pregnancies, compounded by malnourishment and poor or nonexistent medical care. Large families lack even the most basic services such as running water, and need constantly to make do and mend. Together, these pressures create the archetypal Latin American mother who never rests. Cooking, cleaning, changing diapers, looking after children through frequent illnesses, queuing for scarce food, mending clothes or making food to sell outside the home: these activities consume every waking hour. In rural areas fetching water or firewood and the long haul to sell leftover produce in the local market impose further strains on women's workload.

While this still describes reality for millions of Latin American women, their lives are changing fast. By the turn of the twenty-first century, women had made considerable strides in education and politics, and in family and fertility. The size of the average family has dropped at a startling rate over the last sixty years. In the 1950s, the average Latin American woman had six children. By 2003 this had dropped to 2.5 children and was still falling. The causes of such a rapid fall in childbearing include the more widespread availability of contraception, the increase in girls' education, and the rate of urbanization. In the shantytowns, large families can be a liability: women have to go out to work as maids or in the markets and since they have left their extended families in the countryside, there is often no one at home to look after the children.

Diversity has increased both within and between countries. Poor countries such as Bolivia, Haiti, and Guatemala still have large families, while Argentina, Cuba, and Chile more closely resemble "northern" family models. Within each country, family size depends greatly on income and women's education: poor, uneducated women have much larger families than better-off or more educated ones.

In recent years there has been a sharp increase in the number of female-headed households, which now stands at over 20 percent in most countries and above 30 percent in many. These are often among the poorest families, with women forced to perform a grueling combination of housework and wage earning, often in the informal sector, to keep their children from starvation. According to one study men are increasingly seen as shadowy figures, drifting in and out of the family and avoiding responsibility. Latin Americans put it more bluntly in the often-heard phrase "You've only got one mother—your father could be any son of a bitch."

Access to contraception has transformed many women's lives. In the 1980s the number of couples using contraception varied widely from 23 percent in Guatemala to 70 percent in Costa Rica, but by the turn of the century the average for the region was among the highest in the world, at 71 percent. The commonest form of contraception is female sterilization, followed by the pill and intra-uterine devices (IUDs). Nevertheless, the issue remains far more controversial than in the United States or Western Europe. Not only is the Catholic Church hostile to all forms of contraception, but the health problems provoked by the often unsupervised use of the pill, IUDs, and injectables such as Depo-Provera have created widespread suspicion. Contraception is anathema to many Latin American men, who see their wives' regular pregnancies as proof of their virility. In only 6 percent of couples do men take responsibility for contraception by using condoms or by sterilization. In some notorious historical cases, foreign agencies were implicated in sterilizing women without fully informing them of the consequences. Such incidents led to the expulsion of the U.S. Peace Corps from Peru and Bolivia in the 1970s.

One consequence of suspicion, ignorance, and the shortage of contraceptives is a high abortion rate. Abortion on request is illegal in all Latin American countries except Cuba, forcing women unable to afford a medically safe abortion to resort to back-street practitioners or their own efforts. More than 4,000 women—one in every five maternal deaths—die every year in Latin America during or as a result of botched abortions. Not surprisingly, in view of its more liberal legislation, Cuba has one of the lowest maternal death rates in the region. By one estimate, there are four million abortions performed every year in the region, one for every three live births. Although huge numbers of women undergo abortions, it remains a taboo subject, as this woman from a Chilean shantytown explains:

> Women don't want to talk about abortion because it's against the teachings of the Church and also because it's against the law, but nearly all women have them. The difference is that the women from the *poblaciones* use a knitting needle, parsley twigs or rubber tubes and many end up in hospital or die, while the middle class go to a clinic and walk home afterwards. When we go to the hospital with hemorrhages the doctors slap our faces; they send their wives to the best clinics, but they slap the faces of poor women.
>
> —JO FISHER, *Out of the Shadows:*
> *Women, Resistance and Politics in South America*

Literacy plays a vital role in empowering women, making it easier for them to find better-paid work, and to wade through the avalanche of printed information resulting from almost any contact with the state. Research by the World Bank and others suggests that women's education is also the single biggest factor in determining family size—the more years of schooling a woman has, the fewer children she ends up with. Illiteracy is higher among women than men in every Latin American country, in some cases reaching 90 percent among elderly women. The figure for both sexes is higher in rural than in urban areas, since schools are more scarce, and parents may need the children to work on the farm. Many families prefer to keep girls at home to help with the household tasks and learn how to keep house, while believing that boys must study to prepare themselves for the outside world. However, the situation is improving rapidly due to the massive expansion in primary education, which has absorbed an extra two million children a year since 1950, even during the recession-hit 1980s. Among the middle classes, the situation is already very different. Now half of all students in higher education are women, although a large number of them are concentrated in the traditionally female spheres of teaching and health care.

The ideology of machismo has influenced legislation affecting women. In most countries adultery is sufficient grounds for divorce only if committed by the wife, while divorce is available only in exceptional cases in countries such as Argentina, Brazil, and Colombia. Such double standards were condemned 300 years ago by Sor Juana Inés de la Cruz, a Mexican nun and poet who has become a feminist icon in modern Mexico:

Ignorant men who accuse
Women wrongly
Without seeing that you cause
The very thing you condemn.

Whose is the greater guilt
In a sinful passion,
She who falls to his lure
Or he who, fallen, lures her?

Or which is more rightly reproached
Although both are guilty
She who sins for pay
Or he who pays for the sin?

Thanks to the work of women's lobby groups and the UN Decade for Women (1975–85), many governments have improved their legislation and established agencies to promote the status of women and ensure equal rights. Yet despite such paper safeguards, social attitudes and the implementation of equal rights laws lag far behind. Statutory rights on maternity benefits or equal pay are frequently ignored by both employers and male-oriented ministries of labor, and legislation often appears irrelevant to the poor. Most women work in the unregulated informal sector and so do not have even a theoretical right to maternity benefits. Since formal marriage is the exception among poor families, the niceties of divorce law hold little meaning.

Working for Wages

The number of women officially in the economically active population—a definition that excludes those involved in unwaged work in the home, on the farm, or in the informal sector—more than tripled between 1960 and 1990, though the rate of increase slowed dramatically during the 1990s. In most countries, 30 to 50 percent of girls and women over ten years old now work for money (in both the formal and informal sectors), the proportion being highest among 25- to 34-year-olds. Even these figures are underestimates, as women often do not describe themselves as wage earners when asked during household surveys, even though they may bring in money from selling food or taking in washing.

Despite this rise in numbers, the kinds of jobs have changed little, with a strong emphasis on "women's work," which merely extends their caring role in the home. Proportionally fewer women work for money in rural areas than in towns and cities, where as many as half the women employed are domestic servants, most of them young unskilled migrants from the countryside who have had on average only three years of school education. The other main categories of paid women's work are the informal sector (market women, street sellers), caring professions such as teaching and nursing, and office work. Women's participation in agriculture and manufacturing actually fell between 1960 and 1980, as mechanization reduced the proportion of unskilled jobs traditionally performed by women, although it has picked up in recent years in new export crops such as fruit and flowers, which have been promoted under neoliberal reforms. In manufacturing women are concentrated in industries such as textiles, clothing, and the booming *maquiladora* assembly plants in northern Mexico and the Caribbean basin. Besides being segregated by job, women also earn 20 to 40 percent less than men, even though their educational qualifications for comparable jobs are generally higher.

The Domestic Worker

Usually young unskilled migrants from the countryside, servants are among the most exploited and invisible of the region's women. Ignorant of their rights and of life in the city, isolated in their employer's house, they are on virtual 24-hour standby, and vulnerable to verbal, sexual, and physical abuse by their employers. Young girls emotionally dependent on their employers often absorb their values, feeling self-loathing and contempt for their own families and backgrounds, especially in countries where the employers are white and the servants indigenous:

The old lady explained everything to me, and little by little she made me aware of my class, using words like "Indians" and "Yokels" and saying "You shouldn't be like that, you're going to get civilized here."

When you hear it that often you end up being ashamed and uncomfortable about your own class and finally you find yourself supporting the class of your boss. I thought she loved me because she told me: "I love you like a daughter; here you have everything." And I accepted it all.

The truth is that the bosses use us even through love. Without realizing, we end up loving them and so we say, "Ay, my señora is good, she loves me a lot." We look after her things as though they were our own, and after a while you start identifying totally with her mentality.

—ANA MARÍA CONDORI, *Mi Despertar*

The Street Seller

Market women and street sellers are perhaps the most conspicuous of Latin American women workers, lining the streets of major cities with stalls offering homemade cakes, vegetables, soft drinks, or imported toiletries. Their numbers have been swollen by the impact of neoliberal reforms since 1980. By the early 1990s, there was one street vendor for every three houses in La Paz, Bolivia's chief city. Market women's daily contact with the public and unscrupulous wholesalers has made them self-confident and fiercely individualistic throughout the region. As Anita, a 28-year-old Nicaraguan market woman, explains: "I'm better off working in the market. If I don't want to sell, I don't have to. I can go home whenever I want to, we can bring our children to work and no one bosses you about and tells you when to come and when to leave. I don't want to work for a boss again."

Maquiladoras

Since the mid-1960s, Mexican industry has been transformed by the growth of *maquiladora* plants along its northern border with the United States. Others have sprouted elsewhere in Central America and the Caribbean. These factories, largely owned by U.S., Japanese, and other foreign electronics or textile companies, use cheap local labor to assemble products for export to the United States. In the Caribbean, women are also used to perform cut-price data processing for U.S. companies. About 60 percent of *maquiladora* employees are women, usually single and in their late teens or early twenties. Young women are ideal because, in the words of one plant manager, "They are willing to accept lower wages," and "Girls are educated to obey at home. It is easier to get their confidence . . . they are loyal to the company."

> Martina, like many working-class Mexican women, has a hard exterior, a tough skin of nonchalance until you get to know her. She has worked in various *maquilas* in Ciudad Acuña but dislikes them intensely. Last Monday she started at a Korean-owned *maquiladora* called Kim Toys, where the employees sew small cheap stuffed animals to go inside the iron-claw machines in the American chain of Pizza Huts across the border. "It's the worst place I've ever worked in," she says, while making supper. "Run-down and dirty. And no air conditioning, just a couple of old fans in the whole place. It was so hot. Everybody just sat there sweating so much it looked as if someone had come in and thrown a bucket of water over them. I saw one supervisor get mad at a woman for taking too long in the bathroom. "Five minutes," he was saying. "All you've got is five minutes." She went back to her sewing machine and was crying. Martina decided it wasn't worth US$30 a week and quit after just one day.
> —AUGUSTA DWYER, *On the Line: Life on the U.S.–Mexican Border*

Women's growing role in the workforce has brought them mixed blessings. Although paid jobs have often increased women's economic independence and self-confidence, there has been no compensating reduction in housework, with the result that working women are expected to perform what is known as a double-shift. A study of women in Chile during the early 1980s showed that working women did on average a 12-hour day, seven days a week, between workplace and home. When women did manage to reduce their housework, it was by employing poor women as domestic servants. Men did no more housework than before, despite the decline in their role as breadwinner. For any macho man, scrubbing floors or cooking is the ultimate shame. In Cuba, where women's participation in the paid workforce has grown rapidly over the last twenty years, one writer noted that although male Communist Party militants may offer to do the washing, they insist that their wives hang it out to dry so that the neighbors won't find out.

The Peasant

Peasant women in rural areas labor under many obligations; their duties include child care, maintaining the home, and a number of specialized jobs on the farm. Often women tend the animals and a small vegetable plot, while the men look after the main food crops. Housework in peasant farms can be far more time-consuming than in the cities, since women may have to carry water over long distances, collect firewood, and make long trips to markets in nearby villages.

As commercial agriculture has encroached on the traditional peasant farms, this pattern has been disrupted. Peasant farms have been squeezed by large landowners and by subdivision between members of each new generation, so that they are rarely productive enough to maintain a family. This forces their owners to find work on the big commercial farms. Men's greater access to education and training has meant that they take the permanent jobs on new mechanized farms, and women have been relegated to temporary work at harvest time.

With food in short supply, parents favor boys to stay and eventually inherit the farm, and many young girls are packed off to the city as domestic servants. As a result, young women have outnumbered men in the exodus to the cities that has marked the last fifty years of Latin American history.

Women still supply most of the workers in a number of labor-intensive export industries. They pick coffee, tobacco, or cotton, and produce new export crops such as strawberries in Mexico or peanuts in Brazil. In Colombia the women weed, fumigate, pick and pack carnations for Europe's florists, suffering frequent respiratory problems and miscarriages from the pesticides to which they are constantly exposed.

Latin America's agrarian reform processes have largely failed to benefit women, their apparent "gender blindness" masking discrimination in favor of men. Most reforms hand out land to individuals identified as "heads of household," by custom a man, except for widows and single mothers. Instead of being treated as producers in their own right, peasant women are seen as the equivalent of urban housewives and hence as dependents. In traditional Andean culture, farms are owned equally by husband and wife, so the new reforms marked a step backwards for women. In most cases the reforms helped permanent workers, rather than seasonal workers. When General Velasco expropriated Peru's cotton plantations in the late 1960s, women represented 40 percent of their seasonal workforce, but held few permanent jobs. The reform gave the plantations to their permanent workers who had organized into cooperatives, and as a result women made up only 2 percent of members on the new cotton cooperatives. In Chile and Venezuela, agrarian reform laws specifically decreed that land given out under the reform should be passed to the beneficiary's sons when he died.

Women have integrated rapidly into the workforce in new forms of agriculture, particularly goods designed for agro-export such as ornamental plants and cut flowers (Costa Rica, Guatemala, Colombia) and tropical and temperate fruit destined for North American supermarket shelves. These sectors pay better than traditional forms of agriculture such as sugarcane harvest-

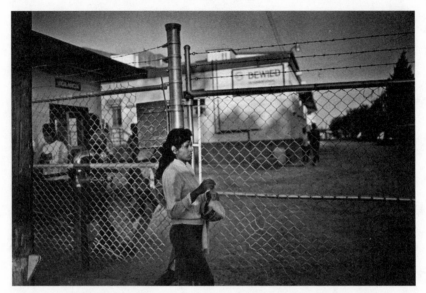

Leaving work outside the gates of a *maquiladora*, Piedras Negras, Mexico, 1994.
(Lina Pallotta)

ing, where the back breaking labor required made them mostly—although by
no means exclusively—the preserve of men.

Neoliberal Reforms

The debt crisis that began in 1982, and the ensuing process of neoliberal
reform, hit women hardest. As employers shed jobs, they preferred to lay off
women, since women are not seen as breadwinners and are generally under-
represented in trade unions. Public spending cuts targeted "female" professions in health and education, and the limited choice of jobs open to women
made it hard for them to find other employment. Poor women increasingly
turned to the informal sector and part-time work to make ends meet. By 2002,
the most common jobs among Latin American women were in the largely
informal service sector.

In their role as mothers, women were hit by price rises in basic foods as
subsidies were cut, making it harder to feed a family. As education and health
budgets were cut, mothers had to find increasing sums for school notebooks
or medicines. Clothes had to be endlessly patched when there was no money
to buy replacements. All these tasks added to the growing burden of keeping
the family afloat. The stress of family life also led to increased cases of alcohol
abuse among men, leaving women to face the frequent domestic violence and

The Price of Structural Adjustment

The tiny adobe house is crammed with gnarled *pailliris* (mining women) in patched shawls and battered felt hats whose calloused hands work breaking up rocks on the surface in search of scraps of tin ore. Outside, the scene is one of high-altitude poverty, all grays and browns in the thin air. The paths between the miners' huts are strewn with plastic bags and human excrement, dried black in the unforgiving *altiplano* sun. Rising beyond the squalid settlement, the barren hills and gray slag heaps of the tin mines complete the bleak panorama. The litany of poor women's woes begins, gathering momentum as it goes:

"Before, it was not too bad, but now we never have a good month. We're mainly widows or abandoned. My husband left to look for work and never came back. Now I have to look after four kids—I can't pay for their schoolbooks and clothes. I've been doing this work for seven years now and my lungs are finished. I've vomited blood for weeks at a time and still had to keep working.

"In the old days, women used to stay at home because the men had work. Now, with the recession, we've had to go out to work. Many of our children have been abandoned. Their fathers have left and there's no love left in us when we get home late from work. We leave food for them, they play in the streets—there are always accidents, and no doctors. I feel like a slave in my own country—we get up at 4 a.m. and at 11 at night we are still mending and patching."

The speaker, Josefina Muruchi, breaks down in a coughing fit. Suddenly, in a mixture of Spanish and Quechua, all the other women burst into speech, unleashing a torrent of pain and suffering. In the gloom, most of the women are sobbing.

"This is *doloroso* for us. We have nothing. Nothing. Only coca [a stimulant leaf chewed to suppress hunger] to keep us going. It's the children; we want them to study, but they're so malnourished and the price of tin is so low. Our kids say 'Mami, I want to help' and don't do their homework, but then they fail their exams and have to repeat the year and the teachers are always asking for money and we haven't got it, and because our children are so ashamed they drop out of school. If I start vomiting blood again, what's going to happen to my children?"

—Duncan Green, *Silent Revolution: The Rise and Crisis of Market Economics in Latin America*, London: LAB, 2003

family breakdown that follow. As one Bolivian miner says: "In my work I am happy. I joke with my *compañeros*, I work in peace. And then I come home and I see my wife and children undernourished, poorly clothed. It is then that I have a sense of the problems in my life and I get filled with rage."

Since the resumption of growth at the end of the 1990s, the situation has changed, with women further increasing their participation in the workforce. A survey in eight leading Latin American countries in 2009 showed that the unemployment rate among women was still 1.4 times higher than the rate among men but that the gap between the two was steadily declining.

Women in Politics

Driven in part by a need to unite to confront the economic crisis of recent years, growing numbers of women have begun to participate directly in political life. In the new social movements such as Mothers' Clubs, Base Christian Communities, and neighborhood associations, women have built a bridge between the traditionally female world of home and family and the predominantly male sphere of political activism.

Before the social movements appeared, women were largely excluded from political life. Although a small suffrage movement of largely middle-class women had won the vote in the whole of Latin America by 1961, this did not lead to the expected upsurge in political participation.

In Argentina, Juan and Eva Perón mobilized women as their foot soldiers in the Peronist Women's Party, led by Evita. Yet despite some progressive legislation, the "father and mother of the nation" never challenged the ideal of wifely submission displayed by Evita herself. The Peronists introduced women's suffrage in 1947 and gave children born out of marriage equal rights before the law. In 1955 Perón's decision to legalize divorce alienated the Catholic Church and helped to bring about his downfall at the hands of the military. It was Perón's second wife, Isabel, who became Latin America's first female president, followed by interim or acting female presidents in Bolivia, Haiti, and Ecuador and latterly full terms for Violeta Barrios de Chamorro in Nicaragua (1990–97) and Mireya Moscoso Rodríguez in Panama (1999–2004). It is in socially conservative Chile that the inauguration of Michelle Bachelet in 2006 marked an extraordinary break with the past. A doctor and single mother of three, Bachelet promptly announced a cabinet in whch half the ministers were women. Elsewhere, few women have reached the leadership of political parties and trade unions. Even in cases where women are politically active at the grassroots level, for example in textile workers' unions, they thin out rapidly further up the union hierarchy.

In Brazil, the rise of the PT (Workers' Party) in the late 1990s blurred the division between social movements (where women play a stronger role) and the political party, allowing women to take a more prominent role in decision making, with several prominent women ministers in the PT government after 2003. In 2010 Dilma Rousseff, who had played a key role in Lula's government, was elected as his successor. The first female president of Brazil, she was the first woman ever to open the UN General Assembly in September 2011. To loud applause, she said she was convinced that the twenty-first century would be the "century of women."

Elsewhere in Latin America, quotas were used to ensure a minimum level of women's representation in elective posts. In Argentina, the electoral law establishes a compulsory 30 percent quota for women candidates for electoral posts, while Brazil has a 20 percent requirement. In Costa Rica, the Law on the Promotion of Social Equality for Women, which aims to protect women's political equality, does not include a quota system but mandates political parties to provide effective mechanisms that will encourage women to participate in elections, particularly to the governing bodies of the parties and to state bodies. Despite such measures, less than 15 percent of parliamentarians were women by the turn of the century.

Table 4.1: Dates of Women's Suffrage in the Americas

United States	1920
Ecuador	1929
Brazil	1932
Uruguay	1932
El Salvador	1939
Guatemala	1945
Panama	1945
Argentina	1947
Venezuela	1947
Chile	1949
Costa Rica	1949
Bolivia	1952
Mexico	1953
Honduras	1955
Nicaragua	1955
Peru	1955
Colombia	1957
Paraguay	1961

Source: J. Nash and H Safa, *Sex and Class in Latin America*, New York: Praeger Publishers, 1980.

During the left-wing Popular Unity government of Salvador Allende in Chile (1970–73), women divided along class lines; middle-class women organized "marches of the empty pots" to protest food shortages and economic chaos, while women in the shantytowns worked in support of the Allende government. In Chile and elsewhere, many left-wing men have been suspicious of an independent women's movement, arguing that it would prove to be a right-wing defender of the status quo, but also unwilling to give up their own privileged status in the home. As Yanci, an activist in El Salvador's women's movement, comments: "In all the key moments of our history,

---

Politics Is Personal

One gets to know people and find out about the problems of others in the neighbourhood. . . . Yes it's a healthy thing to get out of the house to be with lots of people, each talking about their own problems. Getting to know about others' problems you forget your own. Getting out, mixing with people, with different neighbourhoods, but mainly in the struggle . . . one learns, one even learns to talk a bit better.

   I had a lot of activities in the church but at home I couldn't break away from a load of things I felt were my duty because I'm a woman, a mother. I just couldn't break away. I began to be aware of this through the women's group and I said to hell with it all because it wasn't me who should be doing them! At home, when my husband and children had a bath I would get them towels and lay out all their clothes for them to dress. . . . Suddenly I realised that it wasn"t just me, everybody had to change. I think, or rather I thought, that I had to make the meals, clean the house, control household expenditure, pay the bills, it was up to me. Now we divide everything between us . . . it's much better. . . . When I discovered myself as a woman, that I have the same rights as everyone else, my relationship with my children changed, everything changed, and our relationship improved 100 percent. My relationship with my husband got better, I mean it was as if we had just met now, three years later. He wouldn't accept it at first but in time he began to see that it was a need, my need.

—Teresa Pires de Rio Caldeira, "Women, Daily Life and Politics," in *Women and Social Change in Latin America*, ed. Elizabeth Jelin, London: Zed Books, 1990

---

women have always participated, but we have been anonymous. Women have made the coffee so the *compañeros* could think better. Women cook while the men take the important decisions!" Unlike the traditional left, which has often ignored women in its political programs, the right and the military regimes of the 1970s and 1980s stressed the importance of the family, paying homage to the traditional Latin American icon of the long-suffering mother. The names of right-wing pro-military organizations such as Argentina's "Tradition, Family and Property" encapsulated the conservative Catholic message. Such an ideology recognized and applauded women only as long as they remained safely in the "female sphere." When women dared to trespass into public politics, the military's chivalry proved short-lived. In Argentina, 30 percent of those "disappeared" by the military were women. The traumatized mothers of disappeared children, meeting on their fruitless round of the different military barracks in search of news, came together to form the Mothers and Grandmothers of the Plaza de Mayo. Every Thursday under the military government, a small but indomitable band of women wearing white headscarves walked silently around the Plaza de Mayo in front of the Presidential Palace in Buenos Aires, their placards carrying old, fading photographs of their children. As one mother described it, "from washing, ironing and cooking we went out on to the streets to fight for the lives of our children." The human rights movement they created grew to play a crucial role first in forcing the generals to hand power over to an elected government, and then in putting the military's leaders in jail for killing their children.

The Mothers of the Disappeared were able to protest because they did so *as mothers*, effectively preventing the military from using outright repression as they did against virtually all other protest movements. By using the generals' own ideology against them, the women of the Plaza de Mayo opened up the first possibilities of public resistance, which grew into the mass protest movement that helped to remove the military from power.

Military rule forced women to take to the public arena to defend their families in many other countries. In Brazil, opposition to the military took off in the late 1970s with the Cost of Living Movement, made up of women protesting at the suffering being inflicted on poor families by the military's economic policies. In Peru and Colombia, organizations of mothers and relatives of the disappeared have yet to obtain answers from a military that kills their sons and daughters with virtual impunity. In each case the crushing of traditional political parties has enabled women's organizations to expand into the political vacuum, sowing the seeds of the region's new social movements.

The grassroots women's organizations have had a difficult relationship with Latin American feminism. The military period coincided with the rise of feminism in the north, and many returning exiles in the 1980s brought with them feminist ideas from their experiences in London, Paris, or New York. However, they did not find it easy to combine their new beliefs with political activism in the shantytowns, as two working-class activists from Chile recall:

> We were always very wary that we would lose our independence if we let middle-class women in. The difference is that we work with our class identity and middle-class feminism doesn't, they work only with gender. They say women's problems are common to all women. We have things in common with middle-class women but we also have other problems that middle-class women don't have, like the housing shortage, debt problems, unemployment, and we're not going to advance as women if the two things aren't closely linked.
>
> Gender discrimination may be the same but the class situation is different. Working-class culture is more rigid—we've got more brakes. Perhaps because of the influence of religion and perhaps because we've got less choice—we haven't got the economic freedom to do what we want.

Feminism of the upper class or middle class is a long way from our feminism. We've tried to work with middle-class feminists but they talk about a different world from ours. For example, they did a workshop where they told us we've got to value ourselves, stop serving the biggest steak to the men. Of course poor women like us aren't very familiar with steaks! Once we went to a feminist meeting where they told us we should watch blue films to improve our sex lives. That was very shocking to our women. We've been to their women's centers because they have the resources to offer legal advice or psychologists for battered women. It's another world, all carpeted, with pictures on the wall, everything brand-new. We felt uncomfortable. The only time we'd been in houses like that was as domestic servants. We are the ones these women use as their servants.

—JO FISHER, *Out of the Shadows:*
Women, Resistance and Politics in South America

The nature and tactics of the new social movements reflect their predominantly female origin. Stressing the need for internal democracy, social movements aim to improve local communities, usually by putting pressure on local or national governments. They fiercely defend their independence from political parties or the state—both male-dominated. Many of their demands reflect women's immediate needs: campaigns for day nurseries for working women, for better health care, street lighting, running water, or electricity are often seen by the women involved as extensions of the struggles they face as wives and mothers. On occasion, the movements' strengths have also proved to be their weaknesses. Once immediate demands have been achieved —for example, the local authority has agreed to put in street lighting—the movement disintegrates.

After the return to civilian government in Argentina, the Mothers of the Disappeared found it hard to maintain the unity and determination they showed under military rule. New governments often stole the clothes of the women's movement, passing laws to outlaw domestic violence, creating a national women's office (in Chile), or setting up women's police stations (in the case of Brazil). New laws and constitutions did not always translate into changes in real life, but the women's movement has found it hard to move from opposition to the perilous new world of co-option and engagement with professional politicians. Nevertheless, the experience of meeting other women and organizing successful campaigns has transformed many women's lives and could lay the foundations of a new and more democratic politics for the future.

Masculinity, Homosexuality, and Prostitution in Cuba

Fidel Knows Everything

"Fidel" is code for the entire state apparatus in Cuba, so much has the revolution been personalized in him. This young man from Guantánamo explained to me that "Fidel" was far more interested in stopping female prostitution than male. *Pingueros* [male prostitutes] could walk the street "openly," he said. This difference makes sense when sex work is viewed in the context of the nationalist project. Cuban women are used in the same way—and by the same men—who are invading the island economically. The state has been forced by economic exigency to admit capitalist incursion and relinquish some of its economic and ideological autonomy. *Jineteras* [female prostitutes] demonstrate this in their very bodies, and so they are an intolerable reminder of the growing power of external capital in internal affairs. This, "Fidel" cannot abide. But *pingueros*, at least representationally if not also practically, are quite the opposite: they represent the strength of the powerful Cuban phallus conquering the bodies of foreigners. No autonomy has been lost, and symbolically at least, no Cuban body has been defiled. In fact, in a *pinguero*-tourist sex act, the Cuban has invaded the tourist, "screwed" him, as it were. The renowned Cuban phallus, well known in the gay world and about which writers such as Pau-Llosa, Stavans, and Arenas have commented, is perhaps the one entirely Cuban resource that Cuba has left.

—G. Derrick Hodge, "Colonization of the Cuban Body: The Growth of Male Sex Work in Havana," NACLA Report on the Americas, 2001

Masculinities

In a mostly "machista" environment where men and their desires are valued and assigned power over those of women, women have naturally long been the focus of gender studies. But increasingly scholars, activists, and individual women and men are realizing that changing negative attitudes about women and their lives means changing men. Traditional ideas of masculinity, sexuality, and identity are being questioned as never before. A pioneering project by the Nicaraguan popular education organization Cantera seeks to get men to ask what it means to be a "real man" and to question ingrained attitudes toward power, domestic abuse, and personal responsibility.

At the same time, some speak of a "crisis of masculinity" in a region where women's activities are widening, and access to the labor market is growing. There is some evidence that men are beginning to participate a lot more in domestic labor in child care. But if they want to become "new men," Latin American men have their own battles to fight. In Argentina, for instance, a man who does housework is, variously, *dominado* (dominated), *pollerón* (someone who hangs on his wife's skirts), or a *máquina de lavar* (washing machine).

Homosexuality in Latin America

Attitudes and legislation on homosexuality vary enormously across the continent. Latin American machismo appears to have a complex relationship to homosexuality and finds lesbianism incomprehensible.

Countries such as Colombia and Peru have a tradition of transvestite homosexuality stretching back to pre-Columbian times, while studies from Nicaragua and Cuba suggest that heterosexual men break no taboos by having sex with other men, provided they are the dominant partner. Social stigma is reserved for those who behave in an "unmanly" effeminate way. In this sense, homosexuality (for men) is not so much what one is as what one *does*; the importance placed on active/passive roles is also a clear reflection of how sexual relations in Latin America have long been viewed in terms of power. Even so, there is little of the kind of rabid "queer bashing" found in the United States or Europe. Perhaps because of the lower level of discrimination, gays in Latin America do not always identify themselves exclusively in terms of their sexuality, and the gay pride movement is much weaker than it is in the north.

In many countries homosexuality is not specifically outlawed, but more general laws such as "offenses against morality" are used to harass gays and lesbians. Cuba under Fidel Castro has come in for severe criticism over its treatment of gay men, in particular those with HIV and AIDS. In the mid-1980s, the Cuban government was condemned for its draconian initial policy of locking up HIV-positive people in state sanitoriums, sometimes against their will. Closer examination, however, revealed a complex situation: the policy of quarantining patients was the state's normal reaction to previous epidemics such as dengue and African swine fever; the quarantine policy was only possible in the first place because the Cuban health service had the capacity to implement it—in other countries in Latin America, AIDS patients received little or no state support. In any case, by the early 1990s, the policy had been substantially liberalized with most patients free to leave the sanitorium on home visits, and about three in four seropositives were transferred to an outpatient system.

Lesbianism, like other aspects of women's sexuality, is largely considered passive and unthreatening. Many Latin American lesbians feel that the relative invisibility of lesbianism is not so much a condoning of it as active discrimination—more proof that society simply does not take it very seriously. Lesbian movements emerged out of feminist groups and ideology, but are distinct in each country. For example, in Nicaragua, the lesbian and feminist movements were both shaped by a very strong class consciousness, which was itself a product of the Sandinista revolution.

Social Movements and the Struggle for Change

The first sign of the squatters is a huge red flag flapping above a depression in the hills a few hundred yards away. Across two barbed wire fences and an arid, sandy hillside lies the cluster of huts thrown up weeks ago by forty landless families. They have called the encampment *Esperança* (Hope). Already the inhabitants are making the first improvements: tiles are starting to replace plastic sheets on the roofs of the huts, whose walls are made from branches tied together with twine. To provide safety in numbers, 500 people originally occupied the site. When ten armed policemen promptly arrived to evict them, the children stood in front with stones; behind them came the women and adolescents, followed by the men armed with their primitive farming tools. The policemen backed off without a fight, allowing the squatters to get on with planting their first crops of yams and *feijão* (beans).

The red flag belongs to Brazil's Movement of Landless Workers, the MST. The MST leads landless peasants and the urban poor in well-organized invasions of waste land in the cities or uncultivated farmland elsewhere. Standing amid newly plowed furrows thirsty for rain, one of the squatters explains: "People came here for land. We weren't interested in riches—land created people and people must live from it. The owner says the land is his, but if he doesn't even farm it, how can that be?" As he talks, the skies open. Rain sheets across the gray fields and through the torn plastic roofs, onto the dripping but delighted farmers.

By the end of 2000 more than half a million families were living on 3,800 agrarian reform settlements. About one-fifth of the families were members of the MST. Since then about another half a million families have been settled or had their plot land "regularized," that is, legally registered, which is important, as it means the farmer can obtain bank loans. The MST is still mobilizing for a far more radical program of agrarian reform, but just as important are its activities to mobilize support among other sectors—homeless, neighborhood groups, Catholic church groups, hip-hop groups, and so on—for a "national project" to end Brazil's enormous social inequalities. Agrarian reform isn't enough, they say. The MST has become a reference point throughout the world, particularly in South Africa, Paraguay, Uruguay, and Bolivia.

The MST is one of a number of social movements whose political activity, in this case over the explosive issue of land, takes place outside the channels of formal politics. Many of the new movements took off under military rule in the 1970s, when conventional opposition politics was suppressed. Today, in Latin America's shantytowns, women's organizations pressure local councils for food and milk for their children, and neighborhood committees demand electricity or paved roads, while in the rural areas peasant organizations lobby for land reform or bank loans for their farms. In Peru, Colombia, and Central America, human rights organizations demonstrate and protest about the "disappearance" of their loved ones; in Brazil, radical Catholics run "Base Christian Communities" to discuss the Bible and its message for the poor. What such a diverse range of organizations have in common is their use of direct action to improve their lives.

Trade Unions and Social Movements

Trade unions in Latin America occupy a very different place in society than in Europe or the United States, since they represent that minority of workers who have stable jobs in the formal sector of the economy and are therefore relatively privileged compared to the mass of peasant farmers and the urban poor. In countries such as Mexico, Brazil, and Argentina, most of the main trade unions were set up under corporatist governments during the early years of import substitution, and have never had any real degree of independence. Nevertheless, some trade unions have been at the forefront of the radical left. In Chile they were the first to take to the streets to begin the long campaign to topple General Pinochet, and in Brazil from 1978 a new independent union movement led the fight against the military dictatorship.

One side effect of neoliberalism and the debt crisis was the reduction of corporatist regimes' ability to keep the unions on a tight leash. Austerity measures and falling wages have driven a wedge between the union membership and their pro-government leaderships in countries such as Argentina and Mexico, fueling efforts in these countries to establish a new unionism independent of the state.

The period since the 1970s has seen a spectacular growth in so-called new social movements. At the heart of the phenomenon lies the work of the progressive Catholic Church, which through its Base Christian Communities has formed generations of activists and leaders. Shantytown dwellers, women's groups, indigenous and environmental movements, and human rights organizations have joined radicalized trade unions and peasant associations to create a new form of grassroots democracy that involves large numbers of people who previously had little role in the party political process.

Although the social movements form a broad category, they have certain points in common:

- They are often based on a locality rather than a workplace, unlike traditional trade unions.

- They organize around specific and immediate demands, rather than wider appeals for structural change.

- They practice a much higher degree of internal democracy and show a far greater level of women's participation than either left-wing political parties or guerrilla groups.

- They generally demand improvements from the state rather than confront vested interest groups such as landowners, the military, and big business.

So-called catalyst groups, such as radical priests, social workers, progressive non-governmental organizations (NGOs), feminist groups, and political party activists, often play an important role in helping to establish groups by encouraging organization and discussion. The more traditional catalysts often found it hard to let the new groups take control:

> I still thank the Church for having opened my eyes. Working with the mothers' clubs, I learned how important we women are and how important it was for us to get organized. We managed to set up dozens of mothers' clubs. The women were well organized, and were taking on all sorts of activities.
>
> Then all of a sudden the Church pulled the rug out from under us. It stopped the program and took away all our funds. Why? They said there was no more money, but we don't think that's what happened. We think they were afraid of how far we'd gone. It was the Church that first started organizing us women. I'd never done anything before getting involved in the mothers' clubs. The Church forged the path for us, but they wanted us to follow behind. And when we started to walk ahead of them, they decided that maybe organizing the women wasn't such a good idea after all.
>
> —ELVIA ALVARADO, *Don't Be Afraid, Gringo*

The roots of the new generation of social movements lie in the period of military rule that began with the Brazilian coup of 1964. Politics as usual came to a stop in countries such as Chile, Argentina, and Brazil, as the generals banned or severely curtailed the activities of political parties. Opponents of the government or those wishing to press for improvements to their lives had nowhere to channel their protest, and new single-issue campaigns grew rapidly to fill the resulting political vacuum.

Other factors coincided to fuel their growth. The period of military rule coincided with the rise of feminism in the industrialized countries and the sudden expansion of the student population within the region, which provided both activists and direction to the new movements. Military rule also coincided with the heyday of the radical Church, in the wake of the Medellín bishops' conference of 1968. The harsh economic programs unleashed by some of the military governments, notably in Chile after 1973, made necessity a mother of political invention, as women set up soup kitchens to cope with the hunger that suddenly assailed the shantytowns. Grassroots organizations such as Brazil's Cost of Living Movement or Argentina's Mothers of the Disappeared were instrumental in forcing the military to withdraw from power, but their victories in the early 1980s sometimes carried the seeds of future defeat. As dictatorship has given way to democracy, the new social movements have faced difficult choices about how to relate to the political parties and governments that have taken back political life from the protestors. Their central problem, according to the Mexican writer Jorge Castañeda, is that

> without participating in electoral competitions, they run the risk of being rendered marginal, forsaking significant opportunities to advance the aspirations of their members. But by participating, they are immediately subject to the contradictions of any electoral process: whom to vote for, whom to run, what to do if elected, how to govern. There is no solution to this dilemma.

Part of the problem lies in the very nature of social movements. Local needs and their solutions, such as land distribution or greater spending on social services, often require action by the national government.

Recognizing this, many social movements have attempted to link up their vast array of groups into broader district and even national networks in order to lobby the government. In growing to such a size, however, they risk losing the internal democracy that distinguishes them from orthodox political parties. After decades of co-option and betrayal, social movements are understandably wary of ceding power even to elected leaders, and attempts at wider

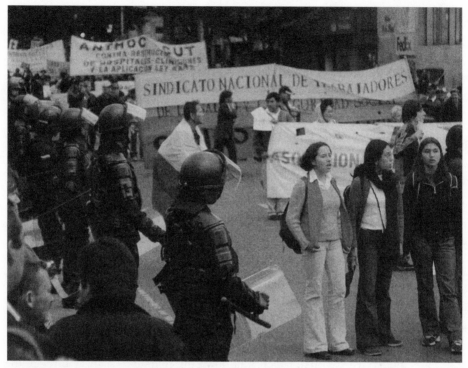

State workers' union protest, Bogotá, Colombia. (Latinphoto)

coalition building have often broken down or been hijacked by populists who promise the earth without ever being able to deliver.

In some countries, recession and neoliberal reforms made survival so difficult and time-consuming for the poor that many had no energy left for activism. In Chile, adjustment created an atomized society, where increased stress and individualism damaged its traditionally strong and caring community life. "Relationships are changing," said Betty Bizamar, a 26-year-old trade union leader. "People use each other, spend less time with their family. All they talk about is money, things. True friendship is difficult now. You have to be a Quixote to be a union leader these days!"

In Brazil on the other hand, social movements survived the transition to democracy rather better, building a strong, vibrant "civil society" and forming the foundations of the region's most impressive left-wing party, the Workers' Party (PT). The PT was set up in 1979 under the military government by the social movements themselves, led by a new generation of radical trade unionists such as Brazil's former president, Luís Inácio Lula da Silva. The trade unionists came together with rural unions, radical Catholics, left-wing intellectuals, shantytown movements, and a number of other currents to try to set up a party controlled by the membership that would avoid being absorbed into the Brazilian political establishment. In an astonishingly short time the PT became a major national force: Lula narrowly missed the presidency in the 1989 elections, and was overtaken at the last minute by Fernando Henrique Cardoso in 1994, eventually going on to win in 2002. Lula was reelected president in 2006, ending his second term with record levels of popular support. With Lula's support, the PT's candidate Dilma Rousseff was elected in 2010. At less exalted levels, the PT has won mayoral elections in many major cities, including São Paulo, and has become a major force in both houses of Congress. The PT made huge concessions to gain power and to govern, even resorting to corrupt political practices, such as the buying of votes in Congress, which has shocked many of its supporters. Even so, the successive PT governments have brought real gains to the poor and its successes and rapid rise to political maturity have given many social movements hope that they can build a national party outside the control of the old political elites.

In Mexico, the Party of the Democratic Revolution (PRD) is a similar ramshackle coalition of fringe parties and social movements. The PRD was formally set up by Cuauhtémoc Cárdenas after he missed coming to power in 1988 thanks to the most blatant of frauds by the ruling Institutional Revolutionary Party (PRI), which shut down the computers halfway through the count. Since then, however, the PRD has struggled. In the 1994 election, it was easily defeated by the PRI, and in 2000 came in third behind both the PRI and the victorious pro-business party, the PAN. Given the unpopularity of the PAN government, led by Alejandro Fox, it seemed that the PRD's new leader, the charismatic former mayor of Mexico City, Andrés Manuel López Obrador, might win the presidential elections in 2006. In the event, in a fiercely disputed election, he was beaten by the PAN candidate, Felipe Calderón, who gained just 0.6% more votes than his opponent. Many PRD supporters believe that their candidate was fraudulently robbed of victory.

The Andean region has seen an explosion of progressive grassroots activism in parallel, though not always in partnership, with the burgeoning indigenous movements of the early twenty-first century. Ecuador suffered a series of constitutional crises as mass protests forced out three of the six presidents who served between 1997 and 2005. In late 2006 a young economist, Rafael Correa, was elected president on the back of a radical program of social, economic, and constitutional reform. He carried out part of his program, introducing a new constitution (which, among other innovations, gave "rights" to nature, the first time any nation has done this) and renegotiating the foreign debt. He was reelected in 2009, winning in the first round. Despite these successes, Correa's relationship with indigenous and social movements has been tempestuous. Like so many other Latin American nations, the Ecuadorean economy is heavily dependent on natural resources (oil provides over half of export earnings) and this reliance on what is essentially a dirty and destructive sector is hard to reconcile with indigenous demands to respect *Pachamama* (Mother Nature). It is a real conundrum that no Latin American government has yet resolved and one that sooner or later Ollanta Humala, Peru's president, will have to face. Elected in June 2011 he was said by one commentator to have inherited from the previous president "a ticking time bomb of disputes stemming in large part from objections by indigenous groups to the damage to water supplies, crops and hunting grounds wrought by mining, logging and oil and gas extraction."

It is in Bolivia, however, that new social movements have had the most impact. The rise of Evo Morales and the Movement Toward Socialism (MAS) at a political level, culminating in Morales's election to the presidency in 2005, has developed in tandem with the organization and radicalization of the *campesinos* throughout the country. Their main point of contention was the proposed privatization and sale—to the United States via arch-rival Chile—of the nation's natural gas reserve. A series of roadblocks and running protests crippled the energy infrastructure and prevented the construction of a pipeline toward Chile. Morales tapped into the discontent and, after a narrow loss in 2002, became president in 2005 in an unprecedented first-round victory. Like Lula, his success was built on the organizational power of a coalition of social movements. Although Morales faced a swathe of problems, from businessmen in the gas-rich eastern lowlands of the country wanting to secede to dissatisfaction from indigenous groups pressing for faster and more radical change, he was reelected in 2009 with a comfortable majority.

Anatomy of a Protest: The Cochabamba Water Wars

Today, Bolivia stands at the vanguard of political change based on the power of social movements. On several occasions in the early twenty-first century, broad coalitions of farmers, indigenous peoples, and workers brought the country to a standstill, demanding better access to resources, and protesting against the sell-off of precious natural assets, mainly water, oil, and gas. Bolivia is also South America's poorest country—the only other Latin American countries where poverty rates are higher are Haiti and Nicaragua.

The use (or abuse) of water has long been a conflictive issue in the politics of the Cochabamba Valley, a verdant, fertile plain poised between the arid highlands and the lowlands. The problem of water shortage in the valley, and the difficulties of managing an equitable distribution among different users, helps to explain the violent response to the Banzer government's scheme in 1999 to privatize Cochabamba's water supply. Existing users found themselves facing huge price increases. Over the years, local organizations evolved around the need to defend what are considered ancestral rights—known in Bolivia as *usos y costumbres* (uses and customs). In what came to be known as the "Water War," farmers joined forces with urban residents and coca growers to mount a lengthy, bitter, and sometimes violent campaign to force the government to retreat from its plan to sell off Bolivia's water to foreign multinationals.

Justice and Truth

As the twentieth century came to a close, retired life for the former military dictators of Latin America looked decidedly less rosy than it once had. General Augusto Pinochet, who had presided over widespread torture, incarceration, murder, and disappearance in Chile, was arrested in London while undergoing an operation in 1998. He was released, but later rearrested in Chile after a court in 2004 ruled him fit to stand trial, a ruling that was later overturned. A long judicial wrangle ensued that had not ended when Pinochet died in December 2006. Argentine military officers did not get off so lightly. After the Argentine Supreme Court denied amnesty to military officers in 2005, several, including former president Jorge Videla, received life sentences. The tireless efforts of human rights groups had paid off.

Truth commissions had initially reported on the atrocities in Argentina and Uruguay as early as 1985, during the transition to democracy, but it was not until the late 1990s that high-profile arrests were made. The first wave of post-transition legal commissions was focused more on the pursuit of truth than of justice. In the 1990s, Latin American governments tried to forget the twin traumas of military oppression and economic crisis and instead promoted reconciliation and national unity.

Guatemala's truth commission was particularly thorough and set new standards for investigation. Details of illegal killings throughout the long civil war shocked many observers, but were able to provide a starting point for some degree of national healing and aided the democratization process. As traumatic as it was to revisit these incidents, it was deemed necessary, as it had been in South Africa, to record—and, in theory, to learn from—the nation's collective trauma.

Peru also attempted a process of reconciliation through truth in the aftermath of the Shining Path's long uprising. The report found that though the guerrillas had been responsible for around half of the 69,000 deaths dur-

The Water Wars

Oscar Olivera is a leader of the *Federación Departamental de Fabriles* (factory workers), but also he was the leader of the *Coordinadora del Agua* (Water Committee), and more recently of the of the *Coordinadora del Gas* (Gas Committee). His office is up two flights of rickety stairs, just around the corner from the main square in Cochabamba. It has a fine view over the leafy plaza, and this is traditionally the place where demonstrations in the city happen. He recounts the story of the "water war":

"During 1999 and 2000 there was an accumulation of public outrage. People felt wholly alienated from the way in which decisions were being made by just a small group of people. The water issue brought us together, because water has been scarce here for 50 years. The political class here is shortsighted and corrupt. The increase in water tariffs would have absorbed about one-fifth of the income of many people in the city. For the *campesinos* it represented the appropriation of a resource which they had always used. The *regantes* (farmers of irrigated land) were the prime movers. They had their own forms of organization and for them water belonged to the community; it could not just be privately owned or managed. The mobilization over water brought together city and country, man and woman, informal worker and formal. It was something completely new. It made people aware of the nature of the economic model. What people want is social justice, respect and health.

"With the water war, people recovered their voice. The issue of natural resources is fundamental in bringing people together. They took the decisions, since there was no *caudillo* out in front. It was a big victory. Water was not privatized in the end, and Bechtel (the foreign multinational company slated to buy the supply) was kicked out. More importantly, people became aware that it was possible to get bad policies changed. If there had been no victory in the water war, there would never have been a gas war. But we have to be like water itself: transparent and always moving forward."

—John Crabtree, *Patterns of Protest: Politics and Social Movements in Bolivia*, London: LAB, 2005

ing the long insurgency, the military or government-sponsored militias had killed or "disappeared" an almost equal number of people. Laws put into place by Alberto Fujimori and backed by another ex-president, Alan Garcia, have ensured that—so far—the conclusions of the truth commission cannot be used as prosecuting evidence. However, as the 1990s came to a close, there were increasingly powerful calls for justice and an end to the culture of impunity that had protected the retired military leaders. In part, this desire

Jimena Vicario

Jimena was born in Rosario, in May 1976. From when she was little she knew that she was adopted. Susana, her adoptive mother, was unmarried and worked as a hematologist at the Pedro de Elizalde Hospital in Buenos Aires:

"I remember the moment when I asked how she had adopted me. I was three years old. I remember that she told me that you could put your name down on a list in the court and when babies appeared the court would call the first person on the list and they got the baby."

Jimena's parents were called Juan Carlos Vicario and Estela Maris Galichio. Juan Carlos was kidnapped in Rosario on 5 February 1977. On that same day Estela Maris was with Jimena in Buenos Aires applying for their passports. Both were kidnapped while carrying out the application in the Central Department of the Federal Police. Jimena was nine months old.

In 1984 two elderly women knocked at the door of Jimena's house. Both were members of the Abuelas [Grandmothers] de Plaza de Mayo. They'd received a report and were following it up. Susana wasn't in at the time.

"I had already noticed that over the previous few months lawyers started turning up every day. I remember that Susana was on duty at the hospital and one night she called me to ask me to tell her the number of a lawyer from her address book, which she'd left at home. She had an older brother who was in charge of things since their father died. I saw that the brother was coming round a lot, they used to shut themselves away in her room to talk and I realized that something was up.

"One evening she sat me down in my room and said, 'The thing is this, you know you're adopted, and that there is a woman who says she's your grandmother. You're going to go to court with a judge, they're going to call you to do a blood test . . . '

"I asked who the family was, so she showed me a photo that had been published in the national daily *Clarín,* along with an interview with my grandmother, a photo of me when I was a baby and a photo of my parents. The photos in the newspaper were very dark and I said no, that can't be me."

—Andres Jaroslavsky, *The Future of Memory: Children of the Dictatorship in Argentina Speak*, London: LAB, 2004 for prosecutions was related to the political shift toward the left throughout the region. In particular, Nestor Kirchner in Argentina had suffered personally at the hands of the military juntas and this may have inspired him to tackle impunity with more vigor. Days after his election, Kirchner purged the Argentine military of officers with links to the juntas and cleared the way for prosecutions to take place.

The Struggle to Regain a Lost Identity

After the demise of the military governments, amnesty laws, and pardons allowed those responsible for the disappearance of some 30,000 people in Argentina to walk the streets freely. But in the late 1990s, a protest movement emerged in the shape of the Daughters and Sons for Identity and Justice against Forgetting and Silence (HIJOS). This organization of children of the disappeared, exiles, and political activists demanded that amnesty laws be repealed. They took to the street, performing "*escraches*"—from *escrachar*, an Argentine slang word for "uncover"—to root out and publicly denounce human rights violators. The protestors would gather outside the homes of known torturers in an attempt to publicly expose and humiliate them.

Another related struggle is that of the children kidnapped from their parents, often in captivity, and given to "adoptive" military families. In some cases, children were unknowingly brought up by their parents' torturers and murderers, who kept their true identity secret. In recent years groups such as the Grandmothers of the Plaza de Mayo have led the fight to have these children's kidnappers prosecuted, as immunity for such crimes was not bestowed by the original amnesty laws.

That the story of these kidnapped children has taken so long to emerge— and to be dealt with by the Argentine authorities and by society as a whole—is testament to the pervasive legacy of silence that terror bestows, but it is also a sign of a new era in which the law is being used to redress impunity. A more difficult task is restoring identity to these children, whose reactions to the news that not only are they adopted, but that their "parents" might be their biological parents' murderers, are ambivalent and complex.

Latin America today bears little resemblance to the simple divisions portrayed by the warriors of either the Cold War or the class war of previous decades. Identity is fragmented, shifting, and multiple. Individuals define themselves along the axes of ethnicity, gender, politics, age, and consumer preference. These dimensions of identity are interwoven with notions of human rights as a central part of citizenship. All this grew up despite the stark economic Darwinism of the last two decades of the twentieth century, as neo-

liberalism incubated new, complex, and challenging social and political movements and ideas that provided the basis for a post-neoliberal order that is still
being forged.

5.
Culture and Religion

Writing on the Wall: Culture, Identity, and Politics

Every evening the suburbs and shantytowns of Latin America grind to a halt as anyone with a television settles down in front of the latest *telenovela*, or soap opera. TV-less neighbors drop by for the show and an animated discussion about the latest twist in an often bewildering plot. Afterward, telenovela addicts can go online for an extra fix of gossip and opinion on one of the hundreds of dedicated websites that cater to Latin America's 216 million Internet users. And addicts they are: when the last episode of *Cradle of Wolves* was shown, a lurid account of a ruthless heroine with an eyepatch who committed a series of gruesome murders, Mexico's underground drivers refused to go to work and the public transport system closed down.

In Europe and North America, Latin America is better known for its literature and music than for its soaps. Salsa and merengue are favorites on European dance floors, like the tango and bossa nova before them. Latin American literature has become so popular that, in the words of critic and translator Nick Caistor, it "has become the equivalent of the Amazon rain forest, providing oxygen for the stale literary lungs of the developed world." Latin American novelists such as Mexico's Carlos Fuentes, Argentina's Jorge Luis Borges, Chile's Isabel Allende, Peru's Mario Vargas Llosa, or Colombia's Nobel Prize–winning author, Gabriel García Márquez, have become international celebrities, periodically joined by rediscovered greats such as Pablo Neruda. In the United States, Allende and García Márquez received the ultimate literary accolade (at least in sales terms) of being selected for the Oprah Winfrey Book Club. Yet at home the audience for one episode of the top Mexican or Brazilian soaps exceeds the entire continent's readership of classics such as *One Hundred Years of Solitude*, which has sold twenty million copies worldwide and is considered by Fuentes to be the greatest novel in Spanish since *Don Quixote*.

In his work, García Márquez draws heavily on the traditional "popular culture" of his native Colombia, filling his books with the tales of traveling singers and storytellers remembered from his childhood. He has turned his hand to other genres, from journalism to film to writing soaps, and challenges those intellectuals and critics who have in the past derided telenovelas as cheap, tacky melodrama churned out by Latin America's media giants. Such critics frequently hark back to a "pure" popular culture in the countryside, free of the taint of capitalism and technology, yet such views risk reducing the idea of "popular culture" to a quaint but increasingly irrelevant folklore destined for the museum. Popular culture would paradoxically cease to be the culture of the people, with its constantly evolving mix of traditional and modern styles.

Ever since the Conquest, Latin America's dispossessed peoples—indigenous villagers, descendants of African slaves, and poor mestizos—have developed varied and unique cultural forms by constantly absorbing new influences into a bedrock of tradition. The indigenous people of the Andes and Central America kept alive pre-Conquest textiles and pottery, while adopting Spanish stringed instruments and combining them with their own panoply of flutes and drums. Traumatic events such as the Conquest and murder of the Inca emperors are today recalled through the cultural memory of street theater and dance, yet traditional styles are still evolving. In Guatemala, widows of men killed or "disappeared" by the military during their counterinsurgency campaigns in the early 1980s now include stylized images of helicopters in their traditional weaving patterns, where they join images of Spaniards on horseback from the time of the Conquest. In Brazil the Kayapó people expertly wield imported video cameras to record their traditional dances and rituals for future generations. The Kayapó explain that they find their own ceremonies more interesting than Brazilian national TV. The cameras also come out at meetings with the Brazilian authorities, to be played back to the bureaucrats should they try to renege on a promise.

The survival of ancient cultural traditions was frequently achieved in defiance of the colonial authorities' attempts to impose European ways. The greatest battleground for the defense of tradition was religion. Traditional indigenous religion and culture are inseparable; music, costumes and dance are part of an annual round of rituals and feast days linked to the seasons and the agricultural cycles of sowing and harvest. To the Catholic Church, charged with a mission to convert the heathen, the pantheon of indigenous deities had to be crushed, the temples overthrown and practices such as ancestor worship stamped out. In order to appease the authorities, indigenous communities adopted Catholic forms, but subverted their content. The Christian saints took on the characters and powers of the different indigenous gods, and All Soul's Day, known in Spanish as Día de los Muertos (Day of the

Dead), became an opportunity for ancestor worship. Every year on November 2, Mexican families still go to the cemeteries to picnic with their dead. Throughout the continent the cycle of fiestas, carnivals, and saints' days plays a central role in community life:

> In all of these ceremonies the Mexican opens out. They all give him a chance to reveal himself and to converse with God, country, friends or relations. During these days the silent Mexican whistles, shouts, sings, shoots off fireworks, discharges his pistol into the air. He discharges his soul. This is the night when friends who have not exchanged more than the prescribed courtesies for months get drunk together, trade confidences, weep over the same troubles, discover that they are brothers, and sometimes, to prove it, kill each other.
>
> —OCTAVIO PAZ, *The Labyrinth of Solitude*

In Mexico, visions of the Virgin Mary began to occur soon after the Conquest, the most famous being the Virgin of Guadalupe, who appeared to a poor villager at Tepeyac, north of Mexico City, the site of a traditional indigenous shrine to Tonantzin, the Aztec earth goddess. A flow of miracles forced the disapproving Church authorities to recognize the event, and the Virgin of Guadalupe's shrine became the most important holy place in the Americas. She also became a symbol of emergent Mexican identity, representing both earth goddess and dark-skinned Virgin Mary, who had chosen to appear to an indigenous person rather than to a member of the white elite. In Bolivia, paintings by mestizo artists of the colonial period transformed the Virgin into Pachamama, the Andean earth goddess. Sometimes the subversion of Catholicism was even more deliberate. The Mexican muralists of the 1920s were particularly influenced by contemporary accounts of a religious dance around the statue of the Virgin in a Puebla village, during which the statue toppled over to reveal a small stone carving depicting the goddess of water, hidden beneath the Virgin's skirts for centuries, and surreptitiously worshipped throughout that time.

In the Bolivian mines, Catholic and pre-Columbian beliefs are fused in the figure of the *tío* (uncle). The *tío* is the god of the underworld whose domain includes the tin mines where, for five centuries, many of Bolivia's indigenous people have toiled in unhealthy and dangerous conditions. Since the Christian God resides in heaven, the *tío* has become equated with the Christian devil, but without the qualities of evil normally ascribed to him. In the mines, the *tío* must be placated and asked for help to avert the all-too-frequent rockfalls and explosions. His statue glares out from niches cut into the walls of the mines, but the miners seem on affectionate terms with him, handing him cigarettes or coca to chew. At carnival time they offer him the blood and heart of a llama. As they prepare to cut the llama's throat, the miners, their cheeks bulging with coca, cry out "for the health and prosperity of our section," "may there be no more accidents." Blood collected in a chipped china plate is then smeared on the walls of the mine to bring good luck for another year.

Above ground, the carnival brass bands and "devil dance" of young men dressed in the elaborate horned and multicolored masks of the *tío* have moved down from the mines to the town center and become a tourist attraction. These days it is the shopkeepers and middle classes who dance in the masks, which have become too elaborate and expensive for a miner to buy. In the dance the Archangel Gabriel, a pink-skinned, blue-eyed European representation of good, fights the devils in ritual combat. The god of the mines, like the miners he protects, comes off worst in this clash of cultures.

In traditional indigenous beliefs, sacred properties were not confined to a god, but filled everyday objects, which could themselves be worshipped or asked to bring good luck. Everything from a hill to a tree or a carving could be seen as holy. To the Catholic Church, these practices were idolatrous, and public worship of objects (other than saints) was stamped out, but many of the beliefs were passed down through the family, principally from mother to daughter. Along the way, they were fragmented and transformed into what became known as "folk magic," involving faith healing and other "magical" practices. Today, throughout Latin America, such beliefs as *mal de ojo* (evil eye) and the sale of love potions are commonplace among indigenous people and mestizos alike. Even such eminently rationalist, Western figures as "The Liberator," Símon Bolívar, have been turned into quasi-religious icons. Stores throughout Venezuela sell "Liberator" aphrodisiacs and his name is invoked in faith healing. This interweaving of the sacred with everyday life is one reason why writers such as García Márquez insist that their style, often labeled "magic realism," is merely an accurate portrayal of the life and stories of their native world. In Latin America everyday "magic" and "reality" are so interwoven as to be inseparable. García Márquez has particular trouble separating life from art: in 1996, hours after he had sent off the final proofs of his latest book, *News of a Kidnapping,* real-life kidnappers abducted the brother of ex-president César Gaviria. Their main demand? That García Márquez take over as president to "save the fatherland."

In Brazil, the African slaves on the sugar plantations of the northeast managed to retain their cultural identity through music and dance. Plantation owners even encouraged erotic dances to keep up morale among their slaves. Today on Rio's beaches young black men can still be seen performing *capoeira*, a traditional slave dance combining both expressive performance and ritualized martial arts. In recent years, as the Brazilian community in

Blessing Cars in Bolivia

"Bless this vehicle. May the driver drive in a Christian way. May the motor not use too much petrol." So goes the much-repeated blessing by the old Irish priest as he totters along a line of new cars, jeeps, and trucks decked out in garlands of yellow and red flowers.

At Copacabana, on the shores of Lake Titicaca, the highest lake in the world, the cars have come from all over the country to be blessed at the shrine of the country's favorite Virgin.

The priest sprinkles holy water on the driver, the upholstery, and the engine and moves on. After the blessing the owners shower petals over their new (and now sanctified) cars. Next comes the beer, shaken vigorously then squirted over wheels, upholstery, and down expectant throats. Off go the firecrackers, as the smells of gunpowder and beer blend in the clear Andean air.

On the outskirts of the town another ceremony is taking place halfway up a small rocky outcrop topped by another shrine to the Virgin. Here, overlooking the silver-blue expanse of the lake, Bolivia's indigenous traditions take over from Catholicism. A family arrives with a toy pickup swathed in bright paper streamers. An elderly indigenous priest blesses them and their cherished vehicle, mumbling in a mixture of the Spanish Mass and the native Aymara language.

Little bells ring. There is a fizz and a splat as the priest sprays beer to the four points of the compass. A palpable sense of calm and spirituality ensues. If the blessing wins divine approval, the family will get their dream car and bring it to the church below to be blessed.

The services mix prayers to Pachamama, the indigenous Earth Mother, with invocations to God and the Virgin Mary; Pachamama and God; petrol consumption and incense. In Bolivia there is no dividing line between "traditional" and "modern."

Europe has begun to assert itself, *capoeira* has spread in popularity to non-Brazilians as a leisure activity. As increasing numbers of blacks left the sugar plantations and moved to the shantytowns and tenements of the cities, African religions resurfaced in the shape of *Candomblé*, which is based on the personal relationship between an individual and a pantheon of African deities, each with a different personality and tastes. As in the Andean religions, music, dance, and worship are inseparable. The gods appear through the possession of chosen "sons and daughters" and receive ritual offerings, songs, and dance. African and Portuguese cultures combined to produce samba and carnival, a joyous three-day euphoria of dance, music, sex, and beer that has become synonymous with Brazil:

> In the official parade grounds—the Sambadrome—I thought the silence eerie until I realized it was in fact a solid wall of sound, a percussive din that did not sound like music and advanced gradually towards the spectators on an elaborate loudspeaker set up on either side of the central "avenue," or parade space. At the head of the noise was a gigantic waggling lion's head that floated down the avenue and overtook us, giving way to dazzling hordes in red and gold. A marmalade-thick river of people swept past; outlandish dancers in feathers and capes, ball gowns and G-strings, hundreds of drummers, thousands of leaping princes singing at the top of their lungs. Drowning in red and gold, I struggled to focus. In the ocean of feathers and banners faces emerged: brown, white, pink, tan, olive. Young men bopping in sweat-drenched suits; old women in cascades of flounces whirling ecstatically; middle-aged men and women with paunches and eyeglasses bouncing happily in their head-dresses and bikinis.
>
> —ALMA GUILLERMOPRIETO, *Samba*

Carnival's origins lay in festivals brought from Portugal, messy affairs in which the populace pelted each other with flour and water and indulged in gargantuan feats of eating and drinking. Over the years dance and music acquired increasing importance, and local carnival associations grew up to organize floats for processions through the streets of Rio. The center of carnival culture moved from the rich European suburbs to the poor black favelas, provoking one well-to-do reader of the *Jornal de Notícias* in Bahia to write in 1901:

> The authorities should prohibit those [African drum] sessions and *candomblés* that in such quantity are overflowing on our streets these days, producing such great cacophonous noise, as well as those masquerades dressed in [typical black costumes] singing their traditional samba, because all of that is incompatible with our current civilized state.

The associations metamorphosed into the samba schools, enormous permanent organizations based in Rio's favelas that each year take on the task of building the increasingly monumental floats, and organizing thousands of drummers and costumed dancers into their various "wings." The vast expense of carnival and the elaborate costumes have so far not forced the samba schools out of the favelas, but there has been a slow erosion of the poor communities' involvement in carnival as a whole. Outside designers and

Magic Realism

The real as magical—electricity comes to Macondo:

Dazzled by so many and marvelous inventions, the people of Macondo did not know where their amazement began. They stayed up all night looking at the pale electric bulbs fed by the plant that Aureliano Triste had brought back when the train made its second trip, and it took time and effort for them to grow accustomed to its obsessive toom-toom. They became indignant over the living images that the prosperous merchant Bruno Crespi projected in the theatre with the lion-head ticket windows, for a character who had died and was buried in one film and for whose misfortune tears of affliction had been shed would reappear alive and transformed into an Arab in the next one. . . . When someone from the town had the opportunity to test the crude reality of the telephone installed in the railroad station, even the most incredulous were upset. It was as if God had decided to put to the test every capacity for surprise which was keeping the inhabitants of Macondo in a permanent alternation between excitement and disappointment, doubt and revelation, to such an extreme that no one knew for certain where the limits of reality lay.

The magical as real—Macondo is stricken by a plague of insomnia:

With an inked brush [José Arcadio Buendía] marked everything with its name: *table, chair, clock, door, wall, bed, pan.* He went to the corral and marked the animals and plants: *cow, goat, pig, hen, cassava, caladium, banana.* Little by little, studying the infinite possibilities of a loss of memory, he realized that the day might come when things would be recognized by their inscriptions but that no one would remember their use. Then he was more explicit. The sign that he hung on the neck of the cow was an exemplary proof of the way in which the inhabitants of Macondo were prepared to fight against loss of memory: *This is the cow. She must be milked every morning so that she will produce milk, and the milk must be boiled in order to be mixed with coffee to make coffee and milk.* Thus they went on living in a reality that was slipping away, momentarily captured by words, but which would escape irremediably when they forgot the values of the written letters. At the beginning of the road into the swamp they put up a sign that said MACONDO and another larger one on the main street that said GOD EXISTS.

—Gabriel García Márquez, *One Hundred Years of Solitude,* trans. Gregory Rabassa, London: Jonathan Cape, 1970

artists are now hired to create the floats, costumes are farmed out rather than made by the women of the favela, and each school's procession is now fronted by TV stars, usually white.

Two Cultures Clash

In Latin America culture and politics have been inextricably linked since Pizarro's conquistadores ransacked the temples of Cusco and melted down the Inca Empire's finest-wrought gold and silver into ingots to be sent home to Spain. After the Conquest the Spanish authorities initially banned fiction, fearing it would excite the minds of the locals and fan subversion. During the colonial period the social and economic divide between the white ruling elite and the dark-skinned masses was mirrored in the gulf between their two cul-

---

Latin America's Melting Pot

Little Tamales from Cambray

Two pounds of mestizo cornmeal
a half-pound loin of Spanish immigrant
all finely chopped and cooked
with a packet of ready-blessed raisins
two tablespoons of Malinche's milk
one cup of troubled water
then fry the conquistador's helmets
with three Jesuit onions
one small sack of multinational gold
two dragon's teeth
add one presidential carrot
two tablespoons of pimps
the fat from Panchimalco Indians
two Ministry tomatoes
half a cup of televised sugar
two drops of volcanic lava
seven pito leaves
(don't get me wrong, it's a soporific)
set it all to boil
over a slow fire
for five hundred years
and you'll discover its unique aroma

—Claribel Alegría, "To Make 4,200,000 Small Tamales," in *Lovers and Comrades: Women's Resistance Poetry from Central America*, ed. Amanda Hopkinson, London: Women's Press

Note: 4,200,000 is the population of El Salvador, of which tamales are the national dish. Malinche was the name of the indigenous mistress of Cortés, who betrayed the Aztec emperor Cuauhtémoc to the Spaniards.

tures. In their art academies and concert halls Latin America's elites pursued a purely European aesthetic and made regular visits to its cultural capitals of Paris or Rome. Werner Herzog's 1982 film, *Fitzcarraldo*, recounts one particularly bizarre example of the forced implantation of European culture—a rubber baron's folly in the shape of a 2,000-seat opera house in Manaus, in the heart of the Amazon jungle. After it opened in 1897, opera companies from Milan, Paris, and Madrid sailed up the Amazon to sing at the theatre, which boasted curtains from Alsace, stone from Portugal, Venetian crystal. and English-wrought ironwork. When the rubber boom came to an end, the theatre closed down until its restoration in 1990, when Plácido Domingo sang in *Carmen* to a full house. Meanwhile, away from the paved streets of the city centers, a rich and separate popular culture was actively combining ingredients of indigenous, African, and European culture into a uniquely Latin American cocktail.

Many nineteenth-century writers, notably Argentina's essayist and president, Domingo Faustino Sarmiento, portrayed popular culture as a form of barbarism that must be fought through the introduction of civilized (that is, European) values, described by one author as "the civil war between the swallow-tailed coat and the poncho." Yet popular culture also offered middle-class writers and artists an apparent solution to a conundrum that has dogged the continent's intelligentsia since the Conquest: the riddle of Latin America's identity. As Simón Bolívar lamented, "We are not Europeans, we are not Indians, but a hybrid species between the aborigines and the Spaniards." After independence, and particularly as modern nation-states began to form toward the end of the nineteenth century, the search for a national and continental identity played an essential role in the formation of a common sense of nationhood. The influence of European Romanticism made writers and artists look for such an identity in Latin America's own version of the "noble savage," an authentic innocent untainted by tawdry modernity. In Argentina the romantic figure of the *gaucho*, the self-reliant cowboy of the Pampas, spawned a series of novels and poems in the dying years of the century, glorifying rural life at a time of massive migration to the cities. Although a caricature, *gauchismo* offered a sense of belonging to a distinctive culture, playing much the same role as the glorification of the cowboy and the "winning of the West" in the United States.

The search for a Latin American identity and debate over politics and art took on greater urgency in the political and cultural ferment that followed the Mexican Revolution of 1910–17. The revolutionary Mexican government set about forging a new national consciousness. Under the patronage of a dynamic education minister, José Vasconcelos, a group of Mexican artists began to cover the walls and ceilings of public buildings with murals

depicting scenes from Mexican history and allegorical portraits of the revolution. In preferring walls to canvas, the muralists sought to make art the
property of the people, not a commodity for sale to the highest bidder. The
movement came to be dominated by the "big three," Diego Rivera, José Cle-
mente Orozco, and David Alfaro Siqueiros. Between them, they developed
what has been called the greatest public revolutionary art of the century, a
maelstrom of unforgettable images of indigenous villagers, conquistadores,
heroic workers, and bloated capitalists. Rivera, in particular, drew heavily
on pre-Columbian designs and the popular artists of his time, notably the
skull images of José Guadalupe Posada, who had earned fame prior to the
revolution for his satirical cartoons.

Although perhaps unintended by the artists, the murals helped the state to
establish enduring myths of a new Mexico that had thrown out the rich white
capitalists and now belonged to the poor mestizos and the indigenous peoples. The muralists' combination of revolutionary zeal with an unquestioning
faith in technological progress both excited and enraged the U.S. art establishment. In California in 1933, Rivera's patron, John D. Rockefeller, ordered
his *Man at the Crossroads* destroyed because Rivera refused to remove the
figure of Lenin from an allegory of progress in the modern age.

The work of the Mexican muralists has inspired political street art throughout Latin America ever since. In Nicaragua following the Sandinista Revolution of 1979, the walls of the cities were quickly adorned with revolutionary
iconography. Figures like Che Guevara, Sandino, Allende, and Zapata joined
Bolívar and others in the roll call of Latin America's secular saints. When
the Sandinistas fell from power in 1990, one of their opponents' first actions
was to whitewash the walls of Managua; in 2005 Ecuador's capital, Quito,
became the scene of a graffiti battleground between the various factions vying
for power in the wake of the flight of President Lucio Guitérrez.

The Mexican experience was the first example of a phenomenon repeated
throughout the continent in the following years. Populist governments took
power in major nations such as Mexico, Brazil, and Argentina, combining
limited social reform with a drive to turn them into industrial powers. By promoting a sense of patriotic identity with its own myths and symbols, populist
leaders such as Brazil's Getúlio Vargas and Argentina's Juan Domingo Perón
could build the national unity needed to implement their model of development and ensure the legitimacy of the state. In Brazil, Vargas seized on samba,
carnival, and football and used state money to turn them into national icons.
Vargas built the Maracanã stadium, the biggest football field in the world, and
transformed carnival into a major international event. Both samba and football were ideal for the purpose, being poor people's pastimes that the state
could use to weld people together at both local and national level.

The political importance of literature and art also showed in the great political weight acquired by the intellectual, a figure of far greater status in Latin America than in Britain or the United States. In the nineteenth century, poet José Martí fought for Cuban independence, while Sarmiento played a key role as president in forging modern Argentina. Rómulo Gallegos, author of Venezuela's classic novel, *Doña Barbara*, was also that country's president. In this century, two accomplished historians, Joaquín Balaguer and Juan Bosch, spent several decades vying for the presidency of the Dominican Republic, while writers and poets such as Chile's Pablo Neruda, Mexico's Carlos Fuentes and Octavio Paz, and Guatemala's Miguel Angel Asturias have served their countries as ambassadors. In 1987 Peru's Mario Vargas Llosa unwisely decided to abandon the pen for the campaign trail and run for president against Alberto Fujimori in 1990 before returning, chastened, to literary life. Even musicians got in on the act when top salsa singer Ruben Blades unsuccessfully ran for Panamanian president in 1994.

Mexican political scientist Jorge Castañeda believes that intellectuals fill serious gaps in Latin American political life, acting as a conduit for ideas from abroad and speaking on behalf of groups in society: "Intellectuals are nearly always substituting for someone or something. . . . They fight for labor rights in lieu of unions and denounce human rights abuses in the place of judges or the courts. They decry injustice, oppression and electoral fraud on behalf of weak or nonexistent political parties, and write pamphlets revealing and condemning corruption, substituting for a fettered, often marginal press."

Electronic Ambassadors

The rapid pace of urbanization since the turn of the century has had a seismic impact on popular culture. Towns and cities act as the entry point for foreign influences, while the most remote rural areas remain repositories of traditional culture. As the rural poor flocked to the shantytowns around the major cities, they brought with them traditional customs, which blended with the new influences. In Peru this melting pot has produced what is known as *chicha* culture, named after a potent local brew. *Chicha* music has combined the traditional wailing lament of the Andean *huaynu* with tropical music and electric guitars to become the sound of Lima's shantytowns.

Salsa, probably Latin America's most successful musical export in recent years, is itself a mongrel mixture of Cuban dance styles such as *son, rumba,* and *chachacha*. In the late 1960s, Fania Records, a Latin record label in New York, had the inspired idea of repackaging this baffling range of musi-

Teenagers in Mexico's Chapultepec Park. (Latinphoto)

cal styles as "salsa," and the music took off, becoming a central part of the Latino identity movement.

The introduction of new electronic media has transformed popular culture in the present century. Film, radio, TV, and increasingly, the Internet have become the main channels of public communication in society, thereby acquiring a central role in creating and passing on cultural values. The mass media have also become a battleground in the struggle to define Latin America's identity. Increased dependence on Western technology has given huge influence to foreign film and TV exporters, with the film industry in particular dominated by Hollywood. Other media, such as radio and TV, have shown greater success in becoming largely Latin American in character, playing an important role in forging national identities.

It is difficult to overestimate the importance of the United States as a purveyor of mass culture. The record shops of Latin American cities blare out the latest musical genres, both from the United States and, increasingly, home-grown versions. Middle-class youth covet the latest jeans or sneakers just as much as their North American or European counterparts. Dubbed or subtitled U.S. films of the *Speed* and *Terminator* school form the staple diet of scruffy cinemas throughout the continent. Especially since the Cuban Revolution of 1959, many artists and writers have come to see North American influence in the media as another facet of U.S. political and economic domination of the continent. They argue that its domination allows the United States to instill its values in Latin Americans, acting as a subliminal ambassador that can reach into the poorest home with a dazzling image of the giant to the north. Latin America's intellectuals have stressed the political importance of creating and sustaining a separate Latin American culture in the mass media, as a means of finding a political alternative to U.S. domination.

Historically, the high cost and advanced technology required in film-making has meant that Latin America's cinema has lived in the shadow of films from the United States and other industrialized nations, but at different moments it has managed to produce high-quality films that have challenged the Hollywood monopoly. Until the 1960s most Latin American cinema consisted of low-budget musicals, comedies, and melodramas whose characters and themes were summed up by the critic John King as "good women who bear the stigma of fate, weak men caught in the trap of a man-eater, rooms and brothels reeking with smoke and moral turpitude, eyes bloodshot with alcohol and grief, innocence, violent death."

Yet Latin American cinema has also been intimately involved in politics since the days when the Mexican revolutionary Pancho Villa signed an exclusive contract with the U.S. Mutual Film Corporation, granting it exclusive rights to film his battles. For US$25,000 he agreed to fight in daylight whenever possible, to rerun scenes of battle if the cameras had missed the real thing, and to reschedule firing-squad executions from 4 a.m. until after dawn.

The Cuban Revolution marked a watershed for the continent's filmmakers, as Havana quickly became the center of a politically committed "New Cinema," dedicated to portraying Latin America's conflicts, especially with the United States, through a brand of social realist cinema and documentary. The 1960s and early 1970s saw young radical filmmakers using a low-budget, hand-held-camera style to film life, warts and all, in favelas and villages across the region, producing classics such as *Blood of the Condor* (Jorge Sanjinés, Bolivia) and *Battle for Chile* (Patricio Guzmán, Chile). Havana became the host of an annual Latin American Film Festival and invited filmmakers from every corner of the Third World to come and study at its international film school.

The New Cinema dominated the 1960s, but soon afterward the optimism began to wear thin as military dictatorships in the Southern Cone drove film directors into exile and the Cuban government started to show growing intolerance toward dissident writers and directors. Cuba illustrates a problem that has beset the Latin American cinema since its inception. In the absence of private capital, it has frequently had to rely on state support, leaving it open to manipulation and censorship, or simply asphyxiation by a state bureaucracy that cares little for artistic innovation. In the 1980s and 1990s, government austerity programs cut state funding and led to a slump in film production in many countries. Since the final years of the twentieth century, however, Latin American cinema has experienced a dramatic rebirth. In Argentina, the economic crisis of 2001 coincided with the beginning of a flowering in home-grown cinema, with the vast success at home and abroad of crowd-pleasing films such as *Nueve Reinas* and *El Hijo de la Novia* and art-house films such as *Mundo Grúa* and *La Ciénaga*. In Mexico some joint ventures of private and public capital scored initial successes with films such as *Danzón* and *Like Water for Chocolate*. More recently, *Amores Perros* and *Y Tu Mama También* provided back-to-back hits for Mexican heart-throb Gael García Bernal, before he went on to collaborate with the feted Brazilian director Walter Salles in the film adaptation of Che Guevara's *Motorcycle Diaries*. *Y Tu Mama También's* director, Alfonso Cuarón, struck gold when he was asked to direct the third Harry Potter movie. Cuba, on the other hand, remains cash-strapped and now produces few films—the success of the 1990s being *Strawberry and Chocolate*, a mild critique of gay issues directed by Tomás Gutiérrez. The film that perhaps more than any other summed up the new global appeal of contemporary Latin American cinema was *Cidade de Deus* (City of God) by Fernando Meirelles and Katia Lund. European and North American audiences are at last prepared to watch challenging subtitled films, a sea change that has helped many budding directors to obtain investment. The problem for new filmmakers lies in distribution, where Hollywood has a stranglehold throughout Latin America. It is a sad truth that many young directors score success at foreign film festivals while awaiting a release for their films at home.

Latin America's film audiences are nevertheless dwarfed by those for its TV networks. Heavily patronized by the state, which recognized its political potential, Latin American TV has grown rapidly. Latin Americans watch an average of just under five hours of television each day, and this figure is rising. There are more than 100 million TV sets in the region, reaching more than 90 percent of the population, and their favorite viewing is the telenovelas that dominate prime time. Brazil and Mexico have even become TV exporters, breaking into the U.S. market to build a large following for their soaps among the growing Hispanic population. Harder to understand is Russia's fascination with Latin soaps. In 1992 Televiza's *Los Ricos También Lloran* (The Rich Also Weep) broke all viewing records, while Boris Yeltsin's successful bid for reelection in 1996 was partly credited to his brainstorm of engineering a special scheduling of TV Globo's *Tropicaliente* to dissuade Russians from leaving town on polling day. At the turn of the century, popular titles included *Maria la del Barrio* (Maria from the 'Hood), *Corazón Salvaje* (Savage Heart), and *Abrázame mas Fuerte!* (Hug Me Harder!)

Walter Salles on Contemporary Brazilian Cinema

I come from a country and also a continent whose identity is in the making. We're a very young culture, and I think that things are not yet crystallized. So the films that are made in our latitudes, I think, carry that sense of urgency. It's as if the people that you meet on the street and the stories that they bring can influence you directly. Imagine trying to do that in Los Angeles—it's impossible because there's no one in the streets! So little by little, I think my generation became very porous to that. But I think it's not all that different from what the Italian neo-realists did 50 years ago, by taking the camera out of the studio and taking it closer to the faces in the street.

—Walter Salles, interview with Geoff Andrew, National Film Theatre, London, 2004

From the mid-1960s, when the first national telenovela was filmed, Latin America's soaps have built on the melodramatic tradition in popular theater and film, developing rapidly into a major cultural commodity dominated by Brazil and Mexico and their giant media conglomerates, TV Globo and Televiza, which rank fourth and fifth in the world-league table of media giants. They have become increasingly global, notably in the United States where they produce much of the content for the growing U.S. Hispanic cable channels.

No other company consistently produces as many popular Spanish language novelas as the Mexican giant Televiza, which is known as *la fábrica de los sueños* (the dream factory). Its soaps are often variations on a fairly standard formula: a struggle between good and evil; an obligatory love story; a baroque plot that only addicts could disentangle; and an emphasis on individual emotion and melodrama. Compared to European or U.S. soaps, Latin American telenovelas are more likely to use historical settings and are time-bound, using intense 100–200 nightly bursts to tell a full story from beginning to climax to end.

In recent years, more social and political content has found its way into the telenovelas. In *Dos Mujeres y un Camino* (Two Women and One Road), a popular Mexican telenovela, the star played an assimilated Latino who returns from the United States to live in Mexico. Characters poke fun at him because of his limited command of Spanish. In Colombia, *Adrian Está de Visita* (Adrian Is Visiting), released in 2002, broke new ground by casting a black leading man with a white woman as his love interest. This is nothing short of revolutionary in a telenovela industry accustomed to featuring only white actors in leading roles. Brazil's SBT dealt with an even more taboo subject—repression after the 1964 coup. Called *Love and Revolution*, it told the story of left-wing militants and students tortured by a sadistic police officer. The soap wasn't aired until 2011, almost fifty years after the events, but even so some incensed retired military officers lobbied unsuccessfully to have it banned.

An analysis of telenovela plots in Brazil showed that the affair usually takes place between lovers from different classes. In a country as profoundly unequal as Brazil, where social mobility is minimal, the soaps raise important issues but, unlike real life, they provide a happy ending as love triumphs over class barriers. In recent years, telenovelas have taken on a number of political issues such as landlessness and the environment in *O Rei do Gado*, in Brazil, or the highly topical question of government corruption in Mexico's *Nada Personal* or Venezuela's *Por Estas Calles*. TV Globo's *Mujeres Apasionadas* (Passionate Women) dealt with alcoholism and gender equality. Unfortunately, the ratings for such programs have not always lived up to expectations, as script writers have struggled to reconcile the conflicting demands for escapism and social comment. One exception was *Yo Soy Betty la Fea* (I Am Ugly Betty), a Colombian series that challenged telenovela orthodoxy by casting its lead as a distinctly unglamorous woman struggling to stay honest in Colombia's fashion business. The series was twice as popular as rival shows and triggered national debates in the press. The English-language show was also very popular in the United States.

The founding of Telesur in 2005 marked a new step for Latin American TV. Paralleling the Arab Al Jazeera (not least in being underwritten by oil money, in this case from the Venezuelan government), Telesur is a pancontinental news channel broadcasting from a Latin American perspective: perhaps it can be thought of as *Al Bolívar*. Aram Aharonian, the Uruguayan journalist who was the general director of the channel for the first three years, described it as "the first counter-hegemonic telecommunications project known in South America." Telesur is broadcast in full on terrestrial television in Venezuela and Ecuador and, on a much more limited scale, in other countries, including Cuba. In 2008 a Portuguese edition began to be broadcast on a few stations in Brazil and then, a year later, on stations in Portuguese-speaking Africa. President Chávez hopes Telesur will one day become a strong competitor to CNN and Univisión but for the moment that seems a distant dream.

Latin America Online

As elsewhere, the digital and Internet revolution is transforming the way Latin Americans use the media. By March 2011, 216 million Latin Americans (36 percent of the population) were online, and numbers were rising faster than in the more saturated markets of the United States and Europe. TV billionaires such as Mexico's Carlos Slim and Venezuela's Gustavo Cisneros are investing billions in moving into multimedia and Web-based activities, as well as slugging it out over control of the lucrative cable and satellite TV markets (one in ten of the region's homes already pays for cable TV, rising to as many as four in ten in Argentina). The battle shows both the risks and potential benefits of the new electronic age. Although the big players may dominate the main stations, the proliferation and fragmentation of communications channels create spaces for other voices that in the past had no way of making themselves heard. New media increasingly make use of audience participation (one U.S. Spanish-language channel now allows the audience to vote online on its preferred ending to the latest telenovela), while the proliferation of weblogs and dedicated sites allows new generations of Latin Americans to find a voice and a virtual community of like-minded people.

The political impact of such changes has barely begun to be felt. Until the *New York Times* published Herbert Mathews's Sierra Maestra interview with Fidel Castro in 1957, the revolutionary movement in Cuba was virtually unknown to the rest of the world. In 1994, the Zapatistas' charismatic Subcomandante Marcos was issuing lyrical communiqués on the Internet within hours of their uprising. Anyone with a laptop and a modem could follow the struggle in the depths of the Lacandón jungle, and there was nothing the Mexican government could do about it. While the site had its fair share of communiqués and *"denuncias,"* Marcos's laconic postings were a long way from the traditional puritanism of the Latin American revolutionary leader. In an idle moment in 2005, he wrote to the Inter-Milan football team to challenge them to a game against the Zapatistas. "Given the affection we have for you, we're not planning to submerge you in goals," the letter promised. "As we wait for your reply, we'll continue with our rigorous training regime." Inter-Milan, one of Italy's biggest and most famous clubs, have built links with the Zapatistas by funding sports, water, and health projects in their part of Chiapas. Inter's captain, Javier Zanetti, said he was willing to consider the challenge.

Football might help with writer's block. In 2004, Marcos joined the tradition of novelist/politician crossovers when he wrote to Pablo Ignacio Taibo II, a successful writer of detective stories set in Mexico City, proposing that they team up to write a detective story in alternating chapters. The writer accepted coauthorship with a hunted guerrilla leader because "it had the enormous attraction of insanity."

The impact of the Internet on the popular movement extends far beyond the Lacandón jungle, of course. Neighborhood assemblies in Argentina, following the financial crash of December 2001, were organized through email and websites. Email has drastically cheapened communication costs for pressure groups and social movements across the region. At a global level, the

Internet provided the basis for the organization of the eleven World Social Forums held so far, over half of which were in Latin America, mainly Brazil, gathering thousands of international participants from every part of the globe.

Other activists, however, warn against overhyping the political potential of the Internet. Access remains dominated by the middle class, and the digital divide could easily become another driver of inequality. One activist in Peru talks about the new underclass of the *"desenchufados"*—the "unplugged ones."

Intellectuals and the Left

The cultural impact of the Cuban Revolution spread far beyond the cinema. In a continent preoccupied with its identity, Cuba became a symbol of resistance to U.S. domination and the search for a new Latin America, where culture was at the service of the people. In the early years of the revolution, the Cuban National Ballet performed classical and folk dance in factories during the lunch breaks; mobile cinema vans took film to isolated villages for the first time; and Havana became an international center for writers, poets, filmmakers, and musicians. According to García Márquez, "The definition of a Latin American 'intellectual of the left' became the unconditional defense of Cuba."

In the 1960s everything was new: "New Song" in Chile blended traditional Andean music with folk ballads and revolutionary lyrics, "New Cinema" recorded real life rather than cinematic fantasies, and the "New Novel" established a worldwide readership for writers like García Márquez, Fuentes, Cuba's Alejo Carpentier, and the Argentine Julio Cortázar. While the 1960s phenomenon in Europe peaked in 1968, Latin America's cultural boom reached its zenith a year earlier. In 1967 the Guatemalan author Miguel Angel Asturias became the first Latin American novelist to receive the Nobel Prize, Gabriel García Márquez published *One Hundred Years of Solitude*, and Che Guevara was killed in Bolivia. With Che died the optimism of a generation who had grown to believe in imminent revolution. In Cuba the beginning of the 1970s saw the government curtailing cultural freedom and arresting the dissident poet Heberto Padilla, leading many prominent figures such as Mario Vargas Llosa to part company with the revolution after fiercely criticizing Fidel Castro.

Gloom settled over much of Latin America in the 1970s. Coups in Chile and Uruguay (1973), and Argentina (1976), coupled with the growing intolerance in Havana, led to repression and exile for many intellectuals, and a climate of hostility, fear, and censorship for those that remained. The clampdown's best-known victim was Victor Jara, Chile's top exponent of "New Song." Jara was murdered, along with thousands of others, in Santiago's infamous football stadium shortly after the coup. In an act of extraordinary malice, the soldiers crushed the guitarist's fingers before killing him. In exile, other musicians such as the Chilean group Inti Illimani toured the world giving concerts aimed at raising awareness and money for the Solidarity movement. Safeguarded by exile and international fame, established writers responded with novels of dictatorship: Paraguay's Augusto Roa Bastos published *I the Supreme*, and García Márquez produced *Autumn of the Patriarch*.

The Nicaraguan Revolution of 1979 brought a chink of light to an otherwise somber panorama. In that country, poetry workshops sprang up in such unlikely places as the secret police and army barracks; a national literacy crusade brought the printed word for the first time to hundreds of thousands of peasants; an internationally acclaimed writer, Sergio Ramírez, became vice president; state-sponsored musicians, dancers, and circus performers sought to recover national traditions, and revolutionary murals adorned the walls of even the smallest village. In Ramírez's words: "Once we lifted the Yankee stone that weighed Nicaragua down, everything that was fundamental and authentic had to surface again: dances, songs, popular art and the country's true history."

In the Southern Cone, the 1980s brought the military's slow retreat from power. In Argentina, war over the Falklands/Malvinas forced the military to treat youth as the saviors of the country rather than potential delinquents. Radio stations were ordered to stop broadcasting music in English, giving "national rock" access to the mainstream media for the first time. The military invited rock stars to take part in pro-war concerts, but instead an antiwar movement sprang up, whose anthem became León Gieco's song, "Sólo le pido a Dios":

> I only ask God
> not to make me indifferent to war
> It is a great monster that tramples on
> the poor innocence of the people

Following defeat in the Falklands, the end of the dictatorship led to a new cultural flowering, for example, in Argentine cinema. But the widespread joy at the departure of the generals was tempered by the impact of the recession and the identity crisis of the left, leaving progressive musicians without the sense of grand purpose that marked the revolutionary 1960s or the struggles against dictatorship in the 1970s.

Life after Magic Realism

Latin America's literary establishment remains dominated by the grand old men of the 1960s boom, but new novelists and poets have also emerged. One of the most important developments has been the rise of a generation of women writers, after centuries in which recognized authors were almost exclusively male. Writers such as Chile's Isabel Allende, Brazil's Clarice Lispector, and Mexico's Elena Poniatowska and Laura Esquivel are gaining growing readerships both within Latin America and abroad. Allende's *House of the Spirits* became the first genuine bestseller by a woman in Latin American history, and since the 1980s she has cemented her reputation as one of the most commercially successful Latin American authors.

Elena Poniatowska has developed a style of documentary narrative to provide a "people's eye view" of key moments in modern Mexican history, such as the social impact of the earthquake of 1985 and the 1968 Tlatelolco massacre of student protestors by the government. She has pioneered a form of writing in which middle-class women journalists and anthropologists work with working-class and peasant women to produce memorable life stories such as *Let Me Speak*, by Domitila Barrios de Chungara and Moema Viezzer, and *I, Rigoberta Menchú*, by Rigoberta Menchú and edited by Elizabeth Burgos-Debray. In recent years Central America has also produced some renowned woman poets, notably Claribel Alegría (El Salvador) and Gioconda Belli (Nicaragua).

Interest in new Latin American writers has grown along with the booming interest in U.S.-based Latino writers such as Cristina García (*Dreaming in Cuban*), Julia Álvarez (*In the Time of the Butterflies*), Oscar Hijuelos (*Mambo Kings Play Songs of Love*), and Francisco Goldman (*The Long Night of the White Chickens* and *The Ordinary Seaman*), all of whom have created a hybrid U.S./Latino genre.

Through novels such as *Betrayed by Rita Hayworth* and *Kiss of the Spider Woman*, Argentina's Manuel Puig challenged the radical orthodoxy of the 1960s, with its scorn for Hollywood and cheap mass entertainment. Puig argued that writing off the cultural preferences of a large percentage of the population is an elitist mistake by intellectuals from the traditional left. Instead, they should be embracing mass culture. His characters belie the idea that Latin Americans are passive recipients of whatever the media throw at them; they are quite capable of indulging themselves with Hollywood fantasies while keeping a clear sense of their own identities. Puig also deals with issues of gender and sexuality in a way that has moved some women critics to describe him as the best creator of female characters in Latin American fiction.

In recent years, magic realism has started to seem stale to new generations of writers, who have instead portrayed the grimy drug- and violence-filled reality of Latin America's shantytowns and city centers, rather than the sleepy rural world of García Marquez's Macondo. Chilean author Alberto Fuguet ironically brands the new genre "McOndo," yet another Latin American syncretic combination of old and new, external and internal influences.

Although the euphoria of the 1960s was lost in decades of militarism and economic crisis, its cultural impact lives on in the continued quest for a truly Latin American identity. While Latin America continues to import its political and economic models from outside, often with disastrous results, the arts, especially music and literature, have always been more successful in finding words and rhythms that are authentically Latin American. If the region is to find its own way out of the recession and confusion of the late twentieth century, its rich variety of cultural forms is bound to play a central role. García Márquez, as always, is in the vanguard, writing *The General in His Labyrinth* about Simón Bolívar in 1990. "For me, what is fundamental is the ideology of Bolívar: the unity of Latin America," he says. "That is the only cause I'd die for."

In his best-selling album *Buscando América* (Searching for America), Panama's salsa maestro Ruben Blades sums up the pressing challenges that lie ahead:

I'm searching for America and I fear I won't find her
. . . I'm calling America but she doesn't reply
those who fear truth have hidden her
. . . while there is no justice there can be no peace
. . . if the dream of one is the dream of all
let's break the chains and begin to walk
. . . I'm calling you, America, our future awaits us
before we all die, help me to find her.

Latin America and Sports

Historically, football (soccer) has played a political role in Latin America, particularly under the military dictatorships in Brazil and Argentina. The 1964 military coup came at a time when Brazilian football was at its height, the national team having won two successive World Cups and turned their stars—many of them black—into national heroes. But the generals could not resist the temptation to gain political capital from this opium of the people. A military official was appointed as the head of the Brazilian Confederation of

Soccer is Latin America's most popular game—and cultural export. (Latinphoto)

Sports; he sought to impose greater discipline and teamwork on the individualist style of Brazilian football. The national team promptly went into decline until the players' anarchic genius was unfettered once more. The 1978 World Cup took place in Argentina in the midst of a wave of human rights violations and disappearances two years after the military coup. The military junta used the national team's victory to seek both national and international legitimacy.

Latin America has always exported its commodities to rich consumers in the north, and sporting talent is no exception. European football teams import new generations of highly talented Latin American players, and many North American baseball teams depend on Latino talent for success. Despite local fanaticism for spectator sports, the finest talents are often prised away by the lure of fame and riches in the north.

U.S. marines involved in the spate of gunboat diplomacy of the late nineteenth and early twentieth centuries left baseball behind them as one of their more positive legacies. European visitors to revolutionary regimes in Nicaragua and Cuba were suitably startled to find baseball the national game, with huge pride attached to players from all three countries who made it in U.S. teams. In New York there is no rivalry as fierce as that between the Amazin' Mets and the Yankee "Evil Empire," and this multimillion-dollar contest is underpinned by Latin American talent. Disparaging commentators have criticized the Mets for using Spanish as their everyday clubhouse language, and the Yankees have sought to expand their marketing operation throughout the Western Hemisphere. Pedro Martínez, Carlos Beltran, and José Reyes against

---

Football, Corruption, and Politics

In the 1978 World Cup no expense was spared to present the best image of Argentina to the world. Despite inflation running at 165 percent, three new stadia were built, at Mendoza, Córdoba and Mar del Plata. Television, telephone and telex facilities had to be completely overhauled. A U.S. public relations company, Burson- Marsteller, was given a million-dollar contract to buff up Argentina's tarnished image. The finance minister, Juan Alemann, put the cost of the project at US$700 million, much more than the subsequent cost of the 1982 cup in Spain. He called it "the most visible and indefensible case of non-priority spending in Argentina today." Mindful of Perón's example, the generals decided that it was worth it, but only if the national team were successful.

The generals had put their faith in a talented young manager, César Luis Menotti. They also took out a little insurance. Eight years later the *Sunday Times* published what it said were details of how Argentina bribed Peru on the eve of a crucial match. Argentina needed to beat Peru by at least four goals to overtake Brazil and so reach the final. The Argentinians knew the precise scale of the task in front of them, because Brazil's match against Poland had conveniently been scheduled for earlier in the day. Peru had looked a decent side but on the night in Rosario they were torn apart 6–0. Some Peruvian players were dropped, others played out of position. Peru's Argentinian-born goalkeeper was a flimsy barrier. The newspaper's anonymous sources said that Argentina's central bank released US$50 million in credits to Peru and that Argentina shipped 35,000 tons of grain, and possibly weapons as well.

—Chris Taylor, *The Beautiful Game*, London: LAB, 1998

Alex Rodriguez, Jorge Posada, and Mariano Rivera? This is not simply an inter-borough rivalry—it is a truly inter-continental contest. U.S. and Canadian players now head south to the Dominican Republic, Mexico, Puerto Rico, or Venezuela for the Winter League season—a way of keeping fit, but more importantly raising the profile of major league baseball in those countries from which the next generation of superstars will be drawn.

Thy Kingdom Come: The Church

In the main square in front of Guatemala's national palace, a paunchy preacher in a shiny new bomber jacket is haranguing the crowd. Grinning as he shouts into a fat blue microphone, he talks of drought, disease, and salvation, exhorting everyone to praise the Lord. An "Alleluia" rises from the largely female audience. The preacher is an Evangelical Protestant, and he is standing outside the capital city's Roman Catholic cathedral. Inside, everything is cool and white after the dust and heat of the square. The smell of candle wax fills the air as a line of indigenous worshippers of all ages wait to pray to and kiss the wounds of a dark-skinned statue of Christ, his legs worn shiny from the stroking of thousands of hands. Catholicism has the cathedral, but the Evangelical preacher has the crowds. The crusading zeal of the Evangelicals is winning millions of new converts every year, threatening the last bastion of global Catholicism. Even so, by 2010 just under half (49 percent) of the world's Catholics lived in Latin America. In Guatemala, as in most of Latin America, old belief systems are breaking down, producing a kind of religious supermarket where worshippers shop around between Catholicism and the different Evangelical churches. But there are other, more exotic offerings on the shelves: in the church of a lakeside town in the indigenous highlands, the townsfolk, both Protestant and Catholic, also worship Maximón, an enigmatic Mayan combination of St. Peter and Judas, with a penchant for cigars and liquor. In Brazil, African spiritist religions such as Candomblé and Umbanda, which arrived with the slaves, are also doing battle for the souls of the poor.

Christopher Columbus had a triple purpose when he set sail for what he imagined would be Asia in 1492. In the words of Bernal Díaz del Castillo, a comrade of Hernán Cortés in the conquest of Mexico, Columbus and the conquistadores who followed went "to serve God and His Majesty and also to get riches." In the year that Columbus "discovered" America, the Spanish, led by Ferdinand and Isabella, finally drove the last Muslim king out of

Granada, bringing to an end the 500-year war to expel the Moors from Spanish soil. That same year, a royal decree expelled all Jews from Spain. With Spain united, the Vatican looked to the Americas as the next great crusade. Two years after Columbus landed, the Pope decreed in the Treaty of Tordesillas that Spain and Portugal could divide the New World between them, with a mission to convert the heathen.

Despite well-intentioned efforts by the Crown and the Church to restrain the worst excesses of the colonists, evangelization took second place to the mass extermination of the indigenous people through disease and slavery. When Columbus dispatched 500 indigenous slaves back to Spain, he commented in his diary, "Let us in the name of the Holy Trinity go on sending all the slaves that can be sold." Under the *encomienda* system, Spanish officers were granted large numbers of indigenous laborers in return for bringing them to Christ. It is not clear how many were successfully converted before dying in the mines or on the haciendas. From the start, there were dissident friars who expressed their revulsion at the treatment of the indigenous people. Just nineteen years after Columbus first landed, a Dominican named Antonio de Montesinos, on the island of Hispaniola (today divided between Haiti and the Dominican Republic) outraged his Christmas congregation with his questions: "By what right do you keep these Indians in such a cruel and horrible servitude? . . . You kill them with your desire to extract and acquire gold every day. . . . Are these not men? Have they not rational souls? Are you not bound to love them as you love yourselves?" Five centuries on, many Church workers are still asking the same questions of Latin America's elites.

The sermon changed the life of one young landowner in Montesinos's congregation, a man by the name of Bartolomé de las Casas. Shortly afterward, Las Casas gave up "his Indians" and traveled to Spain to begin a lifetime's crusade to persuade the Spanish Crown to end the extermination of the continent's native peoples. First as a Dominican friar, then as a bishop, Las Casas became the indigenous inhabitants' foremost defender, and his book, *A Short Account of the Destruction of the Indies,* gives a graphic portrayal of their suffering under the conquistadores. In one famous debate in 1550, the 76-year-old bishop took on the leading Spanish scholar of his day, Juan Ginés de Sepúlveda, to argue that the enslavement of the indigenous communities was theologically unacceptable, and that indigenous civilization was in many ways superior to that of the Europeans.

Not only the Dominicans, but also the Franciscans and the Jesuits brought with them a more enlightened version of Christianity. In the early seventeenth century the Jesuits set up vast *reducciones* (missions) covering much of Paraguay, where Guaraní communities could live and work, safe from the depredations of Portuguese slavers. In these sanctuaries, the Guaraní developed their skills in working metal, stone, and wood to levels of artistry matching anything in Europe. In the end, however, the burgeoning Brazilian state drove out the Jesuits and the Guaraní were enslaved. From its earliest days in Latin America, the Roman Catholic Church supported the colonial authorities in return for being made the official religion and receiving the tithe—a levy on all wealth generated in the Indies. In consequence, an increasingly complacent and materialist priesthood lost touch with the poor. In 1748, one report to the Spanish king commented:

> It seems relevant to mention here what a priest from the province of Quito told us, during his visitation of this parish, in which—between feasts and memorial services for the dead—he received each year over 200 sheep, 6,000 poultry, 4,000 Indian pigs and 50,000 eggs. Nor is his parish one of the more lucrative ones.

The independence wars of the early nineteenth century threatened this cozy relationship and split the Church between pro- and anti-Spanish factions. Usually the upper echelons of the Church supported the empires, and local priests like Miguel Hidalgo and José María Morelos in Mexico went as far as taking up arms in the independence cause. Both were captured and executed. Despite these schisms, independence leaders subsequently swore allegiance to Rome, and soon came to a series of agreements with the Vatican that maintained Catholicism as the state religion. Later in the century, the Church paid the price for backing the most backward sections of the elite, usually via the conservative parties, when liberal reformers severed the Church–state relationship in Ecuador, Brazil, Cuba, Honduras, Nicaragua, Panama, Chile, and Mexico. Liberal governments limited Church control over education and confiscated its property.

The countries where the Church was disestablished later became the most fertile ground for the growth of the radical Catholic Church and the Evangelical Protestants. Anti-clericalism reached its height in post-revolutionary Mexico, where the tensions between Church and state following the Mexican Revolution of 1910–17 led the Church to suspend public worship for three years from 1926. Ninety priests were executed during the ensuing Cristero Rebellion of Church militants, whose name came from their battle cry, *"Viva Cristo Rey"* (Long Live Christ the King). A wartime speech by one Mexican general, J. B. Vargas, encapsulated the virulence of anti-clerical feeling:

> It is enough to have some idea of the terrible history of the Inquisition for one to realize that priests and cassocks reek of prostitution and crime. Confession is an industry invented to seduce maidens, to win over Catholic ladies and

San Sebastian feast day procession, Diriamba, Nicaragua. (Ben Smyth/Grand Opening)

transform fathers and husbands into chaste replicas of Saint Joseph. . . . The
Pope is a crafty foreigner who accumulates wealth in collaboration with the
exploiting Friars who swindle the foolish people for the benefit of a country
quite other than their own. . . . Nowadays, if Jesus Christ were to come down,
the first thing he would do would be to hang them like rabid dogs.

The rebellion ended when the government backed down and allowed
limited autonomy for the Church, though with greatly reduced influence.
Though Catholicism remained essentially European at the top, cultural cross-
fertilization was occurring at a local level. From the earliest days of the Conquest, many traditional indigenous beliefs and practices were incorporated
into a "folk Catholicism," where Catholic saints rub shoulders with Andean
gods in the niches and on the altars. In Bolivia's historic mining town of
Potosí, the wild baroque carvings of the San Francisco Church look distinctly
pagan. Bare-breasted goddesses are interwoven with the ubiquitous symbols
of sun and moon, and at the very top of the building an Inca warrior looks out
sternly over the city. A small, red-cheeked indigenous boy explains, "We built
this for ourselves when we Indians weren't allowed in the Cathedral." Folk
Catholicism has come in for particular criticism by the Evangelicals, who see
it as even more pagan than the pure Roman version. "We take the Cross up to

see our crops grow," says an indigenous peasant woman in Peru's Sacred Valley. "That's our belief. We worship the Catholic religion. Pachamama (Mother Earth) as well. Only the Catholics still believe in Pachamama and the Cross. The other religions, the Evangelicals, don't worship these anymore."

The Modern Church

The social turmoil of the 1930s, with broader suffrage, the beginnings of urbanization, and the rise of mass politics in the cities, brought home the growing irrelevance of the Church's traditional allies, the conservative parties and landowning elites. The Vatican began to wake up to the disastrous condition of its Latin American operation. Grown fat and lazy through its links to the rich, the Church had only the shallowest roots among the poor majority with which to confront a new era of change and mass involvement in politics. Paradoxically, in a continent where the overwhelming majority declared themselves Catholic, few went to church and the ratio of priests to parishioners was far lower than elsewhere in the Vatican's empire.

The Church embarked on a crusade, loosely termed Catholic Action, to organize its lay members and extend its influence within groups such as students, peasants, women, workers, and the middle classes. The new emphasis was on social issues, and the movement grew with the emergence of Christian Democratic parties after the Second World War. Church leaders saw such organizations as a bulwark against the expansion of communism, and religious organizations in the United States contributed funds and personnel as the Cold War gathered momentum in the 1950s. Yet, although the Church acquired renewed political influence, it failed to increase significantly the numbers of active worshippers and reduce its social isolation. In the 1960s only 20 percent of baptized Catholics regularly attended Mass, compared with 80 percent in Poland or Ireland; there was only one priest for every 5,700 believers compared to a ratio of 1:830 in the United States. In addition, the first signs of the imminent explosion of Protestant Evangelicalism were beginning to alarm the bishops.

As the 1960s wore on, events threatened to overtake the Vatican. The Cuban Revolution in 1959 and the failure of Christian Democrat governments to deliver reforms led to the radicalization of many grassroots Church workers and activists. Some student sections even split off from the Christian Democrat Party to become the nuclei of guerrilla organizations. In Colombia, a radical young priest, Camilo Torres, took up arms to fight with the National Liberation Army (ELN), declaring, "The Catholic who is not a revolutionary is living in mortal sin." Torres died in a shootout with the army in 1966.

The course of events in Latin America gave an added urgency to the Second Vatican Council, a massive shake-up ordered by Pope John XXIII to drag the worldwide Catholic Church into the modern era. In four years of meetings with 2,500 bishops from across the globe, the council charted a new direction. It changed its vertical chain of command for a looser structure based on consultation with local churches. It redirected its attention to life in the contemporary world, especially emphasizing issues like human rights, justice, freedom, and peace. The Church had a duty to pass moral judgments on the state when it contravened basic human rights.

Vatican II, as it became known, had a seismic effect on the Latin American Church, leading in 1968 to the meeting of Latin American bishops in Medellín, Colombia. Medellín took the Latin American Church far beyond Vatican II. In new teaching that embraced the newly emerging Latin American "liberation theology," it identified unjust social structures as sinful and called for radical change. Despite its fundamental focus on peace, it came close to justifying popular insurrection as a response to "institutionalized violence":

> One cannot help seeing that in many parts of Latin America there is a situation of institutionalized violence, because the actual structures violate fundamental rights and this situation demands global changes of a bold, urgent and deeply new kind. We should not be surprised that "the temptation for violence" arises in Latin America.

The bishops then went on to establish a new organizational model to implement these revolutionary new ideas. They suggested setting up Base Christian Communities (CEBs), grassroots groups of working-class or peasant Catholics who would study and reflect on the Bible and use it as a basis for

---

The God of the Poor

You are the God of the poor,
a human and a simple God.
The God who sweats in the street,
the God of the withered face.
That's why I speak to you,
just like my people speak,
because you are the worker God,
the laboring Christ.

—"Miza Campesina" (Peasant Mass) by Nicaraguan singer Carlos Mejía Godoy

Base Communities in Brazil: A Critical Perspective

Deep down, pastoral agents thought that base communities would be the spearhead of a social revolution, a social transformation, a new society. So working in base communities was a way of preparing for the new Latin American society. At that time the base communities were seen as the spearhead of the opposition. They were the alternative. People said that basic change might take time, even into the next century, but base communities were the alternative. But the laypeople who entered the base communities had no intention of engaging in social revolution or changing the Church. . . . They didn't have such vast ambitions. What they wanted was greater independence, a community life with more independence from priests. And that's still what they want, but the priests aren't interested. Laypeople do not need complicated courses, they need a "strong initial spiritual push," a very strong message. The Pentecostals do that and so do the charismatics. But if you begin with very intellectual meetings, things are going to be slow. What is required is entering into the people's psychology. It has to be a conversion moment, like the early Baptists and the Methodists.

—Phillip Berryman, *Religion in the Megacity: Catholic and Protestant Portraits from Latin America,* Maryknoll, NY: Orbis Books, 1996

action. This pastoral expression of liberation theology was called the "preferential option for the poor."

Medellín was a political and theological explosion. The Church abandoned nearly five centuries of largely cozy cohabitation with Latin America's elites in favor of an active commitment to the poor and oppressed. The picture varied enormously between countries; in Chile the Catholic Church became a center of opposition to the Pinochet dictatorship, and through its *Vicaría de la Solidaridad* played a vital role in documenting and publicizing the armed forces' violation of human rights. Radicals also gained substantial influence in Brazil and Central America, whereas the Colombian and Argentine churches remained true to their conservative past.

The CEBs became a crucible for a process known as *conscientización* (consciousness raising) whereby the poor became conscious of injustice and organized to change their lives. As one Salvadoran peasant leader recalls, many went on to lead social movements or even guerrilla organizations:

What made me first join the farmworkers' union was when I compared the conditions we were living in with those that I saw in the Scriptures; the situation of the Israelites for example . . . where Moses had to struggle to take them out of Egypt to the Promised Land . . . then I compared it with the situation of slavery in which we were living. Our struggle is the same: Moses and his people had to cross the desert, as we are crossing one right now, and for me, I find that we are crossing a desert full of a thousand hardships, of hunger, misery and exploitation.

—JENNY PEARCE, *Promised Land*

CEBs treated the Bible as a manual for action. The story of Jesus throwing out the moneylenders acquired enormous political impact when brought up to date through a CEB Bible study group. The groups also had a democratizing effect, since the shortage of priests meant that many groups were led by local lay catechists, both men and women, many of whom went on to become popular leaders in their own right. One of them was Rigoberta Menchú, a Guatemalan indigenous woman who became a peasant leader and went on to win the Nobel Peace Prize in 1992. In her autobiography, *I, Rigoberta Menchú*, she describes the impact of becoming a catechist:

> When I first became a catechist, I thought that there was a God and that we had to serve him. I thought that God was up there and that he had a kingdom for the poor. But we realized that it is not God's will that we should live in suffering, that God did not give us that destiny, but that men on earth have imposed this suffering, poverty, misery and discrimination on us.

CEBs took firmest root in Brazil, where they were instrumental in starting the protest movement that helped to drive the military government from power in 1985. They also formed an essential part of the social movements that went on to challenge for power through the Workers' Party (PT). They played a vital role in Nicaragua, where the radical Church supported the insurrection that overthrew the Somoza dictatorship. In El Salvador, the CEBs were at the forefront of the upsurge in the protest movement that ended in a bloodbath in the early 1980s and a prolonged civil war.

Yet the Church paid a high price for its "option for the poor." Within the Church hierarchy, conservative bishops began to backtrack on the Medellín commitments almost as soon as the conference was over. With the advent, in 1978, of Pope John Paul II, an uncompromisingly anti-Communist Polish prelate, the backtracking in Rome was quickly transformed into a full-blooded hue and cry against the perils of liberation theology. It led to the marginalization, investigation, and silencing of its leading clerical figures; it brought two formal Vatican documents fiercely critical of liberation theology and its exponents, both under the signature of Joseph Ratzinger, today Pope Benedict XVI. There was additionally the disowning of the "popular Church" and the expulsion from their religious orders of three progressive priests who had taken ministerial posts in Nicaragua's revolutionary Sandinista government. The Vatican counterattack was intense and resonated well with U.S. policy in Latin America under President Ronald Reagan.

The progressive Church also became a target for military repression. "Be a patriot, kill a priest," ran one death-squad slogan in El Salvador in the late 1970s. Dozens of clerics were killed, the most celebrated being Archbishop Oscar Romero, shot while saying Mass in the capital, San Salvador, in 1980, and six Jesuit leaders, together with their housekeeper and her daughter, all gunned down in 1989. An even greater slaughter awaited the lay preachers, who died in the hundreds. As a result, the Salvadorean CEB movement was devastated.

By the mid-1980s, doubts were starting to surface among radical Catholics about the effectiveness of the CEBs. Field research revealed that most CEB members were not the poorest but often had steady jobs, and that many were much less socially active than had been imagined. Other studies suggested that the numbers had been greatly exaggerated: instead of the two million active CEB members routinely claimed for Brazil in the mid-1980s, 250,000 seems a more realistic estimate. In Latin America as a whole, CEBs only existed in a maximum of 10 percent of parishes, and even there such communities were small islands in a sea of Catholics that the Church scarcely touched.

The research also showed that, far from representing a lasting handover of power from the Church hierarchy to the laity, successful CEBs were heavily dependent on the goodwill of sympathetic bishops, the active involvement of priests and nuns at the local level, and funding from a range of foreign (usually European) agencies.

Partly, the CEBs were a victim of their own success in forging generations of leaders for the new grassroots social movements. As those movements took off, many of the most dynamic CEB leaders went with them. In Brazil, large numbers of the best CEB activists devoted themselves to building up the Workers' Party; in Nicaragua, the Sandinista Revolution had a similar effect on a hitherto dynamic CEB movement. In the twenty-five years of John Paul's papacy, the Latin American Church leadership was transformed, gradually and systematically, from a socially committed and pastorally audacious episcopacy into a rather cautious conservative body hugely dependent once more on the word from Rome. The mechanism was the Vatican's most potent weapon—the power to appoint bishops. Every single bishop is appointed by the Vatican from a short list provided by the local Papal Nuncio, the Vatican's ambassador. Anyone openly sympathetic to a liberation theology view of the world and the Church was simply barred from consideration.

That said, once the Cold War was over in the 1990s, the Catholic hierarchy was freed from anti-Communist preoccupations, enabling it to take on

Archbishop Romero of El Salvador

The progressive Catholic Church's most famous martyr, Oscar Arnulfo Romero, was an essentially conservative man who was radicalized by his contact with El Salvador's poor and the worsening violence of the army and its associated death squads. As Archbishop of San Salvador, Romero publicly attacked both the economic system and human rights abuses in weekly sermons that were picked up on dilapidated radios in peasant huts and shantytowns throughout the country.

On the economy:

"The cause of all our ills is the oligarchy—that handful of families who care nothing for the hunger of the people but need that hunger in order to have cheap, abundant labor to raise and export their crops."

On violence:

"Profound religion leads to political commitment, and in a country such as ours where injustice reigns, conflict is inevitable.... Christians have no fear of combat; they know how to fight but they prefer to speak the language of peace. Nevertheless, when a dictatorship violates human rights and attacks the common good of the nation, when it becomes unbearable and closes all channels of dialogue, of understanding, of rationality: when this happens, the Church speaks of the legitimate right of insurrectional violence."

On 23 March 1980 he signed his death warrant by appealing directly to the soldiers carrying out attacks:

"In the name of God, and in the name of this suffering people whose laments rise to heaven every day more tumultuous, I beg you, I ask you, I order you in the name of God: Stop the repression."

The next day he was killed with a single shot while saying Mass at a local hospital chapel.

many demands formerly put forward by the progressive Church, particularly in response to the social impact of neoliberal reforms. The idolatry of the market and the unacceptable face of globalized capitalism became a regular part of Rome's discourse and were echoed and amplified in Latin America. "Neoliberal capitalism carries injustice and inequality in its genetic code," proclaimed Honduran Cardinal Oscar Rodríguez. In 1995, Latin America's bishops concluded, "We cannot remain indifferent to the extreme poverty, growing unemployment, uncontainable violence, and corruption and impunity that sink millions of families in anguish and pain." But by then the grassroots movements, which might have given teeth to such statements, were in decline.

Brazil's Universal Church of the Kingdom of God

Latin America's fastest-growing Evangelical church was established in 1978 by Bishop Edir Macedo, a former lottery-ticket vendor. It now owns a weekly newspaper with a circulation of 700,000, a TV network, and dozens of radio stations. Its churches operate in 35 countries worldwide. The Universal Church's annual income is estimated at US$750 million, on a par with Volkswagen Brazil.

The Church runs two-hour services that focus on different issues each day: family problems, health and sickness, prosperity, the presence of the Holy Spirit, and the expulsion of demons. Macedo claims to have cured AIDS and brought people fortune. He has certainly made himself rich—he is a brilliant fund-raiser. Tithes are seen as proof of belief. In one of his many books for the faithful, he cites famous people who have paid tithes and become millionaires, such as "Senhor Colgate, Senhor Ford and Senhor Caterpilar."

When John Paul II died early in 2005, the ensuing speculation about his successor was in great part focused on Latin American figures who were *"papabile."* Brazilian, Honduran, Mexican, Argentine, and Chilean cardinals of very different hues in theology and pastoral practice were certainly in the frame. It looked for a brief moment as if the Latin American Church might actually inherit the kingdom. But it was not to be—at least not for the time being.

Benedict XVI, the current pontiff, is from Germany and the former head of the Vatican's doctrinal watchdog agency. He has had only limited contact with Latin America, much of it in adversarial combat with its progressive thinkers. So far, his energies have been focused on Europe and his first and so far only trip to Latin America—to Brazil in 2007—was fairly low-key. As expected, he spoke out strongly against abortion.

A New Reformation

One of the principal causes of the disillusionment with the CEBs was the meteoric rise of the Pentecostal Protestant churches over the same period. Evangelicals, as they are commonly called in Latin America, are "born-again" Christians committed to converting others to their own brand of Christianity. Evangelical services typically involve rhythmic clapping, chanting, and swaying, leading to a cathartic mass euphoria. The Pentecostals believe that true Christians are taken over by the Holy Spirit during religious gatherings, culminating in speaking in tongues and faith healing. The name comes from a biblical reference to the Day of the Pentecost, when Jesus's disciples were visited by the Holy Spirit and received the "gift of tongues" to enable them to preach and evangelize in other languages.

The tide of Pentecostalism has rapidly swamped the traditional Protestant churches of Latin America, such as the Lutherans and Presbyterians. These are small groups generally set up by immigrants from northern Europe, and have largely middle-class congregations. In 1936, Pentecostals represented just 2 percent of Central American Protestants; by the turn of the century they exceeded 90 percent.

With the exception of the Assemblies of God, which have at least eight million worshippers in Brazil alone, the Evangelical movement in Latin America is divided up into innumerable separate churches, disparagingly labeled "sects" by their opponents. Often these are the personal vehicle of a single pastor. When a congregation grows, it will often splinter into new churches. Although this reduces the coherence and influence of the movement as a whole, it means that Evangelical churches remain rooted in their communities. Pastors display a zeal rarely encountered in their Catholic counterparts. In the middle of a war zone in Nicaragua in the 1980s, Evangelical pastors could be found three days from the nearest road, walking between peasant huts in search of converts. The Catholic Church was nowhere to be seen.

The social message of the Evangelicals is one of individualism, hard work, and sobriety. Evangelical pastors are fiercely hostile to collective organizations such as trade unions. Critics, especially radical Catholics, have accused them of encouraging political passivity that only benefits the powerful and denies the poor the ability to organize to improve their lot. Evangelicals respond that their focus on immediate steps such as giving up drink and working hard actually has more immediate impact than the search for long-term social change. The proof is that Evangelical churches are far more popular than the Catholic Church among the poorest communities. As one famously barbed quote from a Brazilian Baptist pastor put it, "The Catholic Church opted for the poor, but the poor opted for the Evangelicals."

In any case, Evangelicals believe that true salvation lies in an individual's relationship to God; as one Costa Rican group sings, "I've got nothing in this world, but a mansion in the next." Carlos Chávez, a 46-year-old Evangelical of the Elim Church in San Salvador, explains: "The Lord changes the Evangelical's life. He makes him more patient, more passive, more humble, more loving, more centered in what he does." Carlos showed a typically Evangelical view of El Salvador's bloody civil war:

The war is the fulfillment of the prophecies—the Lord told his disciples there would be wars, plagues, famines and earthquakes, and these would be signs of his coming. As Evangelicals, the war doesn't torment us, it brings us joy, because it's a sign that Jesus is coming soon. We don't intervene in the conflict. What we do is pray to God that things should change. Today God's people don't struggle with arms, but with prayer.

This essentially conservative message contrasts with the more progressive doctrines gradually being adopted by many of the traditional Protestant churches. Grouped together in the Latin American Council of Churches (CLAI), these older groups have built ecumenical links with the more progressive Catholic Church, although not endorsing the full content of liberation theology. The CLAI has attempted to turn Protestant attention to issues such as the drug war and the debt crisis, but remains a small voice with very limited influence.

Protestant preachers and TV broadcasts tap into the anxieties of life in modern Latin America—health, jobs, crime, and family breakdown. Many writers connect the rise of Protestantism to urbanization. Peasant migration to the cities severs an individual's links to the community, resulting in isolation and confusion. In such circumstances, Evangelicalism can offer both a supportive community and a strong sense of purpose and identity. The emphasis on sobriety is particularly attractive to many women whose partners have alcohol problems.

The most recent and fastest-growing Pentecostals have also left behind the more austere side of Protestantism, absorbing the practices of popular religion that were often abandoned by embarrassed Catholic priests in the aftermath of Medellín. In Brazil particularly, the use of faith healing, magic, holy water, song, dance, and possession shows the Pentecostals' readiness to adopt the trappings of the Afro-Brazilian religions, even as they vilify them as devil worship. To the outsider, Bishop Macedo's exorcist priests bear a remarkable resemblance to their counterparts in Candomblé.

African religions and Evangelicals are often in conflict, yet increasingly share similar methods. In Honduras, Evangelicals have made inroads among the black *garifuna* community (descendants of the original Carib people), urging them to abandon their traditional religion. But the converts find the Evangelical services familiar. "I used to dance for the world, now I can do it for the Lord," explains one teenager.

In countries with large black communities, African spiritist religions are on the rise, despite the efforts of the Evangelicals. Edilson is a *pai de santo*, or Candomblé priest, in Brazil's black capital of Salvador, center of the former slave trade. He operates from his house in a well-established *favela*, with two rooms devoted to Candomblé, the fascinating hybrid of African and Catholic influences. In the first room, Christ and the saints hang alongside Candomblé's African gods, or *orixás*, faceless figures of beaten copper. A set of conga drums and a large urn of holy water also stand by ready for ceremonies that combine drumming, drinking, and possession by any one of the pantheon of *orixás* (deities). In the second room, known as the "room of the slave," Edilson intones a prayer in the African Yoruba language before entering to sprinkle cane spirit, or *cachaça*, over the altar and light a candle. "People come to purify themselves when they're sick or have spiritual problems," he explains. "The Evangelicals are always speaking against us," he adds, "but the Catholics are more ready to coexist—many people here have two religions."

Figures on the Protestant explosion should always be treated with caution. The Protestant churches often exaggerate them, while the Catholic Church suffers an equal tendency to minimize them. However, many sources accept that since the 1960s the number of Protestants in Latin America has risen sixteen-fold to 80 million. Although 80 million people represents only about 14 percent of the total population, and most of the rest describe themselves as Roman Catholics, virtually all Protestants are active churchgoers, whereas the rate among Catholics may be as low as 15 percent. In terms of active participation, Protestants may already outnumber Catholics in several countries. A survey carried out in 2009 in Brazil, the largest Catholic country in the world, suggested that, with the number of Catholics steadily dropping and Pentecostalism growing strongly, Pentecostalism could overtake Catholicism as the largest religious affiliation by 2020.

A further source of confusion over the figures is the growing fluidity of people's religious affiliations. One recent study in Costa Rica showed that there were almost as many ex-Evangelicals as current ones. Two-thirds of those leaving returned to the Catholic Church. Others happily shopped around, worshipping at both Catholic and Protestant churches during the course of a week, as well as moving regularly between different Pentecostal denominations.

Evangelicals in Politics

Although the growth of the Evangelical churches has fed on social chaos, suffering and the divisions within the Catholic Church, other factors promoting its growth have attracted severe criticism from progressives of both Catholic and Protestant backgrounds. The Latin American Evangelical movement is financed and heavily influenced by right-wing Evangelical groups in the United States that have sent thousands of missionaries, run aid projects that also serve as recruitment drives, and trained new generations of local pastors to spread the word. "Televangelical" preachers like Jimmy Swaggart and Pat

Robertson are household names in many Latin American nations, where the resources of the multimillion-dollar Bible Belt TV and radio chains buy hours of airtime. A new breed of U.S.-based Spanish-speaking "super preachers," such as Argentina's Luis Palau and Spanish Harlem's Luis Cortés, has now joined their ranks.

Suspicions that U.S. televangelists' agenda in Latin America might not be purely spiritual were heightened in 2005, when Pat Robertson suggested on his TV channel that the United States should assassinate Venezuelan president Hugo Chávez. Although some radical Catholics claim the Evangelical movement is entirely funded and controlled by Washington, many local sects have few ties to the United States, and the astonishing speed of their expansion shows that they meet a real spiritual and social need in the region.

The Pentecostal Church itself has so far shown little interest in politics, with some isolated exceptions to both left and right. Guatemala has provided both Latin America's first Pentecostal dictator, General Ríos Montt (1982–83), and civilian president, Jorge Serrano (although he was forced into exile after trying to seize power in 1993). Even there, however, the fragmented and apolitical nature of the Pentecostals means that the Catholic Church remains a much more powerful political force. In many ways, the Evangelical churches are a more genuine "church of the poor" than their Catholic rival, and they could undergo the same kind of radical political conversion as occurred within the Roman Catholic Church in the 1960s. There are a few signs of isolated changes of this kind. In Chiapas, where Protestants suffered violence and expulsion from indigenous communities at the hands of local bosses of the ruling PRI, Evangelicals came out in support of the Zapatista uprising in 1994, and there have been some high-ranking Evangelicals in Brazil's Workers' Party, such as Benedita da Silva, the country's first black woman senator, who went on to become Minister for Social Welfare in the early years of the Lula government, and Marina Silva, who was Lula's Minister of the Environment (until she resigned in 2008).

In the religious melting pot of today's Latin America, systems of belief and ritual are ever more fluid and intertwined. The disparate influences of Africa, Europe, and indigenous traditions that have so shaped the region's culture are seen equally at work in the religious sphere, producing a range of hybrid religions that are uniquely Latin American.

In this uncertain world, the Catholic Church must fight a war on at least two fronts. First, it must contend with growing secularization, as increasing numbers of Latin Americans, particularly in the middle class, abandon religion altogether. Second, if it does not find a way to revive its withered grassroots and reconnect with the lives of ordinary Latin Americans, it will continue to lose ground to Protestant Evangelicals.

Conclusion

Latin America is in ferment. The signs of modernity and change are everywhere. The Internet, TV, and public transport have transformed the lifestyles and aspirations of all but the most isolated communities. The sharp hustling world of the city has replaced the slow seasonal cycle of rural life. Politically, the region's depressing round of dictatorship and democracy has been replaced by an unprecedented degree of political stability and civilian government. A Catholic continent is going through a breakneck process of conversion to Pentecostal Protestantism.

In the 1990s a battery of external influences—including the IMF, northern governments, and international capital markets—frog-marched the region down the road to unregulated "savage capitalism," an implausible remedy for the continent's social and economic ills. But in the aftermath of the end (outside Colombia) of the guerrilla wars and the collapse of communism, a new generation of center-left political parties and leaders emerged that now govern in South America (with the exception once again of Colombia and, more recently, of Chile). Progress has finally been made in tackling the region's age-old ills, including the shocking problem of economic apartheid, a yawning gap between rich and poor. Indeed, in many countries there have been real advances in the alleviation of extreme poverty.

But scratch the surface, and evidence will be found of continuity beneath the froth of change. Old evils are alive and well, such as the persistence of clientelistic political parties, police and judicial corruption, scarce regard for human rights, and the refusal by the elites to allow local communities to have a say in their own development. But other continuities provide grounds for optimism. Latin America's extraordinary ability to absorb and transform outside influences remains undimmed. Ever since the Conquest, foreign invasions, be they cultural, political, or religious, have been steadily "Latin Americanized" into distinctive syntheses of traditional and modern. All over the region people show a remarkable capacity for creative innovation, often harnessed to promote political change. Just as much as the Arab world, Latin

America has latched on to the possibilities offered by the digital revolution for mobilization.

However, this energy must be more effectively tapped if the squandering of the region's vast wealth is to end. In their mad scramble to achieve high rates of economic growth, governments are exporting oil, coal, iron ore, zinc, silver, soybeans, sugar, and timber, without counting the true cost to local people and the environment. Mineral and oil wealth will be eventually exhausted, quite soon in some countries. Environmental degradation, exacerbated by climate change, is already threatening the region's rich farming lands and its extraordinary biodiversity. As yet, the region's new political leaders have failed to construct a truly sustainable and equitable model of development. While successfully alleviating extreme poverty and reducing inequality, the recent social measures do not add up to a coherent alternative to neoliberalism. Huge challenges, made more difficult by growing social discontent, lie ahead.

Yet it is the very vibrancy of these grassroots community groups that offers some hope for the future. The range of players is impressive—women's organizations, shantytown movements, peasant groups, indigenous federations, trade unions, environmental movements. These movements ebb and flow, not always prospering under progressive governments, which often find it difficult to accommodate their demands. But it is their pressure that keeps alive the hope that governments will eventually speed up the pace of reform and put the well-being of ordinary citizens at the heart of their policymaking.

Chronologies

Part 1: The Curse of Wealth: Economics

1493   Columbus introduces sugarcane in Hispaniola.

1545   Silver discovered in Cerro Rico, Potosí.

1690s   Brazilian gold rush begins in Minas Gerais.

1808–26   Latin American independence: Britain takes over from Spain as the major trading partner and foreign power.

1922   Venezuela strikes oil.

1929   Wall Street crash and ensuing depression in the United States and Europe pushes Latin America into industrialization.

1930s   Great Depression: collapse of commodity prices.

1938   Nationalization of Mexican oil industry.

1958   Brazil becomes Latin America's leading industrial power.

1973–74   First oil price rise leads to wave of loans to Latin America. Foreign debt soars.

Early 80s   Beginning of cocaine boom .

1982   Mexico defaults on interest payments on its foreign debt, swiftly followed by most other Latin American governments. Start of debt crisis and two decades of neoliberal reforms, including renewed emphasis on commodity exports.

1982–91   Latin America pays a net US$219 billion in debt repayments to the north: US$500 for every Latin American.

Late 1980s   Neoliberal reforms gather pace throughout Latin America.

1989   Announcement of austerity package in Venezuela provokes riots in which at least 276 people die.

1994   Start of the North American Free Trade Agreement (NAFTA) between Mexico, the United States, and Canada enables Mexican economy to become effectively cheap labor addition to United States, reducing its dependence on commodity exports. Mexican currency crisis and subsequent economic recession raises fresh doubts over neoliberal model.

1995	Start of Mercosur, or Southern Cone Common Market, composed of Argentina, Brazil, Uruguay, and Paraguay.
2001–2	Crisis engulfs Argentine economy.
2001–3	One-third of Mexico's *maquiladoras* (assembly plants) relocate to China.
2002	44 percent of Latin Americans (221 million people) living in poverty.
2003	Annual wholesale value of U.S. cocaine market reaches $35 billion. Latin America is sole supplier. Only oil is worth more.
2005	Global commodity price boom due to Chinese demand boosts Latin American growth.
2008	33 percent of Latin Americans living in poverty.
2011	Latin America grows by 6 percent, the best result for three decades.

Part 2: Ballots and Bullets: The State, the Military, and Politics

1808–26	Wars of independence free Spanish America from colonial rule.
1889	Brazil abolishes the monarchy and becomes a republic
1910–17	Mexican Revolution.
1926	Augusto César Sandino returns to Nicaragua to begin a guerrilla war against occupying U.S. forces.
1928	*Caudillo* General Plutarco Calles establishes the National Revolutionary Party (later the PRI) in Mexico; the PRI goes on to establish an effective one-party state.
1930s	Urbanization and industrialization produce new political parties, led by populists.
1939–45	Second World War establishes United States as dominant military power in Latin America.
1946	Juan Domingo Perón elected president of Argentina
1948	Costa Rica abolishes army.
1949	Brazilian Higher War School founded, becoming central to spread of Cold War national security doctrine.
1958	The two main parties in both Venezuela and Colombia agree to share power in order to end decades of instability and military rule.
1959	Cuban Revolution marks first successful guerrilla campaign and leads to wave of *foquista* guerrilla insurgencies throughout Latin America. This is seen by military as proof of international communist conspiracy.
1964	Military seize power in Brazil and rule for 25 years. The coup marks beginning of wave of military takeovers.

1967	Death of Che Guevara in Bolivia.
1968	Medellín conference of Latin American bishops galvanizes the left by creating Base Christian Communities across the region.
1970	Peru's Shining Path movement founded in remote Andean province. In Chile, Salvador Allende becomes the world's first elected Marxist president.
1973	Allende murdered during the military coup that brings General Pinochet to power.
1976	Argentina's military seize power.
End 1976	At least two-thirds of people on mainland Latin America live under dictatorial rule.
1979	Sandinista-led insurrection in Nicaragua becomes second guerrilla victory in the Americas. Founding of Brazilian Workers' Party (PT), based on the support of the "new social movements."
1980s	Civil wars in El Salvador and Guatemala marked byunprecedented human rights abuses by military. United States backs Contras in proxy war against Sandinista government.
1982	Argentina loses Falklands/Malvinas war, military government falls and democracy returns; senior officers subsequently imprisoned on human rights charges.
1989	Chile's Christian Democrats lead coalition that wins elections to end Pinochet presidency. General Stroessner ousted in Paraguay. U.S. invasion of Panama. Fall of Berlin Wall marks end of Cold War; difficult times ahead for military in Latin America, and identity crisis on left.
1990	Sandinistas voted from power in presidential elections
1990	Chile's General Pinochet becomes the last of the military dictators to leave office.
1992	Peace agreement in El Salvador following military stalemate between army and guerrillas. Military removed from politics.
1994	Zapatista uprising in Chiapas, Mexico. U.S. troops intervene to oust military government in Haiti.
1998	Hugo Chávez elected president in Venezuela.
2000	PRI loses in Mexican elections after 71 years in power.
2002	Lula and the Workers' Party (PT) win Brazilian presidential elections, beginning center-left realignment across the region.
2005	Every Latin American country except Cuba and Haiti ruled by elected leader.
2005	Colombia only country in South America with an avowedly pro-U.S. right-wing president.

2011   CELAC is created, the first important political organization to
              represent Latin America and the Caribbean without the pres-
              ence of the United States and Canada.

Part 3: Land, the City, and Environment

1519–35   Spanish Conquest: colonizers introduce new animals and
              crops and take back to Europe novelties such as tomatoes,
              maize, tobacco, and potatoes; Spanish hand out land and
              forced labor to their officers through the *encomienda* system.
1538   First slaves brought from Africa to work Latin America's sugar
              plantations.
1881   Communal land ownership by indigenous peasants banned in
              El Salvador, enabling coffee plantations to expand onto indig-
              enous lands.
1899   United Fruit establishes a monopoly over Central American
              banana production.
1917   Beginning of Mexican land reform, the greatest in Latin
              American history.
1920   First shantytowns recorded in Rio de Janeiro.
1930s   Industrialization leads to explosion of shantytowns and
              environmental deterioration in cities. Start of industrialization
              leads to mass migration to the cities.
1950   41.2 percent of Latin Americans live in towns.
1950s   Expansion of commercial agriculture throughout Latin
              America.
1952   Bolivian Revolution redistributes land and ends the near feu-
              dal status of indigenous "serfs."
1959   Cuban Revolution: state farms take over sugar production.
1960   500 people invade land in Lima to found the Cuevas settle-
              ment.
1961   Washington launches Alliance for Progress, which supports
              land reform programs throughout Latin America.
1964   Military coup in Brazil: new government promotes agro-ex-
              ports and the colonization of the Amazon basin.
1966   Brazil's military government unveils Operation Amazonia to
              colonize and industrially develop the rain forest.
1970   Population of Cuevas settlement in Lima reaches 12,000.
1978   Argentine military government bulldozes shantytowns in
              cleanup campaign before World Cup.
1979   Nicaraguan Revolution: half of the country's farming land is
              included in a land reform.

1980	64.7 percent of Latin Americans live in towns. Brazilian government decrees tax incentives for enterprises taking part in the Grande Carajas development program.
1980s	500,000 gold prospectors pour into the Amazon, bringing disease and destruction to the Yanomami people.
1982–	Under pressure from debt crisis, governments try to increase agro-exports, in many cases by giving more power to large landowners. Debt crisis and ensuing neoliberal reforms lead to massive rise in informal sector.
1984	Brazil's Landless Workers Movement (MST) founded. Opening of giant Itaipú dam between Brazil, Argentina, and Paraguay.
1988	Chico Mendes, leader of Amazon rubber-tappers, assassinated by landowners.
1990	Chilean government declares first ever "environmental state of emergency" in Santiago.
1992	World Summit on the Environment and Development held in Rio de Janeiro.
1994	Zapatista uprising in Chiapas, prompted by government's attempts to privatize communal landholdings.
1998	90 percent of all soybeans grown in Argentina are genetically modified (GM).
2005	Less than a quarter of Latin Americans live in the countryside, more than half of them below the poverty line.
2008	Total remittances from Latin Americans living abroad come to $69 billion, more than foreign investment and aid combined.
2010	A fifth of the Amazon rain forest has been destroyed by cumulative deforestation, an area twice the size of France.

Part 4: Identity and Rights

c. 30,000 BCE	First people reach the Americas across the Bering Straits from Asia.
1492	Columbus arrives in the Americas, to be met by the friendly Arawak people.
1519	Cortés invades Mexico with 600 men.
1535	Pizarro completes conquest of Inca Empire.
Mid-16th c.	Arawak population of the Caribbean extinct within 50 years of Columbus's arrival.
1781	Tupác Amaru II lays seige to Cusco, the former Inca capital, in indigenous rebellion; Amaru captured and executed.
1930s–	Mechanization of agriculture and growth of cities encourages young women to migrate from the countryside to the towns.

1960s	Officials of Brazil's government agency for indigenous people use poison, machine guns, and disease to "clear" land for large landowners.
1961	Paraguay becomes last Latin American country to give women the vote.
1971	U.S. Peace Corps expelled from Bolivia, accused of sterilizing indigenous women without their knowledge.
1975–85	UN Decade for Women encourages some improved legislation on gender issues.
1975	Cuban government passes law making child care and house-work equal responsibility of men and women.
Late 1970s	Women in Brazil's Cost of Living Movement lead opposition to military rule.
1976–83	Argentina's Mothers of the Disappeared lead opposition to military rule, inspiring similar movements in Central America and the Andes.
1979	Nicaraguan Revolution: women head health ministry and police and government bans use of women's bodies in advertising.
1982 on	Debt crisis and neoliberal reforms make life harder for women.
1982–83	In Guatemala, 400 indigenous villages destroyed, 40,000 killed in counterinsurgency operations .
1990	Violeta Chamorro wins Nicaraguan presidential elections.
1992	Indigenous groups throughout the Americas condemn the official celebrations of the quincentenary of Columbus's arrival in the Americas. Rigoberta Menchú wins Nobel Peace Prize.
1993	Proportion of female-headed households now stands at one in five across Latin America.
1994	Indigenous rebels from Mayan groups lead Zapatista uprising in Chiapas. In Ecuador, indigenous organizations cut off cities in protest at economic structural adjustment measures.
1995	New quota rules in Argentina ensure that one in four congress members is a woman: one of the highest proportions in the world.
2000	Alejandro Toledo elected president of Peru, after stressing his indigenous origins during the campaign to oust Alberto Fujimori.
2003	Average Latin American woman has 2.5 children, down from 6 in the 1950s.
2006	Evo Morales inaugurated as Bolivian president, the first indigenous head of state in South America.
2008	Ecuador becomes the first nation in the world to grant "in-

alienable rights" to nature in its constitution.

2010   Dilma Rousseff elected as Brazil's first female president.

Part 5: Culture and Religion

1494   In the Treaty of Tordesillas the Vatican divides up the New
            World between Spain and Portugal.

1826 on   Independence leaders sign concordats with the Vatican, main-
            taining Catholicism as the state religion.

1896   First motion picture shown in Buenos Aires.

1910–17   Mexican Revolution begins attempt to construct a new mes-
            tizo consciousness, especially through the work of muralists
            such as Diego Rivera.

1923   Brazilian government sets up country's first radio station,
            which soon bows to popular demand for broadcasts of samba
            music.

1926–29   Mexican Church suspends public worship to protest at state
            harassment. Ninety priests executed during the Cristero Re-
            bellion.

1959   Cuban Revolution promotes attempt to build a radical and
            distinctive Latin American cultural movement.

1960s–   Evangelical Protestant churches begin to expand rapidly
            throughout Latin America.

1962–65   Second Vatican Council commits the Church to work for hu-
            man rights, justice, and freedom.

Mid-1960s   First telenovelas broadcast in Brazil and Mexico.

1967   Gabriel García Márquez publishes *One Hundred Years of Soli-
            tude*, which sells more than 20 million copies worldwide.

1968   Latin American bishops, meeting in Medellín, Colombia,
            adopt a "preferential option for the poor."

1971   Cuban government arrests the dissident poet Heberto Padilla.

1973   Singer Víctor Jara killed by the army following military coup
            in Chile.

1978   John Paul II becomes Pope and leads conservative offensive
            within Church against liberation theology.

1979   Nicaraguan Revolution provides state support for poets and
            artists.

1980   Assassination of radical Archbishop Oscar Romero of San
            Salvador.

1982   General Efraín Ríos Montt seizes power in Guatemala, becom-
            ing the region's first evangelical dictator. García Márquez wins
            Nobel Prize for Literature.

1989	In El Salvador, the army assassinates six Jesuit priests, their housekeeper and her daughter, leading to the withdrawal of U.S. support for the military and the end of the civil war.
1990	Peruvian novelist Mario Vargas Llosa loses presidential election to Alberto Fujimori.
1991	Guatemala's Jorge Serrano becomes the region's first elected Evangelical President.
1992	Columbus quincentenary prompts continent-wide soul searching. Televisa's soap *The Rich Also Weep* takes Russia by storm.
1994	Zapatista rebels in Chiapas use the Internet to bypass government censorship .
1996	90 percent of Latin Americans have access to a TV set.
2005	Pope John Paul II dies, to be replaced by even more conservative Pope Benedict XVI.
2010	No letup in sight for Latin American progressive Church. Estimated number of Protestants rises to 80 million, from 5 million in 1970. 216 million Latin Americans, 36 percent of the population, have access to Internet.

Further Reading

SECTION 1: THE CURSE OF WEALTH: ECONOMICS

Eduardo Galeano, *Open Veins of Latin America,* New York: Monthly Review Press, 2000.

Duncan Green, *Silent Revolution: The Rise and Crisis of Market Economics in Latin America* (second edition), London: Latin America Bureau, 2003.

Jon Hellin and Sophie Higman, *Feeding the Market: South American Farmers, Trade and Globalization,* London: ITDG publishing, 2003.

Gabriel García Marquez, *One Hundred Years of Solitude,* London: Jonathan Cape, 1970.

Miguel Leon-Portillo, *The Broken Spears: The Aztec Account of the Conquest of Mexico,* Boston: Beacon Press, 1992.

Nick Rowling, *Commodities: How the World Was Taken to Market,* London: Free Association Books, 1987.

Rosemary Thorp, *Economic History of Latin America* in *The Twentieth Century: Progress, Exclusion and Poverty,* Baltimore: Johns Hopkins University Press, 1998.

Timothy A. Wise, Hilda Salazar, and Laura Carlsen, *Confronting Globalization: Economic Integration and Popular Resistance in Mexico,* Bloomfield, CT: Kumarian Press, 2003.

SECTION 2: BALLOTS AND BULLETS: THE STATE, THE MILITARY, AND POLITICS

Jon Lee Anderson, *Che Guevara: A Revolutionary Life,* New York: Grove Press, 1997.

Edward L Cleary, *The Struggle for Human Rights in Latin America,* New York: Praeger, 1997.

John Crabtree, *Patterns of Protest: Politics and Social Movements in Bolivia,* London: Latin America Bureau, 2005.

Andres Jaroslavsky, The *Future of Memory: Children of the Dictatorship* in *Argentina Speak,* London: Latin America Bureau, 2004.

Elizabeth Jelin, *State Repression and the Struggles for Memory*, London: Latin America Bureau, 2003.

Subcomandante Marcos, *Our Word is Our Weapon*, London: Serpent's Tail, 2001.

Hugh O'Shaughnessy, *Pinochet: The Politics of Torture*, London: Latin America Bureau, 1999.

Thomas E. Skidmore and Peter H. Smith, *Modern Latin America*, Oxford: Oxford University Press, 2000.

SECTION 3: LAND, THE CITY, AND ENVIRONMENT

Sue Branford and Jan Rocha, *Cutting the Wire: The Story of the Brazilian Landless Workers' Movement*, London: Latin America Bureau, 2002.

Binka Breton, *Trapped: Modern-Day Slavery in the Brazilian Amazon*, London: Latin America Bureau, 2003.

Alan Gilbert, *The Latin American City*, London: Latin America Bureau, 1998.

Duncan Green, *Hidden Lives: Voices of Children in Latin America and the Caribbean*, London: Latin America Bureau, 1997.

Susana Hecht and Alexander Cockburn, *The Fate of the Forest: Developers, Destroyers and Defenders of the Amazon*, London: Penguin, 1990.

Chico Mendes, *Fight for the Forest: Chico Mendes in His Own Words*, London: Latin America Bureau, 1992.

J.J. Thomas, *Surviving in the City: The Urban Informal Sector in Latin America*, London: Pluto Press, 1995.

Bill Weinberg, *War on the Land: Ecology and Politics in Central America*, London: Zed Books, 1991.

SECTION 4: IDENTITY AND RIGHTS

Sylvia Chant with Nikki Craske, *Gender in Latin America*, London: Latin America Bureau, 2002.

Edward L. Cleary, *The Struggle for Human Rights in Latin America*, New York: Praeger, 1997.

John Crabtree, *Patterns of Protest: Politics and Social Movements in Bolivia*, London: Latin America Bureau, 2005.

Eduardo Galeano, *Open Veins of Latin America*, New York: Monthly Review Press, 2000.

Ian Lumsden, *Machos, Maricones and Gays in Cuba: Cuba and Homosexuality*, London: Latin America Bureau, 1996.

Rigoberta Menchu and Elisabeth Burgos Debray, ed., *I, Rigoberta Menchu*, London: Verso, 1984.

Patrick Neate and Damian Platt, *Culture is our Weapon: AfroReggae in the Favelas of Rio*, London: Latin America Bureau, 2006.

Lynne Stephen, *Women and Social Movements in Latin America,* London: Latin America Bureau, 1997.

Peter Wade, *Race and Ethnicity in Latin America,* London: Pluto Press, 1997.

Philip Wearne, *Return of the Indian,* London: Latin America Bureau, 1996.

SECTION 5: CULTURE AND RELIGION

Philip Berryman, *Religion in the Megacity: Catholic and Protestant Portraits from Latin America,* London: Latin America Bureau, 1996.

Alma Guillermoprieto, *Samba,* London: Bloomsbury, 1990.

Alma Guillermoprieto, *The Heart that Bleeds: Latin America Now,* New York: Knopf, 1994.

Alberto Elena and Marina Diaz Lopez, eds., *The Cinema of Latin America,* London: Wallflower Press, 2003.

John King, *The Cambridge Companion to Modern Latin American Culture,* Cambridge: Cambridge University Press, 2004.

Hernando Calvo Ospina, *Salsa: Havana Heat, Bronx Beat,* London: Latin America Bureau, 1995.

Octavio Paz, *The Labyrinth of Solitude,* London and Chicago: University of Chicago Press, 1950.

William Rowe and Vivian Schelling, *Memory and Modernity: Popular Culture in Latin America,* London: Verso, 1991.

Maya Roy, *Cuban Music,* London: Latin America Bureau, 2003.

Philip Swanson, *Landmarks in Modern Latin American Fiction,* London: Routledge, 1990.

Chris Taylor, *The Beautiful Game,* London: Latin America Bureau, 1998.

Index